CRASH PROFITS: MAKE MONEY WHEN STOCKS SINK *AND* SOAR

MARTIN D. WEISS, PH.D.

WILEY

Published by John Wiley & Sons, Inc., Hoboken, New Jersey
Published simultaneously in Canada

For general information on our other products and services, or technical support,
please contact our Customer Care Department within the United States at
800-762-2974, outside the United States at 317-572-3993 or fax 317-572-4002.

Wiley also publishes its books in a variety of electronic formats. Some content that
appears in print may not be available in electronic books.

For more information about Wiley products, visit our web site at www.wiley.com.

Library of Congress Cataloging-in-Publication Data:
Weiss, Martin D.
    Crash profits : make money when stocks sink and soar / Martin Weiss.
        p.   cm.
    "Published simultaneously in Canada."
    Includes bibliographical references and index.
    The broker's hidden agenda–The bubble–The Wall Street hype–The bubble
    bursts–The $17,000 toilet kit–Sell the Stocks Now!–Get your money to safety–The
    ballooning budget deficit–The bond market bubble–The real estate bubble–The
    winning minority–The team–Hidden risks–Deflation!–The fall of the blue chips–
    Move your account!–An appeal to action–Vertigo–The big bailout–The great
    rally–The gap–The blame game–Rock bottom–The darkest day–A true recovery.
        ISBN 0-471-42998-8 (cloth : alk. paper)
    1. Finance, Personal.   2. Investments.   3. Financial crises.   I. Title.
    HG179 .W4644   2003
    332.6–dc21
                                                                    2002153142

Printed in the United States of America

10 9 8 7 6 5 4 3 2 1

CONTENTS

INTRODUCTION

Millions of investors are now living in fear of the future, and perhaps you're one of them.

I, too, see very tough times ahead for the economy. But unlike most investors, fear is the farthest thing from my mind.

Indeed, my father, Irving Weiss, began preparing me for times like these 50 years ago. While other kids and their fathers were playing checkers, Dad and I were playing a stock market game. If I wanted to be the buyer, he'd play the seller, or vice versa. It was his way of teaching me the lessons he learned from the Great Stock Market Crash of 1929.

Dad was one of the great mavericks of Wall Street. He stood virtually alone as a man who correctly anticipated the Crash of '29, who safeguarded his family's money when stock prices plummeted, and who actually *used* the crash to reap large profits.

Dad Borrowed $500 from His Mother and Turned It into $100,000 during the Worst Market Decline in History

He taught me why every major bubble in stock prices must inevitably end in an equally spectacular bust . . . how stock crashes unfold and impact the average citizen . . . how to prepare for market crashes and their aftermath . . . and how to find safety and build true wealth even in the worst of times. I want to share these valuable lessons with you too.

Dad told me that he conquered the Crash of '29 not just once but twice: While stocks were plunging in the early 1930s, he made his first fortune. And when stocks hit bottom, he made a second fortune—buying the shares of America's greatest companies near their lowest prices of the entire century.

He started in 1924, when he went to work as a typist on Wall Street at the "ripe old age" of 16. By 1928, he had risen to the position of customer's man—a broker.

At the time, stock fever was running high on Wall Street. Investors were throwing every penny they could into the market and then borrowing every last dollar to buy even more stocks. But Dad didn't buy into the mania. He could see that business was bad and growing worse across America. He could also see that British and other European markets were plunging. And he knew too many investors were up to their eyeballs in debt.

So when the Great Crash came in October of 1929, he advised his parents to keep their money strictly in safe investments, with nothing invested in the stock market at all. While millions lost everything in the Great Crash, they didn't lose one red cent.

That was the first critical event of his investing lifetime.

The second came when he met George Kato, a Japanese exchange student and analyst who was in close touch with the most astute speculators of the day. George soon became Dad's mentor, teaching him how to short the stock market to actually profit from a crash.

So, in April 1930, with stocks in a temporary rally and Wall Street wags pronouncing the bear market officially over, Dad borrowed $500 from his mother and used what he had learned from George Kato to short the stocks he thought were the most likely to fall.

The Great Crash of 1929 had been only a dress rehearsal for the real event. The longer, deeper decline began in 1930 and lasted for nearly three long years.

Dad told me that by the time the market hit bottom, he had transformed his mother's $500 into more than $100,000—$1.3 million in today's dollars! But he also confessed that he had suffered serious losses whenever the market did not go his way. "I sweated bullets," he often said, "and sometimes it got ugly."

Then, in the days before Franklin Delano Roosevelt's (FDR's) inauguration, Dad tracked statistics from the Federal Reserve that showed exactly how much cash Americans were pulling out of the U.S. banks. They were withdrawing money in huge amounts, and he concluded that a national banking holiday was imminent.

Most people assumed that a banking panic and shutdown would be one of the worst things that could ever happen. They saw it as a sign of an even deeper crash—a time to run for the hills. But Dad felt that it was precisely the opposite. He believed that the looming bank holiday would mark the end of the entire stock market decline.

By March 3, 1932, he was ready to make his move.

FDR would be inaugurated the next day, and Dad assumed that the new president would have no choice but to close the banks and take all the needed steps to revive the markets. No matter what, Dad knew that at those incredibly low prices major blue-chip stocks would sell for bargain-basement prices.

So, as Dad tells the story, "We went straight to our firm's main offices downtown. We didn't stop at the midtown branch. We wanted to get our orders in to the man who talked directly to the floor traders. We bought everything we could lay our hands on. We bought GM, AT&T, GE, and Sears for pennies on the dollar, right near the big bottom."

The rest is history. As soon as he took office, FDR closed all the banks just as Dad expected. Plus, he shut down the stock market, which Dad did *not* expect. Nevertheless, investor sentiment began to change. Confidence in the banking system recovered. Well-heeled investors made plans to start buying stocks again.

When the stock market was finally reopened, prices soared. The recovery was underway, and Dad was in the catbird seat. "I only wish I had held on for decades to come," he said. "Instead, I took a nice profit and ran too soon."

That was 70 years ago! Now, I have dedicated my life to sharing these experiences—both good and bad—with average investors, including what I learned from my father and what I have learned from my own 30 years of analyzing companies and markets.

I have told investors not to expect to transform $500 into $100,000, and you shouldn't count on that much either. However, you certainly have the potential to turn your financial future around, recoup money that you have lost, and build a very comfortable nest egg for yourself and your family.

For the near term, I expect severe troubles. Fundamentally, however, I am an optimist. I am confident in our know-how, our technology, and our long-term recovery powers.

I see a much better tomorrow once the dust of the current crisis settles. Stock market crashes—even economic depressions—are *not* the end of the world. Our country has been through much worse before, and we survived. We will survive this time too. Even better, if we do the right thing, we can use the interlude as an opportunity to correct many of the economic and social ills that plague us.

For you, there are two opportunities: You can make money on the way down and still more on the way back up. Even if you take advantage of just one of these opportunities, and even if you start with a small amount of money, you can be very successful. The more successful you are, the more empowered you will be to invest in the best-managed, most sound, and most profitable enterprises when they need your support the most.

I have written this book to help you maximize your chances of success. The first half of the book is about the current crisis—how we got into this mess in the first place, what dangers are still lurking behind the scenes, and what you can do about it right now. The second half is about worst-case scenarios for the future and my advice regarding the wisest steps to take before, during, and after the crisis. Although I paint a dire picture, always remember that it is never too late—for you as an individual and for the country as a whole—to take protective action. And even in the darkest of times, there will still be abundant hope for a better tomorrow.

Bear in mind that my worst-case scenario is not written in stone. It is designed strictly as a warning of what *could* happen if our leaders continue their present course. It's also my way of alerting you to the outstanding opportunities that an adverse market environment can offer you.

Some of the events ahead are beyond the power of any one individual or group to control. But never underestimate your own ability to change your future.

Palm Beach Gardens, Florida
December 6, 2002

CHAPTER 1

THE BROKER'S HIDDEN AGENDA

*T*o give you a more complete under-
standing of what will happen and why, this book has been written as a
novel, including a few fictional individuals and companies. However, these
are included strictly to help guide you, step-by-step, through the maze of
events and decisions that you will face in the months ahead.

Unlike a novel, this book is about the real world. The advice is solid and
well documented. Step-by-step instructions are offered throughout to give
you a practical guide that you can put to use right now—to get out of danger and achieve your financial goals.

We begin with a focus on the deceptions and dangers you face as an
investor and consumer; plus we give advice on how to get your money to
safety. Advice on how to achieve crash profits will follow.

Linda Dedini, the 30-something daughter of one of the highest-
paid executives in America, didn't like to talk about her father.

She was attached to him emotionally but completely detached
financially. She valued his love but did not want any of his money.

She and her husband, also very independent-minded, wanted
to prove they could make it on their own without a penny of
fatherly assistance. Other than her most intimate friends, she
avoided telling anyone that her dad was a famous CEO. Her world

was teaching physics at an Arlington, Virginia, high school, and she wanted to keep it that way.

FICTION OR FACT?

This book contains information about real companies and their executives. However, as it is written as a novel, the primary characters and their affiliations, including the following, are fictional:

Individuals	Corporations
Linda and Gabriel Dedini	Harris & Jones
James Dubois	MetroBank
Paul E. Johnston	UCBS
Oliver Dulles	CECAR
Tamara Belmont	ABC Corp.
Don Walker	XYZ Corp.

She didn't even want his investment advice. Instead, for almost all her financial decisions, she relied on one of the largest brokerage firms in America: Harris & Jones. The company had over 5 million customers and was among the most widely respected on Wall Street. She felt she could trust them.

The New York broker handling her account, James Dubois, had done very well for her throughout most of the 1990s. So she had a lot of confidence in him too.

One Monday morning, she called him for advice. She had $160,000 in new funds available to invest—the proceeds from the sale of a second home—and she hoped to grow that amount into a fund that would comfortably cover her and her husband's retirement and most of their kids' college tuition.

"I have a great stock for you," declared the broker enthusiastically. "It was selling as high as $64 per share, but it's come down now to $40. The great news is that it's expected to make $2 per share in earnings this year. So at $40, it's selling for just 20 times its earnings!"

"Is that good?" she asked.

"Good? Are you kidding? It's a fantastic bargain! Most companies in this industry are selling for 30 or 40 times earnings. So this company is really worth 30 or 40 times the $2 per share it's gonna make. Multiply it out and what do you get?"

"$60 or $80 per share?"

"Exactly. I'd say it's worth $80. But you're going to get it for just $40! That's the main reason our research analyst has just put out a 'strong-buy' rating on this stock. Were you watching CNBC this morning? No? Too bad. You could have seen our analyst talking all about it just a couple of hours ago."

"What's its name?"

"United Communications and Business Systems—UCBS. I'm sure you've heard of it."

She nodded slowly. After deflecting personal concerns, she decided to invest $80,000 in the company. The broker put her into 2,000 shares at $40 each, and she waited for the shares to go up.

The shares did precisely the opposite. Rumors were flying that UCBS had somehow exaggerated its earnings. Details were sketchy, but according to several sources (some of which seemed credible), instead of making $2 per share, the company was really making as little as $1 per share.

Since most investors still valued the stock at about 20 times its earnings, if these rumors proved true, the stock would really be worth only 20 × $1, or $20 per share. Almost instantly, investors started dumping their shares as the price plunged toward $20. Within days, she lost nearly half her money.

Adding insult to injury, it was also revealed a few months later that some of the great, positive ratings that this company had earned from Wall Street were effectively bought and paid for by the company itself. The analysts were getting huge payoffs to push the company, and they were sugar-coating the company's already-exaggerated earnings outlook. As the bad news hit, some analysts downgraded the company to "hold," which was really a Wall Street code for "sell." The stock promptly plunged in half *again* to $10. Of her original $80,000 investment, all she now had left was about $20,000.

As she pondered her predicament one afternoon, the phone rang and interrupted her thoughts. It was Dubois again. To her utter dismay, he recommended that she buy *another* 2,000 shares in the same company that was now sinking her portfolio like a torpedo.

"Look," he said. "All these bad rumors you hear about the company are a blessing in disguise. They've driven the share prices down to way, way, *way* below what the company is really worth. All you have to do now is throw in a few more bucks and you can cut your average cost down dramatically. In addition to the 2,000 shares at $40, you'll now have 2,000 shares at $10, for a total of 4,000 shares at an average cost of $25 per share. That's what's called 'dollar-cost averaging.' "

She balked. She told him that she was actually thinking of selling.

"*Oh no!*" he responded, jumping several octaves in one breath. "This is the *worst* possible time to do that. Instead, you should buy more! And if you don't have the guts to buy more, then, for God's sake, just *hold!*"

Dubois paused to gauge her response, but she remained silent. "Remember the golden rule of winning in the stock market!" he added with a professorial tone. "*Always invest for the long term.* The market has always outperformed other investments over a long period of time. It always comes back eventually."

She had heard this claim many times before from virtually everyone—friends, financial planners, even TV anchors and independent commentators. It seemed to be backed up with decades of historical evidence. She had never heard anyone say otherwise, so she accepted the claim without question.

For the next few days, she struggled with this decision, and each time she talked to Dubois, he passed on a new piece of investing wisdom to persuade her to "tough it out" and "hang in there."

The broker had a hidden agenda: He wanted to keep her as a customer, and he knew from experience that once customers sell out their stocks, they often give up on the stock market entirely, or worse, they close their brokerage accounts. With this in mind, he was absolutely determined to prevent her from selling in any way he could.

The first tactic he deployed was the "paper-loss" pitch. "Don't worry about your losses," he declared. "They're just on paper right now. If you sell, all you'll be doing is locking them in." He never mentioned that there is no fundamental difference between a paper loss and a realized loss. Nor did he reveal that the Securities Exchange Commission (SEC) even requires that brokers themselves value the securities they hold in their own portfolio at the current market price—to recognize the losses as real whether they've sold the securities or not. He was well aware that, either way, a loss was a loss. It was a fact of life.

When the paper-loss tactic didn't seem to be working, he tried the "don't be a fool and sell at the bottom" argument. He even used a script that a former sales manager had developed for him, which read, "We're very, very close to rock bottom. We may even be right *at* the bottom. If you sell now, three months from now, you'll be kicking yourself. Don't be a fool."

The truth: The broker didn't have the faintest idea where the bottom was. Nor did anyone in the firm. At the same time, he knew from years of experience that *stocks didn't hit bottom just because they look cheap.* In fact, for his own personal portfolio, the broker had decided that he wouldn't start bottom-fishing until most other brokers like himself finally gave up fishing for a bottom.

As often occurred, at midweek the market suddenly enjoyed a very sharp bounce, and Linda Dedini figured that this was her chance to finally get out. She gave Dubois a call to end it then and there, but he had an immediate comeback for that as well. He launched into his "big rally" pitch. "Look at this big rally!" he said, reporting the details of the Dow's action. "Your UCBS shares are starting to come back now. You don't want to get out, do you? You do? I don't believe it! After waiting all this time through thick and thin, you want to run away *now*—just when things are starting to turn around in your favor!?"

The last ace-in-the hole in the broker's arsenal of pitches was the patriotic approach. "Do you realize," he asked her, "what will happen if everyone does what you're talking about doing? That's when the market would *really* nosedive. But if you and millions of other investors would just have a bit more faith in our economy—in our country—then the market will recover and everyone will come out ahead."

Months later she would learn that there are many alternative investments she could use to profit from a stock market decline, and, after a couple of false starts, she would hone her skills at making large crash profits. For now, however, she knew of only three choices: buy, sell, or hold. She decided to hold.

Unbeknownst to the broker, she also had personal reasons for doing so: Her father was the company's CEO.

CHAPTER 2

THE BUBBLE

Paul E. Johnston, the CEO of UCBS, also knew very little about crash profits. In fact, many months earlier, as he stared blankly at the Wall Street skyline from his midtown office, crash profits couldn't have been further from his mind.

UCBS, a one-factory company just a decade earlier, was snowballing in size with a series of acquisitions and emerging as one of the largest technology manufacturers in the United States.

The CEO's most urgent challenge: To raise a ton of money.

Without more money, he would not be able to take the next giant techno-leap forward in advanced fiber optics. He could not buy out the dozens of start-up companies in the United States and overseas that were the leading technological innovators in the industry. He might not be able to protect himself from other global giants that were plotting to buy *him* out. Worst of all, he might not be able to pay off all the debts now coming due—money that was all spent on the first round of acquisitions.

How much money would he need? For the third time in 24 hours, he pondered the shopping list of companies he wanted to acquire and came up with the same round figure—$4.3 billion, much more than had ever been raised in the company's history. Ambitious? Yes. Impossible? No. Other high-tech and telecom giants were doing it. Why couldn't he?

For the quantities Johnston wanted to raise now, however, there was no bank or investor large enough to provide the funds. Even a consortium of the world's largest international banks would not do it. There was only one source: the stock market.

In the 1990s, the stock market had changed dramatically. Earlier, to raise any sizable amount of money you had to be a well-established Fortune 100 company with your shares traded on the New York Stock Exchange (NYSE).

Now, however, almost any company with a great high-tech story could raise a substantial sum by listing its shares on the newer exchange, the Nasdaq, where millions of investors from all over the world were pouring in billions of dollars. In just a 60-month span from January 1995 to December 2000, investors poured $933 million into WorldCom and $258 million into XO Communications. They snatched up shares of Globalstar Telecommunications, Luminent, Prodigy Communications, Internet Capital Group, and many other hotshot stars of the day. Over 2,809 new companies were born. A total of $177 billion was raised, of which $103 billion was raised in 1999 and 2000 alone.

Johnston was intimately familiar with the Nasdaq craze. That's why years earlier he had been one of the first among his peers to join the club—to list his company's shares on the Nasdaq. And that's why he went back to Wall Street time and again to raise ever-larger amounts of capital.

As if that wasn't enough, he also borrowed to the hilt. By late 1999, for each dollar of capital, UCBS owed $5 in debt. What's worse, for each dollar of debts coming due within one year, the company had only 8 cents in cash in the bank. This was another, unspoken reason the CEO was desperate to raise the $4.3 billion now.

He was aware of two companies that had raised that much money before: UPS, which in November 1999 sold 109 million new shares of its stock to investors for $5.4 billion, and Conoco, which in October 1998 sold 191 million new shares for $4.4 billion.

The CEO knew this. He also knew that to raise that much money he couldn't just go to Wall Street with hat in hand and some wimpy, run-of-the-mill numbers to show. He would need an absolutely fabulous tale. He'd have to demonstrate stupendous sales growth, mind-boggling profit projections, dazzling tales of futuristic technological marvels.

The chief executive was also intimately familiar with the target audience for his show-and-tells. It wasn't the tens of thousands of investors who would pour their life savings and retirement funds into his company's shares. Nor was it the hundreds of mutual fund managers who would rush into the shares like a herd of cattle.

No. In fact, he made a point of rarely talking to *those* people, never allowing their particular fear or greed to cloud his vision of the future or mar his concentration on growth. The *only* audience he really talked to were the Wall Street research analysts—the young, hotshot stock pickers who worked for major Wall Street firms like Merrill Lynch, Salomon Brothers Smith Barney, Prudential Securities, and Lehman Brothers.

It was *their* job—not his—to talk to the mutual fund managers and other investors. It was their job to tout the shares of UCBS to the media and to the public. To get them to do that with a real splash, he had to do more than just convince the analysts that the company was doing well. He had to make them drool like panting dogs and shiver with excitement. *Then* they would write up research reports, conveying those same emotions to millions of investors.

Johnston also knew, however, that UCBS's financial statements could rarely be so picture-perfect. Lurking behind all the makeup and glitter were blemishes and glitches in his company's operations. There were ventures on the verge of collapsing, as well as debts that could stick out like a sore thumb.

That's why on this warm Monday morning in August he invited some of the highest-paid business consultants in the world to assist him in finding ways to embellish his financial statements. These consultants were smart. They came from one of the leading Big Five accounting firms in the country. They knew all the latest tools—accounting gimmicks to dress up bad numbers. But would their proposals be enough? Would they be legal?

"PERFECTLY LEGAL" ACCOUNTING MANEUVERS

As the sun rose further over downtown Manhattan, it forced the CEO to turn his eyes away from the window and reminded him that the consultants were waiting in a private conference room adjoining his office suite. He broke out of his reverie and walked deliberately into the room.

Seated before him were three employees from the accounting firm—a 40-something woman with an MBA from Harvard, a younger fellow, also an MBA, and Oliver Dulles, a gray-haired man with many years of experience as a certified public accountant.

"We have a historic challenge before us," said Johnston after only the briefest of introductions. "To reach our goals, we must cease looking at UCBS shares strictly as 'stock in a company we want to sell.' Instead, we must view them as something much grander than that. We have to think of them as a new *currency*—a new kind of dollar or pound or yen. We must make UCBS's shares one of the most *valuable* currencies on earth. We want to see UCBS shares soar to the stratosphere, creating still more wealth. We want to use that strong currency, our stock, to purchase even larger companies.

The CEO paused briefly, and in the second of silence that ensued, he thought to himself, *Plus, we must goose up the value of my own shares and options. They've already made me a rich man. Now, I will be even richer.*

The Harvard consultant responded as if she had heard his last thought telepathically. "The first item on our agenda," she said, "is the overhaul we're proposing in your management team's compensation packages. We think they—you—need to be rewarded and given incentives to achieve even more rapid growth than you're currently experiencing. Right now, even including all your stock and stock options, you'll personally take home no more than $14 million this year. But based on our comparative analysis of executive comp in your peer group of companies, we figure you should get at least 5 times that much, maybe 10 times. Needless to say, the only vehicle that has the potential to make that possible is *options*. So we are proposing to dramatically upgrade your options plan."

The CEO nodded knowingly. Options were the new elixir of corporate America. They gave CEOs the chance to make the killing of a thousand lifetimes, and they never once had to be recorded as an expense or be deducted from the profits that were reported to shareholders. Options made it possible for CEOs to plunder a company and pull out a king's ransom, yet keep shareholders in the dark almost indefinitely.

This CEO already owned a batch of options that gave him the right to buy shares more cheaply than the going price: UCBS shares were selling for $12, and his options gave him the right to buy 1 million shares for an average of $10 each, or $2 less than their worth. If he wanted to cash them in right now, he could effectively buy the 1 million shares for $10 and then sell them immediately at $12, pocketing a profit of $2 per share, or $2 million total. *Not too shabby,* he thought to himself, *but still not good enough.*

What disturbed him most, however, was the key point the consultants were finally trying to address right now: The growing gap between his own compensation package and those of others at the helm of companies in the same size category.

Johnston knew, for example, that Enron, a company in the forefront of this new field of "creative accounting," was especially generous with its executives. Enron's chairman Kenneth Lay received a base salary of $1.3 million and a bonus of $7 million. Plus, in March 2000, he exercised options worth $123 million. Meanwhile, Enron's CEO Jeffrey Skilling received $850,000, a bonus of $5.6 million, and exercised options in 2000 worth $62 million. Around the same time, Andrew Fastow, Enron's CFO, made off with over $30 million for managing two of Enron's "special-purpose entities."

Meanwhile, WorldCom was quickly on its way to becoming the largest telecommunications giant in the world, driven mostly by an aggressive acquisition program like the one at UCBS. Johnston suspected, correctly so, that its executive compensation packages were among the richest of all. Indeed, Bernard Ebbers, president and CEO of WorldCom, received a salary of $41 million in 2000, along with a bonus of $10 million. Plus, he was granted over one million options in WorldCom stock, which at the time were worth as much as $53.4 million. In 2000, Mr. Ebbers exercised over a million WorldCom options on shares worth $23.4 million. Later, by the time he quit, he would also have a loan from the company for an astounding $408 million—not to mention a guaranteed salary of $1.5 million for life.

What Johnston didn't know was that the Enron empire would later collapse in a cesspool of fraud. Nor did he have any inkling of the coming troubles at WorldCom, a fraud and bankruptcy that would make Enron's look like a friendly game of gin rummy.

That outcome was not even conceivable. Instead, the conversation at UCBS focused on the options portion of the executive compensation package, which was pivotal. If you held options to buy your company's shares, known as *call options,* you would have the right—but not the obligation—to purchase the shares at a relatively low price and then immediately sell them at a much higher level. If the company's stock failed to go up, you would lose nothing except the option itself. If the stock soared, the options *alone* could be worth more than 10 years' base salary.

It didn't take a rocket scientist to figure out what would happen if the company's stock dropped, for instance, by 30 percent: The big cheeses would lose one-third, one-half, or even two-thirds of their personal wealth. Depending on the company, that percentage could translate into hundreds of millions of dollars.

These corporate CEOs weren't dumb. They knew that there was nothing better than a positive earnings report to goose up their stock prices. Hence, once each quarter, unscrupulous CEOs massaged the numbers, hid losses in any way they could, artificially inflated revenues, and when all else failed, looked investors squarely in the eye and lied their rich, well-tailored fannies off.

Later, when these stocks crashed and millions of people were burned, the public and the U.S. Congress would bitterly deplore the CEOs who walked away scot-free with Beverly Hills mansions, ocean-faring yachts, and eight-digit bank accounts. Now, however, few people questioned the standard Wall Street rationale for the superfat paychecks and enormous bonuses commonly earned by CEOs. "As long as these managers are making *you* rich," rationalized the analysts, "why should you give a damn how big *their* paychecks are?"

Thus, at UCBS, size was no issue as the woman with the Harvard MBA handed Johnston a spreadsheet with proposed revisions to management compensation packages. On the spreadsheet, his name—plus the names of four other top officers in the company—appeared at the top of each column, while along the left side were various scenarios for UCBS shares, starting from $10 all the way up to $100. "This is a summary sheet showing how much you and the rest of senior management can make with our new proposal, depending on what happens to UCBS share prices," she declared.

Johnston stared down at the spreadsheet while hiding a narrow smile. The bottom-line number for his total compensation was $360 million at $100 a share. Even if the stock made it just half that far—to $50 a share—he could waltz away with a fat $160 million. *Now you're talking!* he thought.

The woman waited for the full impact of the numbers to sink in and then proceeded to explain the underlying basis for the calculations. "First, we are proposing that the total number of options granted to executives should be quadrupled. Second, we are narrowing the program to be weighted more toward you and your top officers—less to middle management and nothing to rank and file. Needless to say," she added parenthetically, "it's not up to me or you to decide on all this—it's up to UCBS's board of directors."

The CEO had little concern about this aspect. He knew the members of the board would rubber-stamp the changes in a heartbeat. Why? For the simple reason that they themselves were invariably granted miniature versions of the same compensation packages granted to top executives. They'd be richly rewarded for their "yes" votes.

"Now," concluded the woman, "the management team will have a truly powerful incentive to do everything humanly possible to boost UCBS shares in the stock market, which leads us to the second item on our agenda—your bottom line. Oliver will pick up from here."

She nodded to the CPA, who pulled out a yellow pad on which he had scribbled several bullet points.

THE SUBSIDIARY SHELL GAME

Oliver Dulles was an old hand at numbers—far beyond the realm of an ordinary CPA. He received a BS degree in social psychology many years earlier at New York University, where the faculty knew him for the heavy doses of statistics he put into every one of his research papers.

In the early 1980s, however, funding for his kind of research, which had been flowing abundantly during the Johnson era, dried up. Teaching jobs were also scarce. So Dulles reengineered his career and ported his number-crunching skills to accounting, where a stable job and income were virtually guaranteed. Accounting often bored him, but he felt that he had no choice.

"We have gone through your operations with a fine-tooth comb," he said. "We have looked at every single line item on your profit-and-loss statement. And we see all kinds of opportunities for making it look a lot better than it looks now.

"First," he continued, "we have put together a list of all UCBS subsidiaries, joint ventures, and partnerships in the U.S. and abroad. It's 27 pages long, very complex but very rich with opportunities—opportunities that we have already taken advantage of. In nearly all cases, UCBS owns no more than 49 percent of these companies. That's very smart. Because, as you know, if you have less than a majority share, you don't have to consolidate their financials into UCBS's financials. This means you can continue to use them to keep their debts off your books forever. Then later, if the subsidiary becomes profitable, we have the option to buy a majority share for a song. That's when we consolidate the numbers, adding them into UCBS's profits, so we can show them off to investors."

"It's tails we win, heads you lose," added the younger consultant with enthusiasm. "If there are losses, we can hide them. If there are profits, we can flaunt them. Either way, we come off smelling like a rose. Everyone's doing it."

Indeed, in the late 1990s nearly every large, multinational corporation took advantage of subsidiaries—especially those overseas—to manipulate its books.

The prime model cited in the meeting was Enron's, easily the world champion in the subsidiary shell game. By some estimates, Enron had over 900 subsidiaries, partnerships, and joint ventures in the United States and overseas, many of them just hollow shells. It employed 245 in-house lawyers, with 145 of these at their Houston, Texas, twin towers—the equivalent of the sixth largest law office in town—working full-time to build a facade of legality around its massive network of companies. Enron was *so* adept at inflating its assets that it was able to convince Wall Street, the entire U.S. government, and millions of investors that it was the seventh largest company in America—larger than Walt Disney, J.P. Morgan Chase, Boeing, 3M, and Chevron Texaco. Later, it was discovered that had Enron's revenues been valued accurately, it would have ranked closer to 69th largest.

The consultants also cited others that were successfully using legal maneuvers to shift around debts and losses—Adelphia Communications, Computer Associates, Global Crossing, Halliburton, Lucent Technologies, Qwest Communications, and Tyco International. Later, it was discovered that, in some cases, illegal maneuvers also played a large role. It was these illegal acts that made headlines; however, it was the so-called legal activities that were at the core of the companies' deceptive strategies.

The CEO of UCBS had heard a lot about creative accounting before, and he could accept some juggling of the numbers here and there. The proposals now on the table, however, were on a much grander scale. Here he was, talking to representatives of one of the most well-respected, traditional accounting firms in America . . . and there they were presenting a plan that would transform his subsidiaries into virtual accounting dumpsters—a place to throw very substantial amounts of bad debts and unwanted expenses. Despite his misgivings, he sat back and listened silently.

"This structure," continued the younger consultant, "will make your profit statements and your balance sheet shine. Based on this alone, instead of selling for $11 per share, UCBS should be selling for close to $18 per share. Instead of raising just a few bucks for you, investment bankers will be able to get you access to financing you couldn't dream of getting before. Investors and bankers will be throwing money at you like there's no tomorrow."

THE GREAT PENSION FUND MANEUVER

There was a moment of silence as the consultant from Harvard asked an assistant to dim the conference room lights and start up a projector connected to her laptop computer. "We've saved the best for last," she announced. "Everything we've told you about so far is small in comparison to what we're going to show you now."

The logo for Microsoft PowerPoint appeared briefly on a large screen on the wall, followed by the first slide. "This is the latest data we have on the UCBS employee pension fund," she declared, stopping abruptly to imply that something dramatic was about to be said. "The first chart answers the first key question: How much money do we need to fulfill all these promises we've made to employees? The answer: $9.6 billion. This second graph answers the next key question: How much money do we actually *have* in the fund right now? Based on the value of the investments at year-end, the answer is $11.1 billion!"

As was often his style, Johnston played dumb to elicit a no-BS response. "Is that a large surplus?" he queried.

"You're not kidding it's huge. It's a whopping $1.5 billion *more* than we need. In other words, the employee pension fund is *over-funded* by $1.5 billion. Why? The stock market has been surging. The bond market has been going up. So the portfolio has been growing far more than projected. This is a gold mine. And it's just sitting there, largely untapped."

The CEO was genuinely puzzled. "I don't get it. This $1.5 billion surplus you're talking about is money that belongs to our employees. It's money that's held in a separate fund that has nothing whatsoever to do with our operations. How can we possibly transfer this money to our own accounts? You know darn well we'd never get away with that. People get thrown into jail for doing that kind of thing." As his anxiety built up, the CEO's forehead began twitching, as often happened when he was either mad or afraid.

"No, no, no. We're not talking about actually raiding the pension funds. All we're talking about here is moving some numbers around. What we're going to do is get those huge unrealized profits in the pension fund—those paper gains—over to our books. Then we're going to report them as profits to investors to make our statements look great, to get investors to bid up UCBS share prices."

The younger man, mostly silent throughout the presentation, jumped in, raising his voice with marked enthusiasm. "Wow! Just wait till that number hits Wall Street! UCBS shares will go through the friggin' roof!"

Johnston thought it was almost too good to be true. But it was happening everywhere in the real world. Indeed, in 2000 and 2001, some of America's largest companies used the paper profits from their employee pension funds to dramatically beef up the profits they reported to shareholders.

Verizon Communications, for instance, had multi-billion-dollar losses in 2001. But just by adding in its projected pension fund gains exceeding $2 billion, the company was able to magically report a net profit for the year of $389 million.

Eastman Kodak lost tens of millions in 2001. But by including its projected $100-million-plus profit from its pension fund, the losses were magically transformed into a $76 million profit.

Another company that lost tens of millions in 2001 was TRW. But by adding in a $100-million-plus projected gain in its pension fund, it transformed the huge loss into a $68 million profit.

Honeywell International's loss of $99 million in 2001 would have been several times greater. But the company counted the projected pension fund gain of hundreds of millions on the corporate bottom line.

And there were many more.

PHANTOM PROFITS

Johnston had no inkling of the huge stock market declines ahead, but he decided to play devil's advocate. "Suppose the stock market goes down. Then what?"

The consultants froze. The only sound in the conference room was the low humming noise from the projector fan. Finally, the woman spoke softly and slowly to underscore the importance of what she was about to say next. "The stock market never goes down for more than a year. And no matter what, according to the rules, you can virtually ignore it."

"How do you do that?" asked the CEO.

"It's actually quite easy. Let's say, for example, that we have $100 million in the fund and we project an annual return of 10 percent. That gives us a projected $10 million return per year, right?"

"Right."

"Now, let's say that we have the bad year in the stock market you're worried about and the pension fund has unrealized losses of 5 percent. How much do you think we'll have to deduct from the company's profit statement?"

"Five percent of $100 million? That's $5 million."

"Guess again. According to GAAP–Generally Accepted Accounting Principles–we can spread out the unrealized losses over, say, 10 years or any other time period."

"Oh, I get it," said the CEO. "We only have to deduct one-tenth of the loss. So we'd show a loss of just a half million."

The woman shook her head. "No, again. We can actually show a *profit* of $9.5 million."

"Huh? How the heck do you get that number?"

"Remember, we're projecting $10 million gains each year. So we can take that $10 million projected yearly gain and reduce it by the half-million-dollar amortized loss from the stock market decline. That's $10 million minus a half million, which equals $9.5 million."

The CEO chuckled nervously. The consultants broke out into uncontrollable laughter. Everyone in the room was astute enough to realize that $9.5 million was purely a *phantom* profit—a mirage created by accounting smoke and mirrors. What struck them as funny was that it was all strictly kosher according to GAAP.

"Like we told you a moment ago," added the woman, "this pension fund accounting is a gold mine. Anytime you need to boost UCBS share prices, anytime you want to raise a new batch of capital, all you have to do to is tweak these numbers a bit . . . and you tap right into this pot of gold."

THE DERIVATIVES GAME

"This next one is probably the least understood vehicle of all," said the younger consultant. "Derivatives! We're gonna . . ."

"Explain to him what they are first, will you?" interrupted the CPA.

"Oh yeah, right. They're bets, bets on virtually anything. Wanna bet that some developing country is going to have to pay no more than 3 percent for a loan beyond what the U.S. Treasury Department pays between Jan. 1 and June 30? No problem. Wanna bet on natural gas, electricity, microchips? Easy."

The CEO knew there was a lot more to it then that, but he wanted to move on. "Suppose we lose?" he asked.

"Win, lose, or draw, there are all kinds of ways to value these derivatives. Plus, there are all kinds of ways to manipulate the precise timing of the valuations. You can do practically anything you want to do. Let's say, for example, that you don't want to trade one of the standard, already-established derivative contracts that are offered on various exchanges. You can just create a custom derivative of your own—in almost any size, shape, or color. Heck, all they are, in essence, is contracts. So you go to some other player in this game—it could be a competitor, a bank, whatever—and you say, 'I betcha this or that is gonna happen.' He says, 'OK, I'll take that bet.' You write up the contract, sign it, and it's done. You're now the proud owner of a new kind of derivative that probably never existed before. Since it's unique, how you price it, how you book it, and how you disclose it to investors is pretty much up to you. At worst, you may have to insert something into the footnotes of the statements, which no one will pay attention to—much less understand."

Paul E. Johnston, one of America's greatest success stories of the 1990s, felt inner pangs of guilt and the subtle proddings of trouble that might occur someday, but these concerns were overwhelmed by a rush—a sudden feeling of power and control he felt over his destiny and the clear path he envisioned toward personal wealth. Moreover, in their concluding remarks, the consultants allayed his fears with three operative words: *all perfectly legal.*

"Everything we've proposed, every single maneuver, is all perfectly legal," the consultants said, almost in unison.

CHAPTER 3

THE WALL STREET HYPE

UCBS's doctored-up numbers first reached Wall Street through a private conference call with about two-dozen research analysts. As was the custom, only a small group of people knew about the call and were allowed to participate—almost all representing major firms.

Johnston presented the new earnings numbers with great fanfare, making it absolutely clear that they far exceeded Wall Street's most optimistic expectations. The research analysts rushed out to issue glorious reports hyping the company . . . investors bought the stock with wild abandon . . . and UCBS surged from $11 to $30 per share.

UCBS's lead underwriter was Harris & Jones, one of the most aggressive investment banking and brokerage firms on Wall Street.

Harris & Jones grabbed the opportunity to raise a big chunk of the capital that the CEO was hoping for. Its top crackerjack analyst, one of the leading tech stock gurus on Wall Street, issued a glowing review, announcing a strong-buy rating on the stock. And large blocks of the shares were distributed to brokers who pushed the stock to their customers.

Harris & Jones had even invested a few million dollars into its own TV studio and satellite hookup at its Wall Street headquarters—so the stock offering could all be carefully orchestrated on CNBC, the nation's premier financial news network. Harris knew that millions of investors would watch the program and that those who didn't would pick up the stock recommendation on Bloomberg, on the Web, or in the *Wall Street Journal* the next morning. With Harris leading the way, UCBS sold over 3.5 million shares for an average of $36 per share.

Within a few short weeks, UCBS's chief executive, Paul E. Johnston, was being hailed as a Wall Street hero, featured on the cover of *Forbes* and even getting invited to spend a night in the Lincoln bedroom at the White House. UCBS zoomed to $50 per share and beyond.

Strangely, neither the analyst at Harris nor the analysts of other Wall Street firms probed UCBS's bloated pension fund profits. Not one bothered to review the company's annual 10K reports—let alone scrutinize its cryptic footnotes for possible hidden time bombs.

Wall Street was absolutely unanimous in its glowing accolades for UCBS shares. In fact, the unanimity was so overwhelming that the few mutual fund managers who *didn't* have some UCBS shares in their portfolios were accused of "missing the boat" or, worse, "failing in their fiduciary responsibility to investors." They, too, soon fell into line, and virtually every institution in the nation—mutual funds, pension funds, churches, university endowments, major trusts, and many German institutions—loaded up on UCBS shares. The stock price surged again, this time to nearly $64 per share.

One analyst, however, was not so happy. She was also at Harris & Jones, and she also researched stocks. But she was really an economist by training. Her name: Tamara Belmont, research assistant to the senior analyst covering UCBS. During the first conference call with the UCBS, she said nothing. In her own notes to her boss about UCBS, she also said nothing.

But later, when it was obvious that the Internet bubble was bursting, she became more vocal about her concerns. She wanted her boss to downgrade the company to a "sell." But he told her the consequences of that action could be catastrophic—for him personally, for the firm, and probably for UCBS as well. He made it repeatedly clear that *any* downgrade at this juncture could send the stock into a tailspin and sabotage an extremely important business relationship.

To voice her frustrations, she picked up the phone and called a former college roommate who also worked in the industry. "You are not in the market, so I can tell you this," she said in a subdued voice, practically whispering into the receiver. "I think UCBS is a disaster on wheels. The company has grown too fast, too soon. It has too much debt. It quickly spends all the capital it raises. Its tangible assets are few and far between—virtually no land, no building, nothing that could be sold off in a cash pinch. Its grossly overpriced in comparison to its earnings. Even those earnings seem to be fluffed up with some gimmicks, most of which I have yet to fully comprehend. Its accounting is complex as hell."

"And your guy is still giving it a strong-buy rating? Do you think maybe that's kind of intellectually dishonest?"

Belmont's whisper was replaced by a firmer voice. "*Kind of intellectually dishonest?* Are you kidding me? It's an outright f——n' lie! It's a prostitution of research, an abominable hoax."

She was silent for a moment; then she said, "I'm not the only one around here who's disgusted with this charade they call 'research.' Quite a few research people feel the same way as I do, but we're stuck, trapped. Just the other day we griped to our boss, the director of research. You remember him, Don Walker. You met him at the holiday party. Anyhow, we were just venting. Nothing ever changes around here—let alone Don. I happen to know he personally hates this thing as much as we do. Out in public, though, he's stone-faced, just does his duty—either too scared or too proud to talk about it."

"How do you know what he thinks?"

"Some of the guys were joking about it the other day. They said they overheard him in the men's room. He apparently has a habit of going in there, taking a leak, and then letting out this loud, guttural grunt, cursing the investment bankers every time. 'Damn bankers!' or 'f——n' IPOs!' Every single time! Plus, I myself saw."

"Forget about him. What are *you* going to do about it?"

"The plan is to alert a few of our best clients—the ones that we first put into the UCBS IPO—several years ago. Some of 'em are CEOs at other companies we do investment banking with. We can't afford to antagonize them."

"But what about your boss's rating on UCBS?" asked the former roommate. "Does he plan to maintain his buy on the stock?"

"For now, yes . . . or at least until the spotlight is off the stock. Then, Don Walker figures we'll just downgrade it quietly to an 'accumulate' and then maybe to a 'hold.' He says we'll let 'em down slow and gentle. Maybe if we can do it while the stock is enjoying a nice rally, not too many people will notice, and the stock won't fall apart that badly. In the end, he figures we can just drop coverage. By then, he says we'll be getting much less business from the company anyhow. Besides, no one outside the firm has to know we're dropping coverage. We'll just do it. We'll stop issuing new reports, leave the old rating hanging out there, and . . ."

"And let thousands of little investors twist in the wind?"

Tamara turned defensive, but her words carried no conviction. "Hey, give me a break. I'm just the assistant. I carry no weight whatsoever. Plus, Don says we're an institutional firm. We don't deal with retail investors. If they bought the stock, that's not our problem. He figures we're doing right by our VIP institutional clients. Then we're downgrading the stock as soon as we possibly can, considering the damn politics. I hate it, but short of quitting, what can I do about it?"

As it turned out, the "nice rally" in the stock was just a short-term bounce, and the Harris & Jones analyst missed the chance to downgrade the stock. Months later, rumors of a cash squeeze and even bankruptcy began to circulate. But neither Harris nor any other firm got around to downgrading the company until it was selling for less than $6 per share . . . and even then the very *worst* rating for UCBS on the Street was still "hold."

The VIP clients of most of the large investment banking firms couldn't care less. They had bought UCBS at the initial public offering (IPO) price of $3 a share. Then, they got personal warning phone calls from analysts and sold their stakes for more than $30 per share—a spectacular 10-for-1 profit. In contrast, average investors, who had acted on the recommendations they'd heard on CNBC or read in the papers, got creamed. Most bought into the stock in its heyday, in the $40 to $60 range. And none of them ever heard or read the word "sell." So they hung on—to the bitter end.

WALL STREET HAD EVOLVED INTO A GIANT EATING MACHINE, AND YOUR WEALTH WAS THEIR LUNCH

In the real world of Wall Street, the same scene was being repeated nearly everywhere.

In April 1999, Morgan Stanley Dean Witter stock analyst Mary Meeker—dubbed "Queen of the Internet" by Barron's—issued a buy rating on Priceline.com at $104 per share. Within 21 months, the stock was toast—selling for $1.50.

Investors who heeded Ms. Meeker's recommendation would have lost 98 percent of their money. They would have turned a $10,000 mountain of cash into a $144 molehill.

Apparently undaunted and unashamed, Ms. Meeker proceeded to issue buy ratings on Yahoo!, Amazon.com, Drugstore.com, and Homestore.com. The financial media reported the recommendation with a straight face. Millions of naive investors nearly trampled each other trying to be the first to follow her advice.

Yahoo crashed 97 percent; Amazon.com, 95 percent; Drugstore.com, 99 percent; and Homestore.com, 95.5 percent.

Why did Ms. Meeker recommend those dogs in the first place? And why did Ms. Meeker stubbornly stand by her buy ratings even as they crashed 20 percent, 50 percent, 70 percent, and, finally, as much as 98.5 percent?

Answer: Virtually every one of Ms. Meeker's strong buys was paying Ms. Meeker's employer—Morgan Stanley Dean Witter—to promote its shares. Morgan Stanley's underwriting department was paid millions of dollars. And Morgan Stanley rewarded Ms. Meeker—with a mind-blowing $15 million paycheck—for helping to do it.

While millions of investors twisted in the wind, Morgan Stanley Dean Witter and Mary Meeker, as well as the companies they were promoting, laughed all the way to the bank. An isolated case? Not even close.

In 1999, Salomon Smith Barney's top executives received electrifying news: AT&T was planning to take its giant wireless division public, in what would be the largest IPO in history. Naturally, every brokerage firm on Wall Street wanted to do the underwriting for this once-in-a-lifetime IPO. And for good reason: The fees would amount to millions of dollars.

But Salomon had a small problem. One of its chief stock analysts, Jack Grubman, had been saying negative things about AT&T for years. A *major* problem? Not on Wall Street of the late 1990s. By the time Salomon's hotshots made their pitch to pick up AT&T's underwriting business, Grubman had miraculously changed his rating to a buy.

Everywhere, big firms were making money hand over fist on the deal. Salomon was named lead underwriter and made millions. AT&T got a positive rating and the supersuccessful IPO it craved . . . and made more millions. Grubman, who had saved the day, got to keep his $20 million annual salary. But about 4.8 million investors got the raw end of the deal. They assumed that Grubman's buy rating was an honest evaluation of the stock. They didn't know what it really was—cheap sales hype.

They trusted Salomon and Grubman. They bought AT&T Wireless. And they were then left to watch in horror as the stock promptly crashed from $29.50 to $14.75—a 49.7 percent loss.

More examples:

- Mark Kastan of Credit Suisse First Boston liked Winstar almost as much as Grubman liked AT&T, issuing and reiterating buy ratings until the bitter end. No surprise there: Kastan's firm owned $511 million in Winstar stock.
- In 2000, an analyst at Goldman Sachs oozed 11 gloriously positive ratings on stocks that subsequently lost investors 71 percent or more of their money. He got paid $20 million for his efforts. One of his *best* performing recommendations of the year was down 71 percent; his worst was down 99.8 percent.
- Meanwhile, Merrill Lynch's Henry Blodget gained fame by predicting Amazon.com would hit $400 per share. It was soon selling for under $11. Blodget also predicted that Quokka Sports would hit $1,250 a share. It went bankrupt. Blodget issued and reissued strong buy ratings for Pets.com (out of business), eToys (lost 95 percent of its value), InfoSpace (crashed 92 percent), and BarnesandNoble.com (lost

84 percent of its value). Yet even while investors lost billions, Merrill Lynch cleaned up—$100 million on Internet IPOs alone.

In each of these cases, all but the investors got rich. Brokerages made millions. The analysts made millions. The companies they promoted raked in millions. But the poor investors lost their shirts.

Tamara Belmont became increasingly conscious of this great Wall Street scam. She knew it was no coincidence. She knew these were not mere "honest mistakes," as many of her colleagues were claiming. They were orchestrated campaigns to fleece the public. They were overt attempts by Wall Street insiders to get rich at the investor's expense.

"Want to do yourself a favor?" she asked her old college roommate during a weekend visit. She handed her a page printed from her home computer. "Tape this to your bathroom mirror so you'll never forget." In 36-point bold type, the text on the page read

THERE IS NO CHARITY ON WALL STREET.
THE BIG FIRMS ARE NOT IN BUSINESS TO MAKE YOU RICH.
THEY'RE IN BUSINESS TO MAKE <u>THEMSELVES</u> RICH.

At the time, this was radical thinking and never discussed in public. Later, however, Wall Street's ugliest secrets would burst into the open.

AN OUTRAGEOUS BETRAYAL

In August 2001, the acting director of the SEC testified before Congress that nearly *all* major Wall Street firms were guilty of serious conflicts of interest. And in the following year, Elliot Spitzer, attorney general of New York, declared that these schemes were "an outrageous betrayal of [investors'] trust and a shocking abuse of the system, perverted to produce greater revenues for the firm."

Wall Street wasn't always this way. In earlier decades, at least *some* research analysts at major firms would look at the company with a skeptical eye, find the fallacies, and disclose the weaknesses.

In Wall Street firms of the 1990s, however, there was a virtual absence of dissenting voices, an unprecedented unanimity of praise, and far more hype in sales pitches.

What was behind this change? The same force that drove CEOs to tell half-truths or outright lies about their sales and profits—*money and greed.*

In the past, Wall Street firms derived most of their revenues from brokerage commissions—from buying and selling stocks on behalf of the investor. Now, they made the bulk of their money from investment banking fees—promoting and marketing the shares on behalf of their corporate clients. Put simply, the major Wall Street firms used to work mostly for investors seeking to buy shares in the companies. Now, they worked mostly for companies seeking to sell their shares to investors.

A similar change swept through the ranks of individual research analysts working for Wall Street firms. In earlier years, most of the analysts' compensation came from a flat salary. Now, most of their compensation came from bonuses *directly linked to their ability to relentlessly promote the stocks.*

Indeed, the ever-present message from Wall Street firms to the analysts was, "The more you can help us sell the stock, the more you'll make." And for those analysts who didn't get this message, an even stronger followup message was "Issue reports that hurt sales, and you're history!"

A classic example: In 2001, well before the Enron collapse, Chung Wu, an analyst at UBS PaineWebber, sent an e-mail to Enron employees warning them that holding the company's stock—then worth almost $37 a share—could cost them "a fortune." The e-mail enraged Enron executives, who complained vehemently to PaineWebber. Chung Wu was fired, PaineWebber hastily issued a new buy recommendation, and the "little matter" was put to rest. Three months later, Enron shares were selling for less than 25 cents.

Not one major firm on Wall Street tied its analysts' compensation to their actual track record in picking stocks. Quite the contrary, analysts could be wrong once, wrong twice, wrong a thousand times, and they'd *still* earn huge bonuses, as long as they continued to recommend the shares and as long as there were still enough "suckers" who continued to buy into the hype. That's how the investment banking divisions wanted it, and that's how it stayed.

What if it was abundantly obvious that a company was going down the tubes? What if an analyst personally turned sour on the company? Would that make a difference? No.

For proof, anyone can visit the Web site of the New York attorney general and check out the text of Elliot Spitzer's original complaint against Merrill Lynch. They can scroll down to page 11 or run a search for the four-letter word "sh––." That's what Merrill's analysts were saying, behind investors' backs, about the very same stocks they were ballyhooing in public. (See Table 3.1.)

For the once-superhot Internet stock Infospace, Merrill's official advice was "buy." Privately, however, in e-mails uncovered by Mr. Spitzer, Merrill's insiders had a very different opinion. They wrote that Infospace was a "piece of junk." Result: Investors who trusted Merrill analysts to give them their honest opinion got clobbered, losing up to 93.5 percent of their savings, investments, and retirement money when Infospace crashed.

Merrill's official advice on another hot stock, Excite@Home, was "accumulate!" Privately, however, Merrill analysts wrote in e-mails that Excite@Home was a "piece of sh––!" Result: Investors who trusted Merrill lost up to 99.9 percent of their money when Excite@Home went under.

For 24/7 Media, "accumulate!" was also the official Merrill Lynch advice. Merrill's internal comments, as revealed by Spitzer, were that "24/7 Media is a "piece of shi––." Result: Investors who relied on Merrill's advice lost 97.6 percent of their money when 24/7 Media crashed.

Why did they do this? Because Merrill Lynch was raking in hundreds of millions of dollars in revenues from the very companies it urged investors to buy. Because its research analysts were rewarded with millions for peddling companies they knew were junk. And, perhaps equally important, because of the severe consequences that almost inevitably struck those who disagreed publicly with the company's opinion.

Merrill Lynch's relationship with Enron was a classic example. In April 1998, two Merrill executives fired off a memo to the firm's president, complaining bitterly about a Merrill analyst who was not a team player. They said that this analyst had made the grave error of giving Enron a "lukewarm" rating and that Enron had developed a "visceral" dislike for the analyst. They concluded that,

Table 3.1 New York Attorney General's Summary of Merrill Lynch e-Mails and Ratings

Company	Date	Contemporaneous Analyst Comments	Published Rating
Aether System (AETH)	03/15/01	"Might have announcement next week . . . which could pop stock . . . but fundamentals horrible" (ML82578)	3–1 (Neutral)
Excite @home (ATHM)	12/27/99 12/29/99	"We are neutral on the stock" Six months outlook is "flat," without any "real catalysts" for improvement seen (ML 37899; ML37956)	2–1 (Accumulate)
Excite @home (ATHM)	06/03/00	"Such a piece of crap" (ML51453)	2–1 (Accumulate)
GoTo.Com (GOTO)	1/11/01	Nothing interesting about company "except banking fees" (ML03806)	3–1 (Neutral)
InfoSpace (INSP)	7/13/00	"This stock is a powder keg, given how aggressive we were on it earlier this year and given the 'bad smell' comments that so many institutions are bringing up" (ML06413)	1–1 (Buy)

Company	Date	Comment	Published Rating
InfoSpace (INSP)	10/20/00	"Piece of junk" (ML06578)	1–1 (Buy)
Internet Capital Group Inc. (ICGE)	10/05/00	"Going to 5" (closed at $12.38) (ML63901)	2–1 (Accumulate)
Internet Capital Group Inc. (ICGE)	10/06/00	"No hopeful news to relate. . . . We see nothing that will turn this around near-term. The company needs to restructure its operations and raise additional cash, and until it does that, there is nothing positive to say." (ML64077)	2–1 (Accumulate)
Lifeminders (LFMN)	12/04/00	"POS" (piece of shit) (ML60903)	2–1 (Accumulate)
24/7 Media (TFSM)	10/10/00	"Piece of shit" (ML64372)	2–2 (Accumulate)

While Merrill Lynch analysts touted these Internet stocks to the public with their widely respected ratings, these same analysts privately disparaged the stocks in e-mails containing the comments you see in this table. In the column "Published Rating" is a two-digit rating code for each stock. The first digit represents the primary rating, as follows: 1 = buy; 2 = accumulate; 3 = neutral; 4 = reduce; 5 = sell. None of the stocks rated by this group received a reduce or sell rating, which represented an "outrageous betrayal of trust," according to New York State General Elliot Spitzer.

Note: The words in brackets were added by the author.
Source: www.oag.state.ny.us/press/2002/apr/MerrilL.pdf.

as a result, Merrill Lynch had lost lucrative investment banking business with Enron. Sure enough, by the summer Merrill had replaced the uncooperative analyst with an analyst who promptly upgraded Enron's rating to a buy. Lo and behold, by early 1999 Enron had rewarded Merrill with a banking deal that netted the firm $45 million in fees.

Merrill Lynch's defenders claimed that Enron was an isolated case and that the analysts who wrote the venomous e-mails uncovered by Mr. Spitzer were just "a few bad apples." But these claims were not true. These companies were just a few of the dozens that Merrill touted. They were able to raise billions of dollars from investors as their stocks soared. Merrill's investment banking division piled up more than $115 million in fees for 52 investment banking transactions awarded them by the very same companies they were hyping. And analysts who issued the phony buy ratings cleaned up too—with huge bonuses tied to sales. Meanwhile, trusting investors got taken to the cleaners.

Wall Street's defenders would say that Merrill Lynch was the worst case, that other firms were not nearly as bad. But, alas, that claim is also false. Attorney General Spitzer himself warned that as despicable as Merrill's actions were, *other big brokers committed far worse financial atrocities.*

Indeed, new investigations of Salomon Smith Barney make Merrill's shenanigans appear tame by comparison. From 1997 to 2002, Salomon Smith Barney, a unit of Citigroup, collected a mind-boggling $809 million in underwriting stocks and bond offerings for telecommunications companies, plus another $178 million providing merger advice. That's close to $1 billion in fees—more than any other broker on Wall Street.

At the same time, Salomon and its telecom superstar Jack Grubman were showering Wall Street with glowing recommendations on the very companies that were the source of this billion-dollar windfall: AT&T, Verizon, WorldCom, Global Crossing, Level 3 Communications, Qwest Communications, and others. Predictably, investors who trusted Salomon were beaten to a pulp—mugged for 77.8 percent of their money on AT&T, 92.6 percent on Qwest, 99 percent on WorldCom, 97 percent on Level 3 Communications, and a staggering 99.9 percent on Global Crossing. In all, 14 of the telecoms that Grubman and Salomon pushed off on investors defaulted on their debt or filed for Chapter 11 bank-ruptcy protection.

Everywhere one looked on Wall Street, the same pattern was apparent. UBS Warburg's Joseph Wolf recommended Optical Communications Products as a buy 10 times from November 2000 to July 2002, as the stock cratered from $18.88 to just $1.19 per share. Linda Mutschler of Merrill Lynch issued her buy rating on Sprint PCS in July 2001, with the stock at $24.80; then she actually raised her rating to a strong buy at the start of 2002, just before the stock crashed more than 50 percent. James Parmelee, Credit Suisse First Boston's analyst, gave Corvis Corporation (one of his firm's underwriting clients) 11 separate strong-buy ratings from November 2000 to October 2001 as its price slumped from $26.69 to $1.77, shedding 93.4 percent of its value in just under a year.

It was the greatest con of all time. Even the Mafia must have been green with envy.

CHAPTER 4

THE BUBBLE BURSTS

Some investors would later discover how to turn the tables on Wall Street to take back the money that virtually was stolen out of their portfolios. But before they learned that, their primary focus would be sweet justice.

Quietly at first but with a growing crescendo as more scandals made headlines, investors began to protest. "These scumbags are getting away with murder!" they exclaimed. "Where the heck is the SEC? Where the hell is the FBI? Someone do something!"

Eventually, the authorities did catch up with some scoundrels of corporate America and Wall Street. They tightened up a few accounting rules here and there. They set new guidelines for research analysts. They even hauled a few people off in handcuffs. John Rigas and his sons Timothy and Michael, the executives of Adelphia Communications, were marched off on July 24, 2002. WorldCom's former CFO Scott Sullivan and former controller David Myers, as well as Tyco's former CEO Dennis Kozlowski, all met a similar fate. Investors cheered with glee.

Unfortunately, for the victims, these government actions were invariably too little, too late. Wronged investors had lost trillions of dollars, and nothing the authorities did would make them feel whole again.

For Wall Street firms, however, it was *too much, too soon*. Investment banking fees for initial public offerings had already plunged from $51.5 billion in 2000 to $8.4 billion in the first quarter of 2002, an 84 percent decline. Merrill Lynch's profits tumbled 85 percent in 2001. Profits also plunged at Morgan Stanley, Lehman Brothers, and Goldman Sachs. Now, just when they needed the revenues the most, regulators and the public were attacking the essence of their marketing strategies—hype and distorted research.

For many of America's largest companies, it was even worse. They still had puffed-up assets on their books, large debts hidden away in foreign subsidiaries, and too many losses covered up by the projected paper profits in their employee pension funds. Now, as the rules began to change, they got caught out on a limb. Indeed, the very slack these companies had taken advantage of in the 1990s became the noose that hanged them in the early 2000s. The events that ensued at UCBS were typical.

THE RETURN OF THE AUDITORS

Many months after his first meeting with the consultants, the chief executive officer of UCBS attended a similar meeting with a similar group of people, also from the same accounting firm.

"We're the auditors—not the consultants," announced one man with a subtle hint of foreboding. "We'd like to raise some questions about a few of UCBS's accounting practices."

Paul Johnston promptly raised his hand in protest. "Wait! I know all about those. They're all perfectly legal."

The auditors sneaked furtive glances at each other, and then one responded: "On the surface, maybe. In reality, no. Take all these partnerships and other subsidiaries, for example."

"Don't give me any flack on those," Johnston countered. "Other major companies I know about have hundreds of off-the-books corporations and subsidiaries in the Cayman Islands, Bermuda—you name it. What we have is petty by comparison. Besides, we own less than 49 percent of every single one of 'em. That's the reason I gave this whole thing my blessing in the first place. That's the rule, isn't it?"

"Yes, but that's only one part of the rule. The rule also states that if you have effective management *control* of the subsidiary, it doesn't matter how little you own. Even if you own just 1 percent, you have to consolidate. The other companies you talked about—Tyco, Enron, etc.—had big teams of lawyers working overtime to create a legal facade that proves noncontrol. You don't even have that facade."

THE PENSION SCAM UNRAVELS

The auditors passed around copies of a large spreadsheet that looked eerily familiar: It was the UCBS employee pension plan. The CEO took a deep breath. He knew what was coming. He had personally feared this all along, and now his worst fears would be confirmed.

"I don't have to tell you," said one of the auditors, "that the great stock market rise of the late 1990s created an unprecedented pot of gold for UCBS, and you tapped into it like never before. Now, the great stock market decline of the early 2000s has transformed your gold into lead, and it's a dead weight that could sink this company's earnings for years to come.

"In 2000," he continued, "the market plunged, driving your pension fund assets into the hole, and we ignored it. The market plunged again in 2001, and we still ignored it. Now, as the market has continued to fall, we just cannot ignore it anymore. We have to start admitting these shortfalls. Yes, we can try to stretch it out over time, but if the market falls further . . ." His voice trailed off, hinting of dire consequences.

Johnston could think of only one defense: that UCBS was just one of hundreds of companies that the stock market decline was impacting in the in same way. He also thought that maybe—just maybe—investors would not single out UCBS for sale. So for the next half hour the discussion turned to the broader pension fund crisis nationwide.

Among 500 U.S. companies surveyed by consulting firm Watson Wyatt, 87 percent said their pension funds were fully funded in early 2000. By early 2002, the number had fallen to 37 percent—

and that was *before* the S&P 500 Index fell by another 20 percent that year. The total shortfall, just among 234 companies in the S&P 500 that had defined benefit plans, was a whopping $78 billion. But even this large number was based on very optimistic assumptions about the markets and the economy.

General Motors, for example, had a net surplus in its pension fund of $4.5 billion in 1999, but flipped to a net deficit of $12.6 billion at year-end 2001. Ford went from a surplus of $8.2 billion in 1999 to a deficit of $2.4 billion. Delta Airlines had a small surplus in its pension fund of $148 million in 1999, but by 2001, it posted a deficit of $2.3 billion.

Almost invariably, when companies calculated the future growth of their pension fund portfolios, they deliberately skewed the underlying assumptions in three ways:

- They typically assumed the stock market would recover in the next calendar year, even if there was no evidence of such a recovery.
- They assumed a steadily growing economy, even if there was a real possibility of another economic decline.
- They assumed high investment returns, even if actual current returns were far lower.

They lived in a dream world from which no one bothered to wake them. But when the paper gains disappeared in a cloud of smoke, there was hell to pay.

The sheer dimensions of the problem were mind-boggling: Two-thirds of the S&P 500 companies reporting pension data were in the red. Of those companies, 13 owed their employees' pension funds more than $1 billion each—General Motors ($12.7 billion), Exxon ($7.2 billion), Ford ($2.5 billion), Delphi ($2.4 billion), Delta Airlines ($2.4 billion), United Technologies ($2.3 billion), AMR ($1.9 billion), Pfizer ($1.3 billion), and Procter & Gamble ($1.1 billion); 4 owed $1 billion each—Chevron Texaco, Pharmacia, Goodyear, and Raytheon; and 32 owed more than a half billion each. More than 100 companies were short by $100 million or more. (See Table 4.1.)

Table 4.1 Many of America's Largest Corporations Owe a Fortune to Their Pension Funds

(millions of dollars, 12/31/01)

Company Name	Symbol	Pension Plan Assets	Pension Plan Obligations	Underfunded Amount
3M Co.	MMM	$8,008	$8,998	$990
Abbott Laboratories	ABT	$2,644	$3,241	$597
Air Products & Chemicals Inc.	APD	$1,091	$1,476	$385
Allstate Corp.	ALL	$2,532	$3,225	$693
American International Group	AIG	$2,385	$2,787	$402
AMR Corp./De	AMR	$5,482	$7,422	$1,940
Bristol Myers Squibb	BMY	$3,508	$3,914	$406
ChevrontexaCo. Corp.	CVX	$5,947	$7,028	$1,081
Cigna Corp.	CI	$2,500	$2,932	$432
CMS Energy Corp.	CMS	$845	$1,268	$423
Coca-Cola Co.	KO	$1,492	$1,906	$414
ConoCo Inc.	COC	$1,185	$1,715	$530
Cummins Inc.	CUM	$1,684	$2,064	$380
Deere & Co.	DE	$5,951	$6,440	$489
Delphi Corp.	DPH	$6,077	$8,444	$2,367
Delta Air Lines Inc.	DAL	$8,304	$10,657	$2,353

Table 4.1 *(Continued)*

Company Name	Symbol	Pension Plan Assets	Pension Plan Obligations	Underfunded Amount
du Pont (E.I.) de Nemours & Co.	DD	$17,923	$18,769	$846
Eastman Chemical Co.	EMN	$697	$1,062	$365
Exelon Corp.	EXC	$6,279	$7,101	$822
Exxon Mobil Corp.	XOM	$12,170	$19,419	$7,249
Fedex Corp.	FDX	$5,510	$6,227	$717
Ford Motor Co.	F	$48,754	$51,214	$2,460
General Motors Corp.	GM	$73,662	$86,333	$12,671
Goodyear Tire & Rubber Co.	GT	$4,176	$5,215	$1,039
Hartford Financial Services Group Inc.	HIG	$1,711	$2,108	$397
Hewlett-Packard Co.	HPQ	$2,409	$3,255	$846
ITT Industries Inc.	ITT	$3,234	$3,617	$384
Johnson & Johnson	JNJ	$4,355	$5,026	$671
Lilly (Eli) & Co.	LLY	$3,182	$3,599	$417
Maytag Corp.	MYG	$881	$1,334	$453
Merck & Co.	MRK	$2,865	$3,612	$747

(continued)

Table 4.1 *(Continued)*

Company Name	Symbol	Pension Plan Assets	Pension Plan Obligations	Underfunded Amount
Morgan Stanley	MWD	$1,057	$1,457	$400
Motorola Inc.	MOT	$3,131	$3,578	$447
Navistar Internationl	NAV	$2,872	$3,384	$512
PepsiCo Inc.	PEP	$3,129	$3,556	$427
Pfizer Inc.	PFE	$5,648	$6,956	$1,308
Pharmacia Corp.	PHA	$2,887	$3,950	$1,063
Philip Morris Cos. Inc.	MO	$11,720	$12,222	$502
Phillips Petroleum Co.	P	$1,113	$1,849	$736
Procter & Gamble Co.	PG	$1,432	$2,567	$1,135
Public Service Entrprises	PEG	$2,228	$2,676	$448
Raytheon Co.	RTN	$10,164	$11,171	$1,007
Sears Roebuck & Co.	S	$2,349	$3,091	$742
Texas Instruments Inc.	TXN	$1,089	$1,771	$682
Tyco International Ltd.	TYC	$2,690	$3,589	$899
Union Pacific Corp.	UNP	$1,931	$2,321	$390

Table 4.1 *(Continued)*

Company Name	Symbol	Pension Plan Assets	Pension Plan Obligations	Underfunded Amount
United Technologies Corp.	UTX	$10,025	$12,354	$2,329
Viacom Inc-Cl B	VIA.B	$4,566	$5,100	$534
Wyeth	WYE	$2,739	$3,316	$577
Xerox Corp.	XRX	$7,040	$7,606	$566

When the stock market was booming, many large companies found various ways to exaggerate their earnings by manipulating the excesses in their employees' pension funds. As the stock market declined, however, this strategy backfired: By year-end 2001, they had large deficits in their pension funds, threatening to greatly reduce corporate earnings, and by 2002, the deficits had grown even larger.

Data: Companies' 10k filings.

HOW THE AUDITORS JOINED THE COVER-UP

Johnston's meeting with the auditors ended in acrimony. They wanted the company to come clean and start making massive adjustments to earnings immediately. He wanted to postpone the day of reckoning. He fully understood all their arguments and even agreed with most of them. But he wasn't quite ready to face what would surely be a financial burning at the stake.

He rushed back to his desk while his secretary put through an urgent phone call to a senior partner at the accounting firm. "First your consultants tell us what to do, how to do it, and why it's all perfectly within our legal rights," Johnston barked at the partner with venom. "Then, months later, your auditors come back and tell us that everything your consultants told us to do was wrong. Well, now it's *my* turn to tell *you* something: Either you tell your little team of bean counters to back off . . . either you okay our books as is or you can kiss all your fat consulting fees good-bye."

And so it was that even *after* UCBS's auditors uncovered serious accounting problems, the only action they took was to quietly write a little memo to the file. In the memo, they blamed management for past accounting gimmicks and raised issues about questionable practices still in place. They filed the memo away in its proper place, and it never again saw the light of day.

Meanwhile, in their official statement to shareholders, the auditors took a very different tack. They gave UCBS a clean bill of health, and they certified that its financial statements presented the results "fairly, in all material respects." They said nothing about their real concerns.

Did they have a duty to correct the problems or to alert the public? Yes, but this didn't seem to concern them. Could they be accused of serious violations of the public trust, even fraud? Yes, but this, too, did not seem to bother them. The auditors simply bowed their heads and joined the cover-up.

A real example: Waste Management executives were named in a major SEC lawsuit for accounting tricks that let the company hide about $1.7 billion in expenses from 1992 to 1997 while two top executives took $28.4 million in compensation. Its auditors, at Arthur Andersen, complained quietly at the time. But when their objections were ignored by management, they approved the company's financial statements nevertheless.

AUDITORS FAIL TO WARN ABOUT ACCOUNTING TROUBLES IN NEARLY ALL MAJOR CASES

Adelphia Communications, the cable television giant, disclosed early in 2002 that it had an extra $2.3 billion in debt that it never included on its balance sheet. Investors watched helplessly as their shares plunged from $25 on March 11 to just $11.83 on April 2, wiping out more than half of their wealth in three weeks. Only a year before the disclosure, the auditors, at Deloitte & Touche, gave the company a clean bill of health. On June 25, Adelphia filed for Chapter 11, wiping out 100 percent of investor wealth.

Xerox announced in mid-2002 that it would have to restate $2 billion in earnings dating back to 1997. It agreed to pay the SEC a

$10 million fine, the largest of its kind in history. Just 13 months earlier, its auditors, at KPMG, had also given it a clean bill of health.

Enron, WorldCom, and at least 29 other corporations involved in accounting irregularities had gotten a clean bill of health from their auditors not long before their accounting problems were revealed. These companies were not small fly-by-nights; they were large, household-name companies with a combined peak market value of 1.8 *trillion* dollars. (See Table 4.2.)

However, even the list shown in Table 4.2 represents just the tip of the iceberg. It does not include companies that managed to hide their manipulations, nor does it include thousands of companies that cooked their books "legally."

The accounting disease was clearly not limited just to the high-profile cases that most people heard about such as Enron or World-Com. It had become a national epidemic that pervaded nearly every aspect of corporate America.

Nor was it limited just to Arthur Andersen, the first accounting firm ever to be convicted of fraud. Quite the contrary, *approving questionable accounting was standard operating procedure at every one of the Big Five accounting firms in America.* That included not only Arthur Andersen, but also Deloitte & Touche, Ernst & Young, KPMG, and PricewaterhouseCoopers. Every single one was responsible for the audits of major companies involved in accounting irregularities. (See Table 4.3.)

Naturally, had the accounting irregularities been minor, the auditors would not have been responsible for overlooking the problems. However, in many cases the discrepancies were so large that subsequent adjustments gutted the companies' earnings and devastated the share prices. So it defies the imagination to believe that the very people charged with the job of thoroughly inspecting a company's books could have been kept in the dark about issues that soon loomed so large.

THE GOVERNMENT'S "SOLUTIONS": A PATCHWORK OF COSMETIC FIXES

Throughout the late 1990s, former SEC Chairman Arthur Levitt tried to fix this problem. He urged Congress to force a clean break

Table 4.2   Companies Involved with Allegations or News of Accounting Irregularities

Company Name	Auditing Firm	Has the Company Filed for Chapter 11?	Did Auditor Issue a "Going Concern" Warning?
Adelphia Communications	DT	Yes	No
Applied Digital Solutions Inc	PWC	No	Yes
CMS Energy	AA	No	No
Computer Associates	KPMG	No	No
Dollar General	EY	No	No
Dynegy Corporation	AA	No	No
Enron	AA	Yes	No
Gerber Scientific	KPMG	No	No
Global Crossing	AA	Yes	No
Great Atlantic & Pacific Tea Company	DT	No	No
Halliburton	AA	No	No
Hub Group	AA	No	No
Kmart	PWC	Yes	Yes
Lucent Technologies	PWC	No	No
Merck	AA	No	No
Metromedia Fiber Network	EY	Yes	No

Table 4.2 *(Continued)*

Company Name	Auditing Firm	Has the Company Filed for Chapter 11?	Did Auditor Issue a "Going Concern" Warning?
Microsoft	DT	No	No
MicroStrategy	PWC	No	No
Nesco Inc	Tullis Taylor	Yes	No
Network Associates	PWC	No	No
Peregrine Systems	AA	No	No
PNC Financial	EY	No	No
Qualcomm Inc	PWC	No	No
Qwest Communications	AA	No	No
Rayovac Corp	KPMG	No	No
Reliant Resources	DT	No	No
Rite Aid	DT	No	No
Supervalu	KPMG	No	No
Trump Hotels & Casinos	AA	No	No
Tyco International	PWC	No	No
Williams Companies	EY	No	No
WorldCom	AA	No	No
Xerox	KPMG	No	No

AA = Arthur Andersen; DT = Deloitte & Touche; EY = Ernst & Young; PWC = PricewaterhouseCoopers.

Table 4.3 All Big Five Accounting Firms Audited Many Large Companies with Accounting Irregularities

Auditing Firm	Companies with Accounting Irregularities (no. of cos.)	(%)	Peak Market Capitalization (mil. of $)	(%)
Arthur Andersen	11	33.3	$623,296	34.4
Deloitte & Touche	5	15.2	$629,508	34.7
Ernst & Young	4	12.1	$37,379	2.1
KPMG	5	15.2	$85,114	4.7
PricewaterhouseCoopers	7	21.2	$437,845	24.1
Tullis Taylor	1	3.0	$52	0.0
Total	**33**	**100.0**	**1,813,193**	**100.0**

In 2002, there were at least 33 public companies involved in or cited for significant accounting irregularities. With just one exception, each of these companies was audited by one of the Big Five auditing firms, and every one of the Big Five was involved in the audits of several of the firms with irregularities. This raised very serious questions about the integrity of all five firms. At their peak, the audited companies were worth a total of more than $1.8 trillion.
Data: Companies' 10K filings.

between the consulting business and the auditing business, but Congress pooh-poohed his concerns and shot down his proposals.

Finally, in 2002, Congress passed the Public Company Accounting Reform and Investor Protection Act, making it more difficult for companies to cook their books. The new law was a step in the right direction but far from a real fix. It did not force a complete separation between the auditing and consulting business—a key source of the problem. It did not remove the richest incentive for CEOs to cheat—stock options. It did not remove the deep and widespread conflicts of interests on Wall Street. It did not even address one of the largest accounting problems of all—manipulations of employee pension funds.

Meanwhile, the SEC also tried to resolve the nation's accounting troubles by requiring the CEOs of hundreds of large companies to personally certify that their financial statements were true and accurate. It was a nice gesture, but it missed the primary target: supposedly "legal" manipulations.

CHAPTER 5

THE $17,000 TOILET KIT

It was long past 2 A.M., but Paul E. Johnston, the CEO of UCBS, couldn't sleep.

It wasn't so much the nagging guilt associated with his company's aggressive accounting. He had learned to deal with that months ago. Nor was it the growing fear that the firm would soon run out of cash to pay bills coming due. He could handle that too.

What gnawed at his insides were the echoes of his daughter's voice from a phone conversation of a few hours earlier. "Are the rumors true?" she had asked as matter-of-factly as she could. "What's really going on?" she wondered out loud. When he began to answer, however, she cut him off, refusing to hear any insider information.

She also revealed that she had bought some UCBS shares. She did not say how many and tried to give the impression that it was "no big deal," but Johnston could sense that it was more. To his dismay, for the first time in many years he found himself doing something he had vowed to avoid: He was talking to an outside shareholder one-on-one, and it was none other than his own daughter.

In the days that followed, Johnston's sleepless nights got worse. He could imagine her seated in the front row at the annual shareholders' meeting, waiting anxiously for him to give his speech. Or he could see her facing him over dinner while her husband eyed him critically.

So he'd stay up late, watching CNN and other news channels. One night his next set of horrors began. One by one, right there on the headline news, his former friends or rivals were being marched off in handcuffs. He scurried to scan the headlines on *New York Times Online:*

> **WORLDCOM SAYS IT HID EXPENSES, INFLATING CASH FLOW $3.8 BILLION** (Andrew Ross Sorkin, *New York Times,* June 26, 2002). WorldCom, the nation's second-largest long-distance carrier, said last night that it had overstated its cash flow by more than $3.8 billion during the last five quarters in what appears to be one of the largest cases of false corporate bookkeeping yet. WorldCom, which had a peak value of $115.3 billion in June 1999 when its shares reached a high of $62, is now worth less than $1 billion. Its stock, which had already been down more than 94 percent for the year before last night's disclosure, plunged as low as 26 cents in after-hours trading last night. The S.E.C. said in a statement released early today that the disclosures confirmed "accounting improprieties of unprecedented magnitude."

Johnston shuddered again a few days later as he read a story by Barnaby J. Feder and David Leonhardt, also of the *Times.* The names of WorldCom's executives and board members were displayed in a prominent table. There they were in black and white, with all the data on the fortunes they had made selling the company's shares. Even while the stock was tumbling, they allegedly engineered the largest corporate fraud in the history of the world while continually urging the public to buy its sinking shares.

There was Bert C. Roberts, chairman of the board, who sold his shares for $22.8 million . . . Scott D. Sullivan, chief financial officer, who got $44.2 million . . . James Quell Crowe, a former chairman, who walked off with $24.7 million . . . and Gerald H. Taylor, former CEO of MCI, who took $21.8 million. CEO John W. Sidgmore did even better, cashing out with $87.3 million, and Lawrence C.

Tucker, a board member, trumped them all, waltzing away with *$110.8 million!*

Soon, investors would also realize how WorldCom insiders got filthy rich while they suffered crushing losses. So they demanded to see the bums thrown into jail. They wanted blood.

2 EX-OFFICIALS AT WORLDCOM ARE CHARGED IN HUGE FRAUD (Kurt Eichenwald, *New York Times,* August 2, 2002). Two former executives of the telecommunications giant WorldCom were charged yesterday with carrying out a multi-billion-dollar accounting fraud that disguised mounting losses and ultimately helped drive it into bankruptcy.

The executives–Scott D. Sullivan, WorldCom's former chief financial officer, and David F. Myers, its former controller–surrendered at 7 A.M. yesterday at the F.B.I.'s field office in Lower Manhattan. They were later publicly escorted in handcuffs to the Federal District Court for a brief hearing. . . .

Night after night, after all his personal staff had gone home, Johnston would collapse into the leather sofa behind his office, grab his TV remote control, and flip the cable news channels nervously–CNN, Fox, MSNBC, and others. One after another, the images of still more acquaintances would appear on the screen–being hauled off by cops, firing angry epithets to reporters, dragged through the mud, doomed to a hellish life of shame.

There was David B. Duncan, the lead auditor of Enron at Arthur Andersen, charged with obstruction of justice, pleading guilty, the entire firm convicted . . . Scott D. Sullivan, former chief financial officer, and David F. Myers, former controller of WorldCom, both charged with securities fraud and conspiracy . . . and Samuel D. Waksal, former chief executive of ImClone Systems, charged with insider trading.

The reporters' words rang in Johnston's ears: "John J. Rigas, 78, the founder and former chief executive of Adelphia, and two of his sons were taken into custody by federal agents at 6 A.M. yesterday at their Manhattan apartment on the Upper East Side. . . ." [See Table 5.1.]

"Prosecutors contend they improperly used company money

Table 5.1 Senior Executives Investigated in 2001/2002

Executive	Allegations
Adelphia Communications Corporation	
John J. Rigas, Founder	Acctg. irregularities, fraudulent partnerships
Timothy Rigas, former CFO	Acctg. irregularities, fraudulent partnerships
Michael Rigas, former executive VP	Acctg. irregularities, fraudulent partnerships
James Brown, former VP	Acctg. irregularities, fraudulent partnerships
Michael Mulcahey, former VP, treasurer	Acctg. irregularities, fraudulent partnerships
Arthur Andersen LLP	
Joseph Berardino, former CEO	Obstruction of justice
David Duncan, Partner	Obstruction of justice
Nancy Temple, Counsel	Obstruction of justice
Dynegy Corp.	
Chuck Watson, former CEO	Acctg. irregularities with energy transactions
Enron Corp.	
Kenneth Lay, former CEO	Acctg. irregularities, fraudulent partnerships
Jeffrey Skilling, former CEO	Acctg. irregularities, fraudulent partnerships
Andrew Fastow, former CFO	Acctg. irregularities, money laundering
Michael J. Kopper, former MD	Money laundering, conspiracy to commit wire fraud
ImClone Systems Inc.	
Dr. Samuel Waksal, former CEO	Insider trading
Martha Stewart Living Omnimedia	
Martha Stewart, Founder	Insider trading, obstruction of justice
Qwest Communications International, Inc.	
Joseph P. Nacchio, former CEO	Acctg. irregularities
Tyco International Ltd.	
L. Dennis Kozlowski, former CEO	Tax evasion, corporate theft, record falsifications
Mark Swartz, former CFO	Corporate theft, record falsifications
Mark Belnick, former Counsel	Records falsification
WorldCom, Inc.	
Bernard Ebbers, former CEO	Acctg. irregularities, securities fraud
Scott D. Sullivan, former CFO	Acctg. irregularities, securities fraud
David Myers, former controller	Acctg. irregularities, securities fraud
Buford Yates, former Acctg. director	Securities fraud
Betty Vinson, executive	Securities fraud
Troy Norman, executive	Securities fraud

In response to rampant corporate crime, authorities charged or investigated these CEOs of major American corporations. However, these represent only a small fraction of those who stole from the American public by using accounting gimmicks that were defined as "perfectly legal."

for everything from personal loans to buy stock, to building a $13 million golf course, to shuttling family members back and forth from a safari vacation in Africa and . . ."

"The sight of top executives facing criminal charges, once rare, has become almost common in recent months. . . ."

"Samuel D. Waksal, former chief executive of the biotechnology company ImClone Systems, was arrested at his Manhattan home and charged with insider stock trading today. . . ."

"Spitzer sues five telecom executives for ill-gotten personal gains—former WorldCom CEO Bernard J. Ebbers, former McLeod-USA CEO Clark E. McLeod, former Qwest chairman Philip F. Anschutz, former Qwest CEO Joseph P. N. Nacchio, plus the founder and chairman of Metromedia Fiber Networks, Stephen A. Garofalo. . . ."

"L. Dennis Kozlowski, former chairman and chief executive of the conglomerate Tyco International, has been indicted . . ."

Johnston suffered another blow when, at 4 A.M. on September 18, 2002, he went to *New York Times Online* and read the following story:

TYCO DETAILS LAVISH LIVES OF EXECUTIVES.
Tyco International, whose former top executives had been indicted on charges of looting the company, said yesterday that it had uncovered a web of deception and personal enrichment that had spread throughout its management ranks.

The Tyco report showed that its former CEO, L. Dennis Kozlowski, had systematically created a corporate culture of greed and excess, secretly authorizing the forgiveness of tens of millions of dollars in loans to dozens of executives. Kozlowski had bypassed his board of directors and, without their approval, gave 51 Tyco managers $56 million in bonuses *plus* $39 million more to pay the taxes on the bonuses. This money, in turn, was clearly destined to wipe out the loans that the company had made to them.

Tyco's dirty laundry seemed to pour out onto Johnston's lap. Right there in the *New York Times*—and paraded before millions of Americans on TV—was a long list of personal items that the CEO bought with the money that investors had entrusted to the company:

- Fee to Germán Frers, a yacht maker–$72,000
- Traveling toilet kit–$17,000
- Dog umbrella stand–$15,000
- Sewing basket–$6,300
- Shower curtain–$6,000
- Two sets of sheets–$5,960
- Gilt metal wastebasket–$1,650

A $1,650 wastebasket! A $17,000 toilet kit! All bought with shareholder funds! He could not bear one more headline or flash news report. He was sick to his stomach.

His stomachache was caused, in part, by fear. He could vividly see his own company—already slammed by the stock market—getting blasted in the headlines, and he could visualize his own face displayed on CNN like a mug shot. At the same time, however, his nausea was driven by a sense of pride. He never did take most of the lavish executive compensation package that had been proposed by the consultants and approved by the board of directors. He never once went beyond the legal parameters that were outlined to him by expert advisors.

Nevertheless, he felt guilty and vulnerable. He regretted having jury-rigged the pension fund numbers. He wished he had never pressured the auditors to overlook their concerns. If he could just go back in time by a few years, he would strike out on an independent path, even if that meant near-term corporate and personal sacrifices and even if it resulted in less capital raised, lower prices for the company's shares, disappointed employees, and reduced gains for shareholders. The long-term benefits of sanity, control, and self-respect would have made all of those issues look petty by comparison.

The final blow came when he found out, through his wife, that his daughter Linda and her husband had fallen on hard times. They had invested $80,000 in UCBS stock and already lost 75 percent of their money, even *before* any more bad news came out. They had invested *another* $80,000 in a supposedly "diversified" portfolio of telecom stocks, including Global Crossing, Qwest, and WorldCom, with even more severe losses.

"Except for the house, Linda and Gabriel are virtually broke," his wife said, with a sour overtone that Johnston interpreted as a subtle accusation of complicity. "As usual," she added, "they're refusing financial help. Maybe they'll take the bare minimum for a college fund for the children. But not a penny more."

Johnston broke down.

In the days and weeks that followed, the CEO of UCBS suffered through each and every one of the phases of a reforming alcoholic: A long struggle with denial, an even longer struggle to admit his own fault in ruining the financial lives of thousands of investors, and, finally, the most difficult step of all—gaining the peace of mind and courage to convert those emotions into meaningful action.

With a shaky hand at first, then with growing resolve, he sketched out a timeline to start the process of exorcising the demons that haunted him. He would make changes—drastic changes, not just cosmetic changes which the PR flacks could paste into press releases or plaster onto *Business Wire*. They'd be fundamental—in corporate structure, in strategies, and in culture.

He observed executives like Warren E. Buffett, who had long ago eliminated options from executive compensation packages. In New York City, he attended a meeting of the Commission on Public Trust and Private Enterprise. He sat in the back row as Buffett, former Fed Chairman Paul Volcker, and others proposed sweeping reforms for corporate America—proper disclosure of executive stock sales, uniform treatment of stock options as expenses, shareholder approval before stock options are repriced, longer mandatory hold periods before executives can sell their own shares, and more.

He wanted desperately to join these business leaders, to be identified by the media and the public as a leader in corporate reform. Even more desperately, he wanted to avoid seeing his name in those damning headlines. As it turned out, it was *not* too late for Johnston to save his reputation. It *was* too late, however, to save UCBS.

DEBTS AND DEFLATION

UCBS problems were not limited strictly to accounting issues. Otherwise, the company would have made the adjustments, the shareholders would have driven the stock down by another 30 or 40 percent, and the crisis would have passed. But accounting issues were just the tip of the iceberg.

The primary problem was that UCBS was caught in a vise between *debts coming due* and *deflation*–falling prices for their primary products.

Had it been just the debts, maybe the company could have survived anyhow. It would have paid off the debts with the cash flow from revenues. Plus, the company would have borrowed from Peter to pay Paul.

Had it been just the deflation–the falling sales and falling prices–UCBS might have been able to get by as well. It would have eliminated tens of thousands of jobs, sold off hundreds of subsidiaries and joint ventures, and even shrunk back to the small, one-plant manufacturing company where it all began.

But no. The two forces–debts and deflation–collided in one time and place. UCBS had close to $1 billion in accounts payable and commercial paper (short-term corporate IOUs) coming due before year-end. At the same time, the revenues it hoped to use to cover those debts had disappeared.

Indeed, the three primary industries that impacted UCBS's largest divisions–PCs, telecom, and wireless–were all sinking like a rock.

Regarding the PC industry, Johnston read an Associated Press story on the Web about a Goldman Sachs survey. Goldman had surveyed 100 IT executives of Fortune 1000 companies, finding that more than half expected to *underspend* their already-slashed IT budgets. Only 8 percent were going to upgrade their companies' computers, and 44 percent were postponing computer upgrades until the following year. Johnston sent the article in an e-mail to his VP of sales and asked for his feedback.

"No wonder our PC sales are falling apart!" the VP said later that day over lunch. "Here, look at these global sales figure we're tracking! Look at this chart–down nonstop for five quarters in a row! Damn. Every time we think the PC market is about to hit bottom, it sinks again. No one wants to upgrade anymore. I can't blame 'em. My own computer is already at least 10 times faster than I need it to be. What am I going to do with a computer that's *another* ten times faster than that? I need it like a hole in the head."

Johnston, again playing dumb, sought to strike an upbeat note. "You're too negative. Look at the positive side. Look at . . ."

The VP of sales shrugged and laughed nervously. "Hah! You

think *I'm* negative. I'm going to quote Brian Gammage—the guy's an analyst for Gartner Dataquest. Here's what he says: 'This is the worsening of a worsening result, the worst since the third quarter of last year, which was the nadir of a bad year.' Tell me: Doesn't that sound like he's sitting right here in our PC division, talking about our business?"

"Let's talk about our telecom division."

"Oh no. Please don't make me talk about the telecom division. Must I? OK, if you insist. The fact is, the telecom sales folks would gladly change places with the PC sales people. Sure, the PC business may be falling into a valley, but the telecom business is getting sucked into a giant black hole of debt, overexpansion, and even fraud. You already know about the megabankruptcies at Global Crossing, WorldCom, and soon, possibly, Qwest. But did you know that at least 82 telecom firms filed for bankruptcy between 2000 and 2002? Did you realize that so much of the telecom industry is on the verge of financial collapse that it could paralyze key segments of the U.S. economy?"

"That bad?"

"Worse!"

"What about our cellular equipment subsidiary?" queried the CEO still playing dumb.

"The cellular industry is on a collision course with a five-car pileup on the freeway. The people running our cell division thought they were smart, spending billions on rights to the so-called Third Generation airwaves. The rights may be worth something in a sci-fi movie or some future techno-era. But today, they're one of the greatest white elephants in the history of mankind. Our wireless subsidiary spent a fortune—almost a quarter billion just for a small piece of the pie. You want to hear how much other companies around the world spent on 3G rights? Yes? OK, here it goes: Telecoms in Europe alone—$260 billion; in the U.S.—$1 trillion. Total profits from these investments: zero. A big, fat, round *zero*."

The CEO had heard these figures before from various other sources. "That's why I encouraged them to focus back on ordinary low-speed cell phone business," he said.

"Good move! But sales are drying up there too. There are just too many manufacturers pouring out too many different models at cutthroat prices. There are too many service providers, too many overlapping networks, too many deals and bargains. It's a classic case of a massive, worldwide *glut!* That's why six of America's nationwide service providers cut capital spending by more than 20 percent in the first quarter of 2002! That's why Nokia and Ericsson are floundering. That's why I've been telling you to dump that subsidiary before it's too late."

Johnston stared, stone-faced, at the VP for a few long seconds. He wasn't sure whether he should confess his innermost fears about the company, as he might with a shrink, or try to put up a solid defense, as he might when talking to Wall Street analysts. He decided to try a mix of the two. "Look, I admit we've made serious mistakes in the high-tech areas. I admit we didn't stop and ask even the most basic questions: Does this company make money? Does this company have real, tangible assets? But that was part of the euphoria. Did we get caught up in it too? Yes, of course. Fortunately, however, we're a broadly diversified company and . . ."

The VP interrupted, shaking his head. "I have just one question," he said.

"Go ahead," replied Johnston.

"They say the recession last year was short and mild, right?"

"Yes."

"They say we're in a recovery now, right?"

"Right."

"Well, if we're running into so much trouble—if almost everyone in our industry is running into so much trouble all over the world, even during a recovery—then can you tell me what is going to happen to us if we fall back into just an average recession? Can you tell me what is going to befall us if, God forbid, we get a severe or long recession?"

The meeting ended, and Johnston was not sure what to do next. He felt like an alcoholic trying to find the right moment to go to an AA meeting. But he finally took the first step.

He called the auditors, apologizing—to no one in particular—for any disdain he had expressed or implied in the previous meeting for the auditing process. Plus, he did something that he had never done before: He called in consultants and auditors to the same meeting at the same time. With everyone assembled, he requested a sweeping internal study of every possible accounting gray area:

executive pay and options, the subsidiaries, the pension funds, the derivatives.

Once the report came back, he called a new press conference with Wall Street research analysts—this time open to the public, as required by new SEC regulations.

Later, commenting on a CNBC talk show, one analyst described the conference this way: "I felt like a priest sitting in a confessional, hearing a long litany of corporate sins. Item by item, piece by piece, the CEO told us what they had done wrong. Then he told us how they were going to fix it. Did it shock the market? Of course. No one had any inkling that UCBS was that far into the accounting gimmicks. Did the stock plunge? Of course. But it cleared the air. If investors can survive today's conference, they can survive anything. As to the company's own financial survival, though, that's another matter. No one knows."

Johnston's second step: to clean house. He finalized his timeline to unravel the derivatives transactions, to sell off or consolidate the subsidiaries, and more.

His third step: to resign.

CHAPTER 6

SELL THESE STOCKS NOW!

lso resigning was Tamara Belmont. She quit Harris & Jones and began searching for new opportunities. She had eight years' experience as a Wall Street research economist. Before that, she spent four years as an assistant professor at Columbia, teaching microeconomics. She loved pure research. She would find some way of getting back into the academic or research world, making up for the lower salary with publishing and speaking engagements.

Her first speaking invitation came from the Columbia School of Business. It was a small, intimate group of investors and staff, all with an academic interest and most with a personal stake in the market as well. It was her opportunity to come out, to confess for the first time what she had been thinking for so many months. From a small desktop podium she said,

I come here today representing myself personally and the corporate world collectively. And I have come to tell you that *we lied!*

At Enron, at WorldCom, at Merrill Lynch, at Arthur Andersen: We lied to you.

Enron, the largest corporate failure in history! We lied about debts, profits, and subsidiaries. We lied to bankers, brokers. We lied to shareholders and employees. We lied to the SEC, the NASD, George Bush, and even to Bill Clinton. Pinocchio would be proud.

WorldCom, nearly triple the size of Enron! We lied to the tune of $9 billion, the biggest of all time.

At Merrill Lynch, the largest and most respected brokerage firm in the world, with over *10 million* customer accounts! We ran a veritable *lying machine.* We turned out a steady stream of falsified ratings to investors all over the world with great efficiency and dispatch.

At Arthur Andersen, one of the most respected accounting firms in the nation! We also lied to you. We have even been convicted in a court of law for obstruction of justice—for lying and attempting to cover up our lies.

But if you have come here today thinking that you have seen the worst of our lies, it's time to wake up and smell the coffee.

Besides Enron, at least 30 others have lied, and those are just the ones that have gotten caught so far. Moreover, for every Enron that committed a crime, there are hundreds more that made sure all of their accounting manipulations were completely within the letter of the law.

Besides Merrill Lynch, there are at least 46 other major Wall Street firms that have lied to you, mine included. These firms recommend the shares in companies right up to the day they filed for bankruptcy, despite blatantly obvious signs that these companies were going under.

Besides Arthur Andersen, there were four other major accounting firms that lied to you. Every single one had the same conflicts of interest, the same tug-of-war between their auditing divisions and their consulting divisions.

You've no doubt heard about many of our lies before. But do you realize how dangerous our lies can be? Do you know how much damage they can do to your family's financial future?

THE LAST PITCH

Linda and Gabriel Dedini certainly knew. They had lost almost all of their money in the stock market. They had already sold their summer home, and now they even talked about selling their primary residence.

That, however, was out of the question. There was no other good place to live. Their two children were still in primary school, and the school itself was just three blocks away.

Their discussion was reaching a heated crescendo when the phone rang. It was Dubois, their broker from Harris & Jones, calling with a new sales pitch for what he called a "great new investment opportunity."

He knew their portfolio was down, so he started on a different tack. He talked about how mortgages rates had fallen and how they could refinance, pull a big chunk of fresh cash out of the home equity, and make that cash work for them in the market. He said everyone was doing it—that is, everyone but the Dedinis. "The Dedinis are missing it!" he said, as if it were the gossip all over town. Sure, he admitted, the stock market had suffered some years, but that was all the more reason to jump back in now, to get in on the ground floor.

Linda listened politely and told him she'd get back to him within 24 hours. One hour later, she called back and fired him; four hours later, she was sitting in the Baltimore, Maryland, office of a financial planner recommended by a mutual friend.

THE ADVISER

She gave the adviser a thumbnail sketch of her financial history and asked for his opinion. Before proceeding, however, he gave her some information about his fees. He said that although the first consultation was free, there would be a charge of $75 per hour for any future consultations.

He made no money whatsoever from commissions. He did not sell insurance, mutual funds, or any other investment product. All he sold was his information and advice—nothing more. He had no incentive to put her in any investments except those that were the best for her. If she wanted to pay him a small percentage to manage her assets, that would be another alternative. The choice was hers.

"Amazingly," he said, "there are 40,000 financial planners registered in the state of Maryland, but there are only a few hundred that are *fee-only* financial planners. I'm one of them. If you don't want to work with me, I'll regret losing the business, but I can show you how to find other fee-only financial planners in the area. Or you can use a special kind of accountant that has specialized training in investments—a personal financial specialist. They also charge by the hour. But please, please, whatever you do, don't go back to anyone who is commission-driven. They are not advisers. They're strictly salespeople in disguise."

"How can I tell the difference?" she asked.

"It's actually quite simple. Everyone you deal with in the financial industry is either a salesperson or an adviser. It is impossible for anyone to be both at the same time. Salespeople will tell you that they are not charging you for the advice. They will tell you that it comes with the service or that it's covered by transaction fees or commissions. That's a dead giveaway."

"And advisers?"

"Totally different. Advisers tell you what fee they are going to charge you, then charge you the fee and tell you what they charged you. It couldn't be clearer."

She saw the wisdom in that but was still unsure. "Aren't there some time-tested, proven principles of investing that are true regardless of the fee structure, regardless of commissions and conflicts of interest? I teach physics. And no matter how I'm paid, it's not going to change the fact that e almost always equals mc squared."

"This is not about relativity, it's about history—yours, for example. You just told me you lost 75 percent on one stock and almost 100 percent on a few others. You told me that a Harris & Jones broker recommended them. Did you know that Harris was the lead underwriter of most of those stocks, that about 90 percent of their revenues were generated from those kinds of deals last year?"

Linda Dedini shook her head. She did not know. "But what about Dubois, the broker? I trusted him. Why did my broker . . . ?"

"Brokers are trained to be the ultimate selling machines. I happen to know a few at Harris. I have friends who work there. Did you know what they make and how they make it? Harris brokers who can place the most shares in those companies get fat six-figure bonuses. They win special contests. They're given three-week all-expense-paid vacations at Club Med. Your Harris broker never told you about that, did he?"

"I see. But it's not his fault the market went down."

"No, but look at all the ways he can hurt you. You paid high stock commissions for the 'service,' and those commissions came straight out of your pocket. You bought investments that were more likely than usual to be underperformers or outright losers. You wound up getting trapped in losing investments."

She still seemed uncertain, so the adviser tried a metaphor. "It's like walking into a ring with a professional wrestler," he said. "First, he socks it to you with commissions. Then, he dumps you into bad investments. And last, he pins you down on the mat and won't let you go. Moral of the story: Never act on so-called free advice."

"But what about the principle of long-term investing?" she asked. "You always make money in stocks over the long term. That's one the main principles I was alluding to earlier. Like the ever-expanding universe."

The adviser laughed heartily. "You know the universe, I know the stock market. Take the bear market of 1929 to '32, for example. If you invested in the average S&P 500 stock at the peak of the market in 1929, how many years do you think you would have waited to get back to breakeven?"

"You tell me."

"At least 25. I don't know your age, but I'm 62. If I had to wait that long, I'd be 87 before I could recoup. Maybe six feet under. Even though you're a lot younger, can you wait that long? Can your children wait that long before going to college? And how many years do you think it would take you to catch up with someone who invests in something that grows while the market falls . . . and then reapplies that money to buy nearer the bottom?"

"Fifty?"

"No, probably never! You would never catch up!"

"I see."

"Look. The whole theory that 'stocks always pay off in the long term' is chock full of holes. It assumes that you buy stocks near the beginning of a bull market when, in reality, only a smart minority get in at the beginning and usually only with small amounts. It assumes that you never buy stocks at the peak of the bull market when, in the real world, most of the money goes into the market near the peak. When did you buy most of your stocks? In the late 1990s, right? So did most people."

"I understand," she said. She knew all about false assumptions. She warned her lab students about them at the beginning of every semester.

"It also assumes," he continued, "that you actually bought 'the market'–all 30 stocks on the Dow, or all 500 stocks in the S&P–when, in reality, you did *not* buy the market. You bought UCBS, Global Crossing, WorldCom, and the others. You bought stocks that may never recover, companies that may cease to exist. So even when the overall market does go back up, you wouldn't be there to reap the rewards. The whole argument about the stock market always going up was totally irrelevant to your situation right from the beginning."

She was livid. She couldn't believe Dubois would deceive her so thoroughly, that so many Wall Street experts could be so deceptive. Did they do it on purpose? Were they themselves deceived by someone else, just like she was? It didn't matter. All that mattered was that she was in near ruin and could not yet find a way out. "OK, but *what do I do now?*" she asked with as much calm as she could muster.

"Do you have any debts?"

"Just the mortgage on the house."

"What mortgage rate are you paying?"

"About 9 percent."

"Do you absolutely guarantee you will make the payment every month, no bones about it?"

"Of course we do, God willing."

"So now let me ask you: Can you find me an investment today–anywhere–that is absolutely guaranteed and pays you 9 percent? You can't, right? It doesn't exit. Yet you can effectively *save* that 9 percent by paying off–or paying down–your mortgage. And remember: A penny saved is a penny earned, right?"

"Sure, but everyone is telling us to do *exactly the opposite.* To refinance, to take cash *out*–not put cash *in!*"

"*Who* is telling you to do that? The mortgage brokers who make the stiff fees? The stock broker who wants to play with more of your money? Even if you're not talking to them, they're the source of the push to refinance. Even if they're not the ones telling you, they're the ones putting the word out there. The truth is, once you factor in all the points and closing costs, you may not save nearly as much as you think. If you do it, make sure you're really saving money and not just increasing your debt!"

"If we don't refinance, though, where do we get the cash to pay down the mortgage?"

"That takes me to the next step. Sell your stocks. Stop the bloodletting. Get the heck out of the market. Get your money to safety. Then, we can start from scratch, to get you on the right track, the right way. I cannot guarantee success. But I *can* guarantee no conflicts of interest, nothing to skew the odds against you."

"But I can't sell now," she said with a painful half-smile. "I can't afford to take the loss."

"The loss is history too. You've *already* taken it."

"I understand that. But suppose I sell now and the next day the market goes up. I'll feel like total nincompoop."

"Sure that could happen. But don't you see? You're talking about companies that are losers in a market that is falling. If you had fresh money today, would you be buying these stocks."

"No way!"

"Then seriously consider selling. Clear out. No matter what the stock is doing right now, no matter how much you may have lost, selling them now may be the most prudent course."

SELLING INTELLIGENTLY

"Do I just call my broker first thing in the morning and flat out say, 'Sell everything—get me out,' and call it a day?"

"No, you should try to sell intelligently."

"Not sure I understand what you mean. But in my case, though—all I've got is a few stocks. They're getting killed. I'm sick and tired of watching them sink." She paused, started to say something, stopped, and then finally went ahead. "But there *is* someone in the family who does have a big portfolio. He's in his nineties and not doing too well healthwise. He's not going to be able to make these kinds of decisions without some assistance. Plus, he's as stubborn as a mule crossed with an ox. He's probably had some of his shares for, I don't know, 30 or 40 years, maybe more. If I push him to blanket 'sell all,' I know exactly what he'll say to me—'over my dead body!' "

"What is his relationship to you?"

Linda didn't answer immediately. Although she trusted this adviser, she was still reluctant to get into a conversation about her family. But this was her mother's side of the family, so she figured it would be OK. "He's my 91-year-old grandfather."

"OK," the adviser said. "Here's what we're going to do for him. Step one: Sell the most vulnerable stocks in America today."

"How do we know which ones they are?"

"The ones with the lowest ratings from an unbiased, independent source."

"Where do I get those?"

The adviser seemed a bit flustered. He told her, as politely as he could, to please hold most of her questions until he could walk her through the basic steps. Then they could add the details. "Where was I?"

"Step one."

"Right. Sell the most vulnerable companies. If you're going to do this right away, I happen to have a list that can get you started. Here, see? It gives you the name, the stock symbol, the exchange, and the rating. All are believed to be very vulnerable to earnings declines and possibly even bankruptcy. If you own 'em, sell 'em. Don't wait." [See Table 6.1.]

"Step two. You probably own stocks that are not on this list. In a moment I'll give you a couple of independent rating agencies you can contact to get that info. If the rating is low, sell those too. [See Table 6.2.]

"Step three . . ." The adviser stopped himself and asked his client how soon she intended to take action—this week, next month? She said she had no idea. It could be right away, it could be years. It wasn't even clear who would be making those decisions or whether the adviser would be consulted at the time.

"That makes it a lot tougher to give you specific advice," he

Table 6.1 The Most Vulnerable Large Stocks in America Today

Company	Symbol (Exchange)	Weiss Investment Rating
3Com Corp.	COMS (NASDAQ)	E+
ADC Telecommunications Inc.	ADCT (NASDAQ)	D–
Alkermes Inc.	ALKS (NASDAQ)	D–
Amazon.Com Inc.	AMZN (NASDAQ)	E+
American Tower Corp.	AMT (NYSE)	D–
Amkor Technology Inc.	AMKR (NASDAQ)	D–
Applied Micro Circuits Corp.	AMCC (NASDAQ)	E+
Ariba Inc.	ARBA (NASDAQ)	E+
AT&T Wireless Services Inc.	AWE (NYSE)	D–
Atmel Corp.	ATML (NASDAQ)	D–
Avaya Inc.	AV (NYSE)	D–
Avocent Corp.	AVCT (NASDAQ)	D–
Ballard Power Systems Inc.	BLDP (NASDAQ)	D–
Broadcom Corp.	BRCM (NASDAQ)	D–
Broadwing Inc.	BRW (NYSE)	D–
Cablevision Sys Corp.	CVC (NYSE)	D–
Checkfree Corp.	CKFR (NASDAQ)	D–
Ciena Corp.	CIEN (NASDAQ)	E+
Conexant Systems Inc.	CNXT (NASDAQ)	E+
Corning Inc.	GLW (NYSE)	E+
Crown Castle Intl Corp.	CCI (NYSE)	D–
Earthlink Inc.	ELNK (NASDAQ)	E+

Table 6.1 *(Continued)*

Exult Inc.	EXLT (NASDAQ)	D–
Gateway Inc.	GTW (NYSE)	D–
Genta Inc.	GNTA (NASDAQ)	D–
Globespanvirata Inc.	GSPN (NASDAQ)	E+
Hollinger Intl Inc.	HLR (NYSE)	D–
I2 Technologies Inc.	ITWO (NASDAQ)	E+
Icos Corp.	ICOS (NASDAQ)	D–
ImClone Systems Inc.	IMCL (NASDAQ)	E+
Level 3 Commun Inc.	LVLT (NASDAQ)	E+
Ligand Pharmaceutical	LGND (NASDAQ)	E+
Lucent Technologies Inc.	LU (NYSE)	E
Maxtor Corp.	MXO (NYSE)	E+
Millennium Pharmactcls Inc.	MLNM (NASDAQ)	D–
Mirant Corp.	MIR (NYSE)	D–
Netiq Corp.	NTIQ (NASDAQ)	D–
Nortel Networks Corp.	NT (NYSE)	E+
NPS Pharmaceuticals Inc.	NPSP (NASDAQ)	E+
Openwave Systems Inc.	OPWV (NASDAQ)	E+
Parametric Technology Corp.	PMTC (NASDAQ)	D–
PMC-Sierra Inc.	PMCS (NASDAQ)	E+
Regeneron Pharmaceut	REGN (NASDAQ)	D–
Retek Inc.	RETK (NASDAQ)	D–
Rite Aid Corp.	RAD (NYSE)	E+

Table 6.1 *(Continued)*

Scios Inc.	SCIO (NASDAQ)	D–
Sepracor Inc.	SEPR (NASDAQ)	E+
Verisign Inc.	VRSN (NASDAQ)	E+
Vitesse Semiconductor Corp.	VTSS (NASDAQ)	D–
XM Satellite Radio Hldgs Inc.	XMSR (NASDAQ)	E+

These stocks are considered weak due to a combination of factors such as excessive debt, inadequate capital and irregular or poor earnings patterns. Among the stocks receiving a Weiss Investment Rating of D– or lower, these are the ones with the largest market capitalization. Scale: A = excellent; B = good; C = fair; D = weak; E = very weak. Plus sign = upper end of grade; minus sign = lower end of grade range.

Source: Weiss Ratings, September 2002. Current Weiss Investment ratings on these or other stocks are available from the Weiss Ratings' *Guide to Common Stocks* available at many public libraries or directly from Weiss Ratings (www.weissratings.com or 800-289-9222).

confessed. "By the time you're selling, we could be at the bottom or even on the way back up! So let me show you just one of the things I will be looking at—something you can hang your hat on if there's no one around to help you."

He picked up a yellow legal pad and handed it to her. She looked down at it with a slight frown, not sure what she was supposed to do with it. "The key question you have to ask all the time is, 'Are we still in a bear market?' Write that down: 'Are we still in a bear market?' "

She pulled out a pen and wrote the words at the top of the pad. He then swiveled slightly in his chair to view his computer monitor and went through a series of steps, stopping after each one to give her time to write it down. By the time he was done, he had created and printed a relatively simple chart. "This will give you a simple yes-no answer. If the chart says 'Yes, this is still a bear market,' that means you should be selling either right now or very soon."

"Even if my stocks are already way, way down?"

"Yes. There's nothing—except a total 100 percent wipeout—that can absolutely prevent them from going down some more. There's nothing you can count on that will stop your losses from getting

---

Table 6.2 Best Sources for Independent Stock Ratings

Morningstar: (800-735-0700 or www.morningstar.com). Covers approximately 7,000 stocks. Ratings attempt to identify undervalued or overvalued stocks. $109 per year.

S&P: (800-221-5277) or www.standardandpoors.com). Covers 2,000 stocks, with two types of ratings—one based on quantitative analysis and another based on an analyst's personal opinion of the stock. $298 per year.

Value Line: (800-634-3583 or www.valueline.com). Covers 1,700 stocks in standard edition, with two ratings on each stock. One reflects the timeliness of purchasing the stock, while the other seeks to measures the safety of the stock. $598 per year.

Weiss Ratings: (800-289-9222 or www.weissratings.com), the author's firm. Covers 8,720 stocks. Reflects a stock's fundamentals, valuation, momentum, and risk. $495 a year for unlimited access; $7.50 per company.

Unlike most ratings issued by Wall Street research analysts, these sources are independent of the investment banking industry and free of conflicts interests. This alone does not guarantee success, but it can have a major impact on your performance. In a bear market, use these ratings to help guide you regarding which stocks to sell first.

worse. If anything, the fact they've been going down steadily means that you're in a long-term down trend—a trend that you've got to assume, until proven otherwise, *will* continue."

"Step four: If this indicator says 'yes, we're still in a bear market,' call your broker and start selling."

ARE WE STILL IN A BEAR MARKET?

If you have access to the Internet, follow the instructions given here. If you do not have Internet access, your broker should be able to help you—either by following the instructions given here or by using another program that provides the same information.

To begin, open your Web browser with Microsoft Internet Explorer, Netscape, or AOL; then do the following:

(Continued)

1. Go to http://finance.yahoo.com.
2. In the lower left corner of your screen, you will see today's stock market chart titled "Market Summary" and, below that, the latest on the major stock market averages. Click on "S&P 500."
3. A chart of today's S&P 500 will appear on your screen. Under the chart, look for the line that starts with the word "Big:" Then click on "5y."
4. A larger, 5-year chart of the S&P 500 will appear. Look at where the market is today as compared to three years earlier. In most circumstances, it should be obvious which direction the market has been trending over the past three years.
5. If it's unclear to you, look a few lines above the chart for text that begins with "Chart: Basic–Moving Average." Click on "Moving Average."
6. You should now see a new chart of the S&P 500 with three lines:
   - The blue line is the S&P 500 index itself, showing daily closing prices only.
   - The red line is the S&P 500's 50-day moving average.
   - The green line is the S&P 500's 200-day moving average.
7. Ask yourself which is higher on the graph–the blue line (the S&P itself) or the green line (the 200-day moving average)?
   - If the green line is higher, the long-term trend in the market is likely (although certainly not guaranteed!) to still be *down*. This indicates that *yes, we are still in a bear market.*
   - If the blue line is higher, it is an indication that the market may be recovering. *Warning: This alone should not be your signal to hold or buy common shares.*

Warning: Web sites *will* change their layout! This book provides very specific directions on using today's publicly available Web sites. However, these sites often change their structure and layout. If so, you'll need to adjust your steps accordingly.

"So *now* I tell him to sell everything immediately, right?"

"Not yet! This is where intelligent selling comes in. If you're a smart seller, you will try to avoid 'selling into a hole.' That's when the market is falling as you sell, when everyone else is trying to sell at the same time as you are."

"What's the solution?"

"Sell about half immediately. Then wait for a good, short-term bounce before selling the balance."

"A good short-term bounce?" she asked.

"Ideally," he said, thinking he was answering the question, "I'd like you to be selling into *favorable market conditions.* I'd like you to avoid selling into panicky conditions or fast-moving markets."

She was not satisfied with the answer. "Let me rephrase my question this way: In certain branches of my field, 'short-term' can mean a million years, while in other branches, 'long-term' can be a millisecond. We don't have the luxury of throwing terms around as loosely as you do in the stock market. What I need is a precise definition of 'short-term bounce.' "

This time, rather than have her take notes, the advisor invited her to come around the desk and view his computer monitor. She put her reading glasses on, stood behind him, and leaned over his left shoulder.

"OK. Let's call this step *five,*" he said. "I'm using the tools that are available free on the Web. You can buy more sophisticated software if you want, but this should do fine. See? Click here and you get the S&P 500 for the last year. Then go over here and you get the moving averages. As soon as the black line is lower than the blue line, I would define that as a good short-term bounce. This is where you start selling. Is it arbitrary? Yes, but it imposes the scientific discipline you are seeking."

As she sat back down, he handed her what appeared to be a photocopy of the instructions he had already prepared for another client. At the top, in bold letters, it read, "Is The Market in Rally Mode."

"If the answer is 'yes,' " he continued, "you can sell the whole shebang with confidence. If the answer is 'no,' sell half now and half later."

"Later? When precisely is 'later'?"

"Check it daily if you want. At least weekly. Once you have it set it up on your screen and you're logged in, all you have to do is click on the "refresh" button in MS Internet Explorer. You know—the box with the two little arrows pointing in different directions."

"Huh?"

"Look. Right here. See? This one between the little "home" and the "stop" icons? Just click it. Then glance at it. Right away you can see that either the market is in rally mode or it's not. But remember, this is entirely arbitrary. Not guaranteed to work; just there to lend you a helping hand."

"Is that it?"

"Yes . . . ah . . . no, wait a minute. One more thing. There are no small-cap or very thinly traded stocks in your grandfather's portfolio, are there?"

"I don't think so."

"Good, because those can be harder to sell. You'll need to work with your broker to . . ."

"Broker? I don't really have a broker anymore. Remember? I fired him a long time ago. Now I do everything online."

"It's fine to trade online, but in times like these, you do need a broker to help you execute trades, especially in panicky markets and especially with thinly traded stocks. With a lot of securities, you will probably need to set a price limit, a minimum you'll accept for the shares you're selling. That's where the real live brokers can help you. Just don't let them talk you out of selling . . . or talk you into setting a price that's so high, you never get out."

When Linda went home and related the gist of the meeting to her husband, he was apparently pleased. He said that he never

IS THE MARKET IN RALLY MODE?

Go back to where you left off in the previous box, "Are We Still in a Bear Market?" (page 67). Your Web browser should still be pointed to the Yahoo! page displaying the larger S&P chart with the index itself (the blue line) and the moving averages. (If it isn't, simply repeat the first five instructions in that box.) Do the following:

1. Two lines above the chart, look for the words "Range: 1d 5d 3m . . ." etc. Click on "3m."
2. You will see a new chart displaying just the last three months of the S&P 500 Index. On the line immediately above the chart, look for text that begins with "Moving Avg: 5 | 10 | 20 |" and click on "20."
3. Displayed on the screen will be the same graph, but this time with an additional line—a black line representing the 20-day moving average of the S&P 500 index. Ask yourself which is higher on the graph—the blue line (the S&P itself) or the black line (the 20-day moving average)?
   - If the black line is higher, it's a sign that no, the market is not in rally mode. Call your broker and say, "Sell half my shares at the market. Park the proceeds in your money market fund for now."
   - If the black line is lower, it's a sign that yes, the market is currently in a rally mode. Call your broker and say, "Sell all my shares at the market. Park the proceeds in your money market fund for now."

Note: Give your broker a chance to provide input regarding an appropriate sell limit price for inactively traded stocks or stocks that are currently suffering erratic trading conditions. (A sell limit is the minimum price you will accept for your shares.) Depending upon the situation, your broker may recommend a somewhat higher or lower limit price. Provided the recommended limit price does not vary by more than, say, 5 percent from the price of the most recent transaction, it is probably within reason. However, make it clear to your broker that although you are flexible regarding the timing and level of the sale, you will not be swayed from your basic goal of selling as soon as possible or as soon as market conditions allow.

For future convenience, add this Web page to your favorites.

trusted her broker to begin with. His parents and grandparents had told him never to trust brokers, bankers, or any financial-sales people. He felt better about this new guy, but Linda was still in shock. "I can't believe Dubois lied to us!" she moaned.

His reply was not exactly comforting. "Who else is lying to us, and what are they lying about?"

CHAPTER 7

GET YOUR MONEY TO SAFETY

"You told us to sell, but you didn't tell us where to put the money," Linda Dedini said at the next consultation with her adviser, this time with her husband Gabriel by her side. "So I just parked the money in the money fund at the brokerage firm."

"I heard about money funds," said Gabriel. "But I have two problems. First of all, I don't understand what the heck they are. Remember, Linda comes from a family of investment and business people. She grew up with this stuff. I just teach Romance languages. To me, 'money' and 'fund' are the same thing."

Linda didn't want to waste the adviser's time, let alone the hourly fee. She wasn't sure if she should shush her husband or butt in and explain it to him in 10 seconds or less. She decided to do neither.

"Forgive me," the adviser said, turning to Linda. "I neglected to show you it was right there in my instruction sheet I gave you—to temporarily park the proceeds in a money fund. But all's well that ends well. You did the right thing."

Then, turning to Gabriel, he added, "It's a mutual fund—in this case, run by a subsidiary of your brokerage firm. But instead of buying stocks for you, they put your money strictly into bank CDs or short-term IOUs called 'commercial paper,' issued by big

Table 7.1 Largest Treasury Only Money Funds with Key Features

Fund Name	Toll-Free No.	Web Address	Minimum Balance to Open Account	Cost to Print Checks
Alliance Treasury Reserves	(800) 247-4154	www.alliancecapital.com	$1,000	No charge
American Capital Presv Fund	(800) 345-2021	www.americancentury.com	$2,500	No charge
American Performance US Treas	(800) 762-7085	www.apfunds.com	$5,000	No charge
Dreyfus 100% US Treasury MMF	(800) 242-8671	www.dreyfus.com	$500	No charge
Evergreen Treasury MMF/Cl A	(800) 343-2898	www.evergreen-funds.com	$1,000	No charge
Gabelli US Treasury MMF	(800) 937-8909	www.gabelli.com	$3,000	No charge
HighMark 100% US Treasury MMF/Retail	(800) 433-6884	www.highmarkfunds.com	$1,000	No charge
Huntington US Treas MMF/Trust	(800) 253-0412	www.huntingtonfunds.com	$1,000	No charge
One Group US Treas Secs MMF/Cl A	(800) 480-4111	www.onegroup.com	$1,000	No charge
Regions Treasury MMF/Cl A/Trust	(800) 433-2829	www.regions.com	$1,000	No charge
Reserve Fund/ Government Fund	(800) 637-1700	www.reservefunds.com	$1,000	First 185 checks free
Scudder US Treas MF/Cl S	(800) 728-3337	www.myscudder.com	$2,500	No charge
T. Rowe Price US Treasury MF	(800) 638-5660	www.troweprice.com	$2,500	No charge charge
U.S. Treasury Securities Cash Fund	(800) 873-8637	www.usfunds.com	$1,000	First 15 checks free
Vanguard Treasury MMF	(800) 662-7447	www.vanguard.com	$3,000	First 20 checks free

These are some of the largest Treasury-only money funds. All provide equivalent safety. If you want to use them actively for checking, you should focus on those that offer checking with no minimum dollar amount per check or a relatively low minimum per check. Funds with a $500 minimum amount per check or more are fine for savings, but are not practical for an active checking account. Take a look also

Maximum Number of Checks without Extra Charge	Maximum Number of Deposits without Extra Charge	Charge for Each Transaction over Maximum Number	Charge for Each Bounced Check	Wire Transfers out of Your Account	Wire Transfers into Your Account
Unlimited	Unlimited	No charge	No charge	No charge	No charge
Unlimited	Unlimited	No charge	No charge	No charge	No charge
Unlimited	Unlimited	No charge	No charge	No charge	No charge
Unlimited	Unlimited	No charge	No charge	No charge	No charge
Unlimited	Unlimited	No charge	No charge	No charge	No charge
Unlimited	Unlimited	No charge	$15	No charge	No charge
5	Unlimited	Not allowed	No charge	No charge	No charge
Unlimited	Unlimited	No charge	No charge	$11	No charge
Unlimited	Unlimited	No charge	No charge	No charge	No charge
Unlimited	Unlimited	No charge	No charge	No charge	No charge
Unlimited	Unlimited	No charge	No charge	$10 if under $10,000	No charge
Unlimited	Unlimited	No charge	No charge	No charge	No charge
Unlimited	Unlimited	No charge	No charge	$25 if under $5000	No charge
Unlimited	Unlimited	No charge	No charge	$10	No charge
Unlimited	Unlimited	No charge	No charge	$5 if under $5000	No charge

at all the special transactions that you can get for no charge. When was the last time your bank did *not* charge you for a bounced check, for example? For more information on how to maximize the benefits of these funds, refer to the *Ultimate Safe Money Guide* (Wiley).

corporations. In other words, you buy their shares, just like any other mutual fund. Then they loan your money to the banks and corporations for a very short period of time, like from 30 to 90 days, for example."

Gabriel smiled broadly, content that he understood the answer. "But you say the broker runs it. I don't trust the broker. So why should I trust the broker's money fund?"

"Your brokerage firm doesn't hold the money in a money fund. Even the money fund management company itself doesn't hold your money. Your money—or, rather, the CDs and IOUs, etc.—are held by the bank that the fund picks as its escrow agent. Then, on top of that, the bank keeps all the money completely segregated from *its own* assets too. So even if the brokerage firm or the fund management company goes under, your money won't be affected. Heck, even if the bank *itself* fails, it will not jeopardize your money fund investment."

Linda rotated her eyes toward her husband without moving her head—an unmistakable "I told you so" gesture that the adviser could not have missed even if he tried.

"Here's where the *true* risk lies," he said, as Gabriel perked up. "It's a very minor, subtle risk right now, but it could become an issue someday in the future. Remember, I told you most of these funds buy short-term IOUs issued by companies, bank CDs, and other money market investments. Now suppose one of those companies or banks goes under? You could suffer a loss of income or even principal."

Despite the relatively low risk, Linda seemed disappointed. She wanted something safer than that. "So where do we go? A bank?"

"You can do that, provided it's a safe bank. But I have an even better alternative for you. Put your cash in a money fund that is specialized strictly in U.S. Treasury securities and equivalent. That's all they ever buy—short-term U.S. Treasuries or some short-term paper that's more than 100 percent collaterized by Treasuries. Their charter doesn't let them buy anything else."

He picked up a book on safe investments that was on his desk and began flipping the pages. When he found the page he wanted, he spread the book open, laid it down in front of the couple, and with his index finger began pointing to some bolded headings. "No investment is perfect, but here are the advantages of these Treasury-only funds: Their yields are competitive with equivalent other money markets. Their fees for all kinds of services are far lower than any bank's fees. You only have to have one account for everything—no shuttling back and forth between checking and savings. There's no limit to the account size—FDIC insurance is not even an issue, since the Treasury guarantees every penny of the securities. Your yield is exempt from local and state income taxes. You get *truly* free checking—none of those penny-ante or hidden charges for checking. You—"

Without averting his eyes from the adviser, Gabriel raised the angle of his head ever so slightly, conveying polite suspicion. "You said no investment is perfect. What were you alluding to?"

"The yields! Since the Fed has dropped interest rates so darn low, the yields aren't just bad—they're absolutely terrible. But what would you prefer: A big loss or a small yield? Many investors would kill to be able to exchange their losses for money market yields!"

ADVANTAGES OF TREASURY-ONLY MONEY MARKET FUNDS

Advantage 1: Competitive yields with equivalent money markets. In recent years, Treasury-only money funds have yielded double the average yield on personal checking accounts, and when compared to a business checking account, the difference is even greater. Furthermore, in a business of fairly average activity, you should also be able to take better advantage of the float (i.e., the funds remaining in your account while checks written against them have not yet cleared).

Advantage 2: Low fees. When a bank quotes you a yield on any kind of account, it always quotes you the yield before it deducts a variety of service fees. With bank charges and fees currently very high, it's almost impossible for most bank customers to collect anything near the advertised yield. In contrast, when a money fund quotes you its yield, it always quotes the yield after it deducts all its expenses and most of its fees. Of course, the past or

(Continued)

current yield is no guarantee of future results. However, the yield quoted *is* the *actual* net yield that investors in the fund are earning.

Advantage 3: One account for both checking and savings. At banks, most customers divide their money between a checking account (where they give up most of their yield) and a savings account or CD (where they give up immediate access and liquidity). No matter what, it's almost impossible to get both optimal liquidity and yield in the same bank account. In contrast, Treasury-only money funds let you keep nearly all your cash assets, whether they're for savings or for checking, in one single account. As a result,

- You have complete access to all your funds at all times.
- You can withdraw the entire amount, with no penalty whatsoever. Just write a check or request a wire transfer, and it's done.
- Your money consistently earns competitive current market yields.
- You never have to worry about leaving too much in your checking account at low rates. The full amount is available for checking at all times, earning full interest.
- You continue earning interest on your money up until the moment your check clears. The longer it takes for payees to cash their checks, the more interest you make on this float.
- If you want to use your account as your most active checking account to pay most of your bills, that's even better. The more you use it, the more you take advantage of the float.
- In short, you are always getting maximum liquidity and maximum yield on your entire balance.

Advantage 4: No limit to your account size. Bank deposits are federally insured up to $100,000–but not beyond. All deposits over $100,000 are at risk, particularly in a financial crisis. So when you use banks for your savings or your checking, you may have to use a series of maneuvers to keep your money safe from failure, including

- Spreading your CDs among various accounts. This means that you would have to keep track of several accounts at the same time.
- Making sure that your initial investment in each CD is actually under the $100,000 limit. Otherwise, the accumulation of accrued interest could put your balance over the limit, and that portion would not be covered by the FDIC.
- Calling your bank regularly to make sure (in the case of large checking accounts) that the account is not over the $100,000 FDIC limit. If there are several large checks outstanding, your bank balance could be over the limit. If the bank were to fail at that time, any excess amount could be lost.

With Treasury-only money funds, insurance is essentially a moot point because your funds are invested strictly in securities that are guaranteed directly by the full faith and credit of the U.S. Treasury Department. There is no limit on the Treasury's guarantee of its obligations, whether you're a beginning saver with just a few thousand dollars or a high-net-worth investor with substantial sums.

Note: There were more than 3,000 bank and S&L failures between 1980 and 2002, causing savers and businesses serious inconveniences and even outright losses. In contrast, there has never been a default on U.S. Treasury securities.

Advantage 5: Exempt from local and state taxes.   The income that you earn on both Treasury-only money funds and bank accounts is subject to federal income taxes. However, when it comes to local and state income taxes, there *is* a difference: The dividends that you earn on Treasury-only money funds are exempt. The income

(Continued)

that is earned on bank accounts and CDs—or on money funds that invest in CDs—is not exempt.

Advantage 6: Truly free checking. One way or another, nearly all banks charge you for your checking privileges. They may charge you a fee for each check you issue. They may charge you a flat monthly service fee. Or they may charge you a combination of both. Most Treasury-only money funds do not charge you any extra fee for check-writing privileges. You can write as many checks as you want, as often as you want.

Advantage 7: Immediate liquidity. There are several ways you can withdraw your money from your Treasury-only money fund:

- You can write a check against the balance in your account to yourself or to another payee.
- You can call or send a fax to your money fund's share-holder service department, giving it instructions to issue a wire transfer. (Before the fund can accept your wire instructions, however, you will have to file a signed authorization ahead of time. This can be done when you open your account.)
- You can request that a check be sent to you directly from the fund. You can also authorize telephone instructions for redemption by check when you open your account.

No other kind of account (e.g., one with a bank, an S&L, a credit union, a broker, or an insurer) can give you this level of immediate access.

For a step-by-step guide on how best to take advantage of your Treasury-only money fund and even how to use it for low-cost do-it-yourself checking, refer to *The Ultimate Safe Money Guide* (Wiley).

CORPORATE BONDS

The couple liked all the advantages, but the whole business about dirt-cheap yields was potentially a deal-breaker. Gabriel seemed much more concerned with safety, while Linda wanted to pursue and explore various ways of getting at least a halfway decent yield. It was one thing to park the funds in a money market temporarily. But to leave substantial amounts there for long periods of time? It seemed like a waste.

"What about corporate bonds," Linda asked. "Are they safe?"

"Not always," said the adviser. "Sometimes they can be just as risky as common stocks."

"Hold it, please!" interjected the husband. "I've heard about stocks and bonds all my life, and I just realized that I don't understand, in depth, what the heck the difference between them truly is."

"It's simple. With a corporate bond, instead of buying a share in a company, you are making a loan to the company. Instead of becoming an owner, you become a creditor. Whether the company makes a profit or suffers a loss, it promises to pay your interest every year and give you back your entire principal at the end of the term, just like any loan. In essence, they get your money. You get a piece of paper—the bond certificate—that says they owe you the money."

"Can you give me an example?"

"Sure. Let's say you buy a $10,000 General Motors 6.75 percent bond maturing in 2028. All that means is that you are making a loan to General Motors for $10,000. GM is promising to pay you 6.75 percent interest per year. They're also promising to return your principal, in full, in 2028."

"We get the bonds directly from General Motors?"

"No. You get them through a broker, just like a stock. And just like a stock, they fluctuate in price in the market—the bond market. If too many people are trying to buy them, they go up in price. If too many are trying to sell them, they go down in price."

"Why would anyone want to sell them?" Linda asked.

The adviser smiled with respect. These were *not* dumb questions! "Let's say you buy a $10,000 bond from a company. Now, instead of $10,000 in the bank, what have you got? You've got a piece of paper that says, in effect, 'IOU $10,000.' Can you take that IOU to Toys-R-Us and buy your kids a couple of new bikes? If you lose your job, can you use it to pay your mortgage? No. So the first reason anyone might sell a bond is *need*–because they need the money.

"The second reason," he continued, "is *fear.* Let's say you bought a bond in UCBS. And let's say, since UCBS is losing so much money, the rating agencies–Moody's, S&P, or Fitch–downgrade the company. What does that mean? It means all three agencies agree there's a greater chance than before that this company will default, that it will miss an interest or principal payment."

The adviser paused for a moment to find a way to bring the point home.

"You seem to be the type of people who would never dream of defaulting on your mortgage payments, but believe me, there are big companies defaulting on their bond payments all the time. That's where the fear comes in. If investors are afraid the company is going to default, they sell. That drives the price down. And if UCBS actually does default, forget it! The value of UCBS bonds can go to 25 cents on the dollar, maybe even down to zero, just like a stock. Their bond is their word, and if they break their word, their bond is next to worthless."

"That's hypothetical," she said with a bit of discomfort as she thought about her father. "Can you give us some real examples?"

The adviser bent over to dig a folder out of his lower left file drawer. Within half a minute, he pulled out a big 11- by 17-inch sheet of paper and placed it before the couple, covering the book on safe investments that he had opened in that same spot a few minutes earlier.

On the sheet, hundreds of bonds were shown, all casualties of the tech wreck, the recession, the bankruptcy crisis, or just bad management. They saw Revlon's 6-year bond, which fell from $975 to $450 following downgrades in ratings. They saw American Airlines' 2-year bonds, which plunged by nearly half. They also saw bonds issued by Kmart, Lucent, Polaroid, AT&T, Qwest Communications, Electronic Data Systems, and many more–all clobbered in value after downgrades in ratings.

"See my point?" the adviser said at last. "A lot of these bonds plunged just like stocks!"

GOVERNMENT BONDS

"What about government bonds?" Linda retorted.

"Yes, of course. The safest bonds are issued by the Treasury Department. They're similar to the securities that the Treasury-only money funds buy, except they're long-term—up to 30 years. Instead of loaning your money to a company, you're loaning your money to the U.S. Treasury to finance whatever it is the federal government wants to spend it on. Their rating is higher than triple-A, and they have never been downgraded. They have never failed—and probably never will fail—to pay their interest and principal on time."

"But can the market price of Treasury bonds go down too?" Gabriel asked.

"Yes. They can go down because of the 'need' factor I told you about. And all bonds—whether Treasury or corporate—can go down for one other reason."

"What's that?"

"I call it the 'envy factor.' "

"Huh?" Linda interjected. "I understood the 'need factor.' Fear I also understood. But envy?"

"Let's say I have put $100,000 into a U.S. Treasury bond that will pay me a fixed 5 percent per year for the next 30 years. How much do I collect in interest each year?

The husband replied, "$5,000?"

"Right. But now things change. Time goes by, and interest rates go up and up. The Treasury issues new bonds that pay a lot more now, say, 10 percent per year. What happens? I suffer from yield envy—I envy everyone who's buying the new 10 percent bonds. I say to myself, 'Darn, if I had only waited, if I had only bought the new bonds paying 10 percent, I could be earning $10,000 per year instead of just $5,000.' "

"Tough luck, eh?" interjected Gabriel.

"You said it! So one day, I go to you like a used-car salesman and say, 'Hey, I've got this great bond I bought not long ago. Check it out. It's paying me a nice, respectable income of $5,000 per year, and it's 100 percent guaranteed by the United States Government.' If I made that offer to you, would you buy it from me?"

Gabriel responded immediately. "You've got to be kidding! Why in the heck should I buy your old 5 percent bond when I can get a brand-new 10 percent bond from the Treasury and make double the income?"

"Because I'll sell it to you cheap."

"How cheap?"

"Make me an offer."

Gabriel pondered what might be a fair price. The old bond was paying $5,000 a year. But to get $5,000 a year from a new 10 percent bond, all he'd have to invest right now is $50,000. So he figured that's what the old bond would be worth—$50,000. "Give it to me for half-price—50 grand. That's all it's worth to me."

The adviser smiled. "Yes, yes. You got it! That's very close to what the price would actually be in the open market. And that's also why the market price on existing bonds invariably goes *down* when prevailing interest rates go *up*. It's why rising interest rates are a major threat to everyone who owns bonds. It doesn't matter who issued the bonds—a rinky-dink company or a Fortune 500 company, a struggling township in a blighted region or the United States Treasury Department—they're *all* driven down by rising interest rates across the board."

Linda was skeptical. "This all sounds very far-fetched. Has it ever really happened before?"

"Ohh! *Ab-so-lute-ly!* In 1980, $10,000 30-year Treasury bonds plunged to $5,500. In 1981, Treasury bonds fell to $4,300. And 1994 was the worst calendar year for bonds in history—all in conjunction with rising interest rates. If you held onto the bonds till maturity, you'd eventually get all your principal back. But in the meantime, you'd be stuck with low yields for years and years."

Linda was despondent. She had come looking for advice on what to buy, but it seemed that all her adviser was doing was giving her advice on what *not* to buy. She came looking for hope, but it seemed all he could give her was more cause for despair.

"You talk all about dangers and disasters," she said. "Is that all you can see?"

He was pensive, then spoke softly.

"You're forgetting the Treasury-only money funds I told you about. With these funds, your income goes up almost immediately as interest rates rise. The more rates go up, the more you make." [See Table 7.1.]

"Besides," the adviser continued, "danger is a reality of our time, but even the worst disaster can be an opportunity. It can be an opportunity for you to build your wealth and for the entire country to fix itself. No matter how bad things get, we will survive and, ultimately, thrive."

"OK, but you even talk about safe investments, like government bonds falling in value. You talk about people selling because of need, fear, envy, and God knows what else. We understand that now. Thank you. But how do we avoid these problems?"

"Just as I told you before. You loan your money only to those who are truly trustworthy, who spend the money wisely, who can almost surely pay back. That takes care of most of the problem right from the outset. Then, to take care of the other problems, you only trust them for a short period of time. For example, instead of lending your money for 30 years, you do it for just 3 years, or 1 year, or even just 3 months. The shorter the period, the less the risk of price fluctuations. If the initial term is from 10 to 30 years, it's called a 'bond.' If it's between 1 and 10 years, it's called a 'note.' Anything under a year from the U.S. Treasury is called a 'bill.' The safest of them all is the Treasury bill, which takes us back to the Treasury-only funds. That's essentially all they invest in."

"But you said their rates are horrendously low right now!"

"Yes. But what do you prefer—a low guaranteed income on Treasury bills or huge losses on common stocks?"

"Low yield, of course. But we can't sit around in low yields forever. What could push them back up?"

CHAPTER 8

THE BALLOONING BUDGET DEFICIT

Paul Johnston had no intention of spending his next years riding up and down on a golf cart in Florida or day-trading a roller-coaster stock market from home. He launched immediately into the next part of his plan—promptly forming a nonprofit research and lobbying group, the Chief Executive's Committee for Accounting Reform, with a small office in Washington, D.C.

The committee would gather prominent executives as spokespersons and put together a research staff to uncover every kind of accounting chicanery in America. It would reveal the problems, cite the facts, and name the names of wanton companies.

He recruited one the nation's best press agents, as well as the best forensic accountants—sleuths specialized in going into companies and ferreting out hidden skeletons. Plus, he also thought about inviting some of the same people who had advised companies on how to distort their earnings in the 1990s. Who would know more about bending and breaking the rules than the people who actually did it in practice? he reasoned.

As soon as word got out, he began getting phone calls from those interested in joining. Oliver Dulles, who lost his job with the accounting consulting firm soon after Johnston had resigned, was among the first—and the most eager. The man was desperate to join the group. He didn't care that he would have to take a big pay cut. And to prove his skills, he had already done some research that he felt would add great value to the project.

At first, though, Dulles seemed apologetic: "Not sure if this is what you wanted. Maybe you'll say it's off track. If so, we can just forget about it . . . but wow! Is it big!"

"What the heck are you talking about?" Johnston asked impatiently.

"Correct me if I'm wrong, but as I see it, your group's mission is to uncover *all* accounting shenanigans in America, right? Well, it just so happens that the greatest accounting fraud of all is being perpetuated by none other than the *federal government*."

"I've heard that kind of talk before, but . . ."

"I'm talking about the federal budget accounting. Listen to this: According to the Treasury Department, in 2000 we had a federal surplus of $236 billion. Remember that? The big windfall of cash the Democrats and Republicans were fighting over, each outdoing the other on how to spend it? Well, here's the shocker—instead of a $236 billion federal surplus, we actually had a federal *deficit* of $137.6 billion that year."

"Are you sure about that?"

"Absolutely, and I'll give you proof in a minute. But it gets worse. For 2001, the Treasury Department declared we had a surplus of $127 billion. Care to guess what the actual figure was?" Johnston was mute, so Dulles continued. "Hold onto your hat. It was a shocking $623.8 billion deficit. Can you believe that? Over $600 billion! And it's even bigger in 2002!" [See Figure 8.1.]

Johnston was skeptical. He had often heard government critics and watchdog agencies talk about the "smoke and mirrors" behind budgetary accounting, but he had never seen any definitive evidence, in black and white, to pin it down with the kind of precision that the CPA's numbers seemed to imply. "Where's the proof? Where do you get your numbers?"

Dulles had nearly two decades of experience as a public accountant. He had developed highly disciplined statistical skills as a psychology major in college. He was not one to make rash statements without backup. So he was ready. "Do you have access to a computer?" he asked softly.

"Sure."

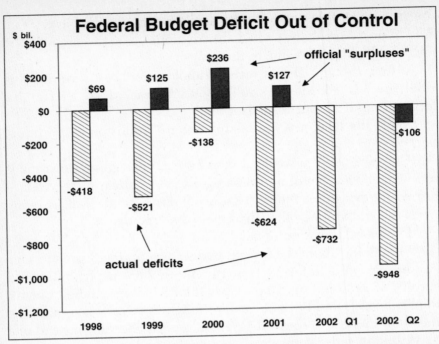

Figure 8.1   The so-called federal budget surpluses of 1999, 2000, and 2001 were purely bogus, based on massive, overt accounting manipulations of the budget. Meanwhile, data provided by the Federal Reserve on the government's actual borrowing of new funds demonstrate that the government was running increasingly larger deficits throughout this period.

Data: U.S. Treasury Department, Federal Reserve *Flow of Funds,* as illustrated in Table 8.1.

"Then when you get this e-mail that I'm sending you now, click on the link. It's www.federalreserve.gov/releases/Z1/Current/z1r-3.pdf. When this file comes up on your screen, scroll down to table F4, 'Credit Market Borrowing, All Sectors, by Instrument.' Then check line 3, 'U.S. government securities.' That's all the proof you'd ever want, right there, from the most unimpeachable of sources—the U.S. Federal Reserve Board." [See Table 8.1.]

Johnston, who had been an ardent student of government while in a Washington, D.C.–area college, was flabbergasted. "You've got to be kidding!" he responded. "You mean the U.S. Treasury Department on Pennsylvania Avenue is saying we had these huge surpluses in 2000 and 2001 . . . while at the same time the Federal

Reserve, just down the street on Constitution and 20th, is saying we have these huge deficits?"

"Exactly. But no one's paying attention to the Fed's numbers. They're poorly distributed, rarely talked about. It's the Treasury's numbers—the doctored-up numbers—that get all the press, get debated before Congress. Do you realize how big this is? Do you realize what the ultimate consequences could be?"

Johnston's interest perked up, but he still wanted to know the mechanisms, how it actually worked. In response, Dulles explained a long series of accounting manipulations routinely used by the government to make the federal deficit look better and more acceptable to voters—measures that were uncannily similar to the gimmicks that UCBS used in the 1990s to make their earnings look better to investors.

"In a nutshell," said Dulles, "here's how it's done. First, the government has a bunch of agencies—the Federal Home Bank, Freddie Mac, Sallie Mae, etc. These agencies are controlled by Congress. They are guaranteed, backed, or at least sponsored by the U.S. government. And, their debts are universally classified as U.S. government securities. Yet their books are not consolidated with the government's books for the purpose of budget accounting. So it's a very convenient dumping ground for bad numbers that might otherwise be a huge embarrassment to a lot of people in and outside the beltway.

"Second," he continued, "there's the Social Security fund. The fund has a surplus that it's going to need in order to cover expected Social Security deficits down the road. That money belongs to the 45 million people that are retired or are going to retire. It has nothing whatsoever to do with the rest of the operations of the government. Yet they're adding those surpluses into the federal budget to help cover up the deficit."

Momentarily, Johnston's thoughts flashed back to another place and time. Then he returned to the present with a new question. "That's the Treasury's numbers. But you said the Federal Reserve does it differently—how does the Fed calculate the deficit?"

"The Fed's numbers show how much the government and government agencies *actually borrow* in new money—over and above the refunding of old debt—each and every calendar year. In 2000,

Table 8.1

F.4 Credit Market Borrowing, All Sectors, by Instrument
Billions of dollars; quarterly figures are seasonally adjusted annual rates

	1997	1998	1999	2000	2001	2001 Q1	Q2	Q3	Q4	2002 Q1	Q2	
Total	1538.5	2172.8	2178.0	1741.3	2020.7	1792.5	1789.5	2286.2	2214.7	1887.5	2461.3	1
Open market paper	184.1	193.1	229.9	207.6	-164.4	-316.8	-215.1	-163.5	37.8	260.2	167.3	2
U.S. government securities	236.0	418.3	520.7	137.6	623.8	373.3	458.8	1027.8	635.1	731.8	948.4	3
Municipal securities	71.4	96.8	68.2	35.3	117.6	102.9	107.3	70.0	190.1	70.7	184.6	4
Corporate and foreign bonds	430.8	563.7	462.2	400.8	653.4	848.8	616.6	416.7	731.5	589.6	638.7	5
Bank loans n.e.c.	128.2	145.0	69.0	112.8	-75.8	19.2	-141.6	-18.6	-162.4	-4.6	-129.3	6
Other loans and advances	93.2	166.3	158.5	142.7	50.3	80.8	103.9	115.3	-98.7	-15.8	65.6	7
Mortgages	337.2	514.6	570.0	565.6	705.6	540.0	783.5	767.9	731.2	704.0	817.0	8
Consumer credit	57.5	75.0	99.5	139.0	110.2	144.5	76.0	70.6	149.9	81.4	101.9	9

Memo:
Funds raised through corporate equities and mutual fund shares

	1997	1998	1999	2000	2001	2001 Q1	Q2	Q3	Q4	2002 Q1	Q2	
Total net issues	185.3	113.7	156.9	197.2	276.9	236.3	41?.?					10
Corporate equities	-79.9	-165.8	-34.3	-37.8	75.5	120.3	138.8	-61.2	104.2	28.0	206.2	11
Nonfinancial	-114.4	-267.0	-143.5	-159.7	-61.8	-25.0	-70.7	-126.6	-25.0	-3.7	62.5	12
Foreign shares purchased by												
U.S. residents	57.6	101.3	114.3	103.6	106.8	86.1	222.9	43.5	74.7	-5.9	80.9	13
Financial	-23.0	-0.1	-5.1	18.3	30.5	59.1	-13.4	21.8	54.5	37.6	62.8	14
Mutual fund shares	265.1	279.5	191.2	235.0	201.4	116.0	273.5	160.4	255.9	386.8	107.2	15

(Callouts circled: 731.8 and 948.4)

For those who might disbelieve the statement made here that the federal deficit was running at a rate of close to $1 trillion, here is the proof: The Federal Reserve's table F.4, available to the public at www.federalreserve.gov/releases /Z1/Current/zlr-3.pdf. This data clearly shows that the federal government borrowed funds at the annual rate of $731.8 billion and $948.4 billion in the first and second quarters of 2002, respectively. These borrowings had only one purpose: To finance a government deficit of equivalent magnitude.

they borrowed the $137.6 billion I just told you about. In 2001, they borrowed the $623.8 billion. In 2002, they borrowed at the annual rate of $731.8 billion in the first quarter and an absolutely shocking $948.4 billion in the second quarter!"

"Where is all that money going?"

"I can assure you, they're not tucking it away under a mattress. They're borrowing it for one purpose only—to finance the deficit. That's why I say numbers are the real deficit, my friend. Not the higged numbers you hear debated in Congress or quoted in the press."

Johnston had heard about these gimmicks before but had never realized, until now, how incredibly huge it was. *My God,* he thought to himself, *In the second quarter of 2002, the government was borrowing new money at the annual rate of nearly $1 trillion! This is so much larger than the official budget deficit, it defies the imagination!*

He also never realized, until now, how uncannily similar the government's manipulations were to the gimmicks he knew so well from his experience with UCBS. The exclusion of the government agencies from the budget sounded just like the subsidiary shell game they used to use to hide losses and debts. The tricks the government was playing with America's Social Security fund seemed virtually identical to the way they used to juggle UCBS's employee pension fund.

For the average person, the threat was huge. Social Security funds could dry up. The government's heavy borrowing could drive up the cost of money—that is, in the form of higher interest rates. Mortgage rates could go up when Americans could least afford them to. Investors in bonds could lose fortunes.

He tried to calm down, but couldn't. Here he was, busting his butt to get some government agencies—like the SEC and the IRS—to support his drive for a cleaner and more responsible corporate America. And there they were, pulling the exact same tricks in their *own* accounting, killing—utterly shattering—any semblance of credibility they might have to help bring sanity to the private sector.

Johnston could just hear the executives now. They'd be saying, "Hey! The government's doing it—so why can't we?" On the other hand, if he buried this issue and just ignored it, he could never live with himself. He decided to recruit Dulles for the project and go forward.

Two days later, with some trepidation and anxiety, the committee issued a press release without hyperbole or sensationalism. Nevertheless, they felt the headline, "Government Fudges Deficit to the Tune of $500 Billion," was sure to make it to the front pages.

The following morning, Johnston walked into the office of his new press secretary and asked, "What's the response been like? Positive, right? No? Don't tell me it's been negative! Geez, don't keep me in suspense. What are they saying?"

"Nothing, sir."

"Nothing? Whaddaya mean 'nothing'?"

"I mean, sir, we're just not getting a rise out of 'em. No response at all. The general press doesn't seem to understand it. The financial press guys do sort of get the point, but they don't seem to care. One financial markets reporter who called about an old UCBS question this morning tells me it's 'a nonissue.' He goes, 'So what if the government cheats? So what else is new?' Besides, he says that 'it has never seemed to have a major impact on the bond market, so why worry?' He said it's old news and implied our press release was naive. That pretty much sums up the general attitude out there."

Johnston was stunned. Why was it, he thought, that when he personally confessed to the accounting manipulations of his company, it hit Wall Street like a bombshell . . . but when someone tried to bust open far more egregious trickery in Washington, it fell on deaf ears? For the next several weeks, he became obsessed with this question. He had his staff talk to economists, and they talked about economic cycles. He had them go to Wall Street government bond dealers, and they talked about government bonds. Step by step, piece by piece, they assembled a picture that Dulles then painted for Johnston in their next conversation.

"First of all," said Dulles, "let's set the record straight. We *are* on the right track. These accounting gimmicks that Washington uses are actually much *worse* than the ones Main Street or Wall Street got smacked for."

"Worse? Why worse?"

The CPA took out his yellow legal pad from the desk drawer and placed it next to a tall glass of ice water he had just brought from the fridge. On the pad, as was his habit, he had jotted down four bullet points. "There are *four* reasons I think it's much worse," he said after a 15-second pause.

"Reason number one. The shenanigans in Washington are clearly on a much, *much* bigger scale. Heck, how much in extra profits were we able to squeeze out of our little shell game with the subsidiaries—$1 billion? Or $1.5 billion at the peak? Well, the Treasury's manipulations with the government agencies and the Social Security fund add up to nearly $2 *trillion* just since 2000. And how many employees did we have in our pension fund? At most, 40 thousand. Well, the government's tricks with the Social Security funds could result in cuts for 45 *million* citizens!

"Reason number two," he continued. "They're not just juggling numbers—it's real money. Remember our very first meeting a few years ago? Remember how I explained to you that we were not actually raiding the employee pension fund?"

"Refresh my memory," Johnston requested.

"We weren't taking actual cash from the pension fund. We were just moving numbers around in the accounting."

"Ah, yes. Now I remember."

"Well, guess what! The government actually *does* raid the Social Security funds. They take that hard cash that's supposed to be earmarked for future Social Security checks, that belongs to tens of millions of citizens, and . . . they *spend* it."

Johnston's forehead began twitching again. He could feel his blood pressure rising as Dulles continued.

"Reason number three. Did you ever wonder why the government let us and other big companies go hog-wild in the 1990s without so much as a faint word of caution? Did you ever wonder why the Fed suddenly stopped warning about 'irrational exuberance' and actually started encouraging the tech boom?"

"No. Why?"

"Because the government was raking it in too, and it didn't want to do anything that might upset the applecart. Never forget—the tax man is the silent, ever-present partner behind every single company in America. When businesses make more money, the government takes in more tax money. Never forget that the government is *also* the silent partner of every company that *exaggerates* its taxable profits. The more the companies exaggerate, the more they have to pay the government in taxes. The result: While corporate America was enjoying the 1990s superboom in profits, the U.S. Treasury Department was having its own superboom in tax revenues. Just in corporate income taxes, the Treasury collected $204 billion in 1998, $213 billion in 1999 and $224 billion in 2000—despite the fact that many companies were finding new ways to avoid taxes, all 'perfectly legal,' of course."

"Of course."

"It was a windfall for the Treasury—a huge, unprecedented windfall. It was like sitting under a bulging money tree, shaking it gently and just letting all the money come pouring down into your baskets. Think about that for a moment. If you were managing the government's cash flow in that environment, wouldn't you have had the common sense to know that the boom could not go on forever? Wouldn't you set aside some of the money for leaner times? Unfortunately, they did exactly the opposite."

"Why's that?"

"They were listening to the government's economists, of course. The economists said the music would never stop and the party would never end."

Dulles was out of breath and took a sip of water, but Johnston was just warming up. "You said there were four reasons the federal deficits could be even more dangerous than the private sector disaster," he said. "What's the fourth?"

"The fourth reason ties back directly to the nonresponse we got when we tried to issue that press release on the budget a couple of weeks ago."

"I don't get it."

"I'm talking about the fact that the world is totally ignoring it! Let me explain. When you confessed the troubles at UCBS, investors reacted right away, right? That was actually good. It meant they got the message. They absorbed it. Anyone who didn't like the truth sold their stock, and that was the rational thing to do. But that ended it. From then on, the stock stabilized. Not so in this case! The truth is not out yet. The government and the people are still living a pack of lies."

"Yes, but . . ."

"Don't you see? It's the bubble psychology all over again. Back in the 1990s, if you talked about accounting problems or earnings exaggerations at major U.S. companies, people would throw you out on your rear end. Or worse, they'd simply ignore you. That was the stock market bubble. Now, what we have is another kind of bubble, a far more dangerous bubble."

"Which is . . . ?"

"The bond market bubble! If you thought the stock market crash was bad, wait till you see what a bond market crash feels like! And remember: When bonds crash, interest rates–and mortgage rates–go up. So think of what that could do to American families in debt."

CHAPTER

9

THE BOND MARKET BUBBLE

Paul Johnston was so deeply troubled by the federal deficits that he wanted to find out for himself what the impact might be. He asked his staff for the contact info for one of the veteran government bond dealers in New York and gave the man a call. He prefaced the conversation with a brief apology for his general ignorance of bonds and interest rates. Then he asked what the future consequences might be of a ballooning federal deficit.

The bond dealer was reticent at first but soon loosened up. "Never mind what might be. It's already happening! It seems like just a few months ago the folks in Congress and the White House were talking about $200 billion surpluses, stumbling over each other to see who could spend it the fastest. Now they're talking about $200 billion deficits! Never in my 30 years in this business have I seen the deficit swing that far that fast!"

Johnston was going to mention the $1 trillion deficits Dulles had just told him about, but then decided not to. "What will that do to interest rates, to bond prices?" he queried.

"There's only one way the government can continue to exist with a deficit—by borrowing. And there's only one way it can borrow—by selling bonds and other government securities to the public. The bigger the deficit, the more bonds they have to sell. It's that simple. How do they convince people to buy more and more bonds than ever before? They pay out higher and higher interest rates."

"And?"

"And soon, people start saying, 'Why in the heck should I give you my money now for your lousy 5 percent bonds when you're probably gonna be issuing new bonds that'll soon pay 7 or even 8 percent?' That attitude makes it even harder for the Treasury to sell its bonds, and interest rates start surging at an even faster clip. And as you know, when rates surge, the price on existing bonds paying lower fixed rates goes down. Bond prices plunge, sometimes just as badly as stock prices."

Johnston used to read the stock market wrap-up columns almost daily, and he remembered the commentaries he occasionally saw about bonds. They seemed to contradict what the bond dealer was saying. "Wait a minute," said the former CEO. "If the economy is falling, isn't that good for bonds? Don't investors take their money out of stocks and put it into bonds? Doesn't that help push bond prices up? And when bond prices rise, don't interest rates go down?" Johnston was proud of himself. He actually knew a lot more about bonds than he had given himself credit for.

"Yeah, that's the theory they teach you in economics 101, but you can push that theory just so far. You say, 'The economy is going down, so interest rates will go down.' OK, I accept that. Then you say, 'The economy is going down some more, so interest rates should go down some more too.' Fine, I accept that too. But sooner or later you reach the edge of the cliff, and you risk pushing the economy—and this whole theory—over the brink."

ONE OF THE MOST DANGEROUS CRASHES OF THE TWENTIETH CENTURY

Johnston had never heard anyone talk like this before, so he pressed for specifics.

"Look," continued the bond dealer. "At some point, the economy falls *too* far, and too many people start running low on cash or going broke. Countless numbers of bond owners rush to sell off their bonds for cash. Plus, millions of ordinary people lose jobs and rush to refinance their homes or borrow more on their credit cards. Companies lose sales and rush to borrow from banks or investors. Cities and states lose revenues and rush to borrow to fill crater-size holes in *their* budgets. Then Uncle Sam, the biggest borrower in the world, desperate to finance the biggest deficit in history, steps in and pushes everyone else aside. He says to all the other borrowers, 'The heck with you guys. I get first dibs. The first few hundred billion is mine.' "

"Then what?"

"Then what? Are you kidding me? By that time, everyone's screaming for *cash now*, but most investors and lenders are backing off in horror, afraid to throw good money after bad. Cash money is as scarce as hens' teeth, yet everyone absolutely *must* have it. What happens? The price of cash—the interest rate—goes through the roof. And you know what happens when interest rates surge. Bond prices collapse! It doesn't matter what kind of bonds you own. They could be bonds in the richest and bluest blue-chip corporation in America. They could be triple-A double-insured, tax-exempt municipal bonds, or government-guaranteed Ginnie Mae bonds, or absolutely safe United States Treasury bonds with gold ribbons wrapped around them. The market doesn't care. When rates go up, your bonds go down. Period."

"But can Treasury bonds really fall that far? How much real risk is there in Treasury bonds?"

"Look back a bit in time," responded the bond dealer. "Look back to 1980. You were around then, weren't you? In 1980, Treasury bonds that investors originally paid $10,000 for were selling for less than $5,000. Things got so bad at one point that in addition to a collapse in bond prices, we began to witness a *collapse in the bond market itself*."

"I don't get it," Johnston interjected.

"Because of the plunge in bond prices, every last bond dealer on the Street was severely wounded, hurting bad. Our firm was running dangerously low on capital. So were a dozen others."

Johnston had heard of something similar—but it was in the stock market, not the bond market. And it happened in 1987—not in 1980. "I've never heard about this happening in the bond market."

"Very few people have. Yet, ironically, the bond market

collapse of 1980 was one of the most dangerous crashes of the twentieth century—maybe even more dangerous than the stock market crash of 1987."

"How's that?"

"Look, the U.S. government is far bigger and more mission-critical for the whole economy than any single corporation. If the U.S. government has to virtually declare bankruptcy and close up shop, you can forget just about everything else. You can kiss good-bye nearly every stock, bond, or piece of real estate you've ever invested in. You can forget about triple-A corporate bond ratings; they'd be meaningless. Agreed? OK.

"Now listen carefully," said the bond dealer more deliberately, "because *this* is the critical link. We are the government bond dealers. We're private corporations, but without us the government can't sell its bonds. We work just like automobile dealers. We buy the bonds from the Treasury or the government agencies at a discount in their big auctions. We put the bonds in our inventory. We mark 'em up a bit; then we sell 'em to investors in the United States and all over the world. Later, when the government auctions off another new batch of bonds, we do it all over again—buy 'em, stick 'em in inventory, mark 'em up, sell 'em."

"OK. So what's the big problem?"

"The problem is, when the bonds are crashing in value, our bond inventories are also crashing in value. We take huge losses. Sure, we try to hedge against those losses, but in 1980 the crash hit so big, so fast, we got stuck with huge losses anyhow. The deficit was out of control. Inflation and interest rates were surging. No one wanted to buy bonds."

"What happened exactly?"

"Would you like a play-by-play description?"

"Yeah, go ahead."

BOND MARKET PARALYSIS

"One day, I'm sitting at my desk in the trading room here at our Water Street offices. I'm staring blankly at the bond quote screen, and I happen to notice the price of the *long bond*—the newest, longest term U.S. Treasury bond. My eyeballs practically pop out of my head. The damn price is down to below the equivalent lows that it hit during the Civil War! I say to one of our senior partners, 'Can you believe this? Our country was split in two back during the Civil War, millions of soldiers falling by the wayside on American soil, and still these damn bond prices were better back then than they are right now!' "

"Amazing!"

"All of us say, 'bonds are so low now, they can't possibly go any lower.' So we take a big piece of the next Treasury bond auction, with only partial hedges. Little do we realize that it's just the *beginning* of the bond market crash! Next thing you know, the Russians are invading Afghanistan, and bond investors are freaking out. They're worried about the Cold War heating up and the federal deficit going totally haywire, even more haywire than it already *is* going. That's when we *really* get clobbered!"

The bond veteran took a short breath. "In those days," he went on, "a truly *bad* day in the government bond market is a plunge of maybe 1 full point—say, from 85 to 84. But in the next few days, we'd pay anything to go back to just 1-point down days. Because the long bond is now plunging 3 points in one trading session, 4 points in the next! Never before—and never again—in my lifetime have I experienced anything like that!

"But it gets worse," he added. "There are no buyers. Just sellers. On one particular day, bond prices fall by close to 10 percent. That's almost as much, percentage-wise, as the worst day of the crash of '29 in the stock market! And we're not talking about risky stocks; we're talking about supposedly supersafe bonds—bonds issued by the U.S. government!" [See Figure 9.1.]

Johnston could hardly believe his ears. He mumbled his acknowledgment and listened silently while the bond veteran proceeded with his story.

"We check our capital—practically zero. We call the authorities—tell them, 'Game over! We give up, we're out. Can't take no more of your bonds. Can't bid in any more of your bond auctions.' Then, we call our colleagues in the industry. They say they're doing the same thing. Practically all of them are shutting down, withdrawing from the market. Finally, the point is reached when everyone's out—everyone except for maybe the two largest bond dealers with the deepest pockets: Merrill and Salomon. One day, a

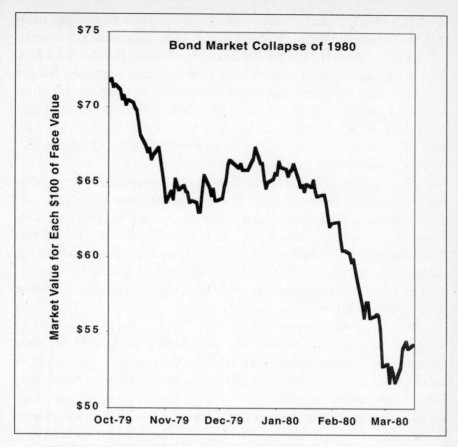

Figure 9.1 In 1980, the price of U.S. government bonds fell so swiftly, many bond dealers were forced to withdraw from the market, making it difficult for the government to sell its bonds to the public—an extremely dangerous situation which prompted drastic action by the Carter Administration. Unless the government takes steps to gain control over its ballooning budget deficits, a similar crisis is possible in the future. *Data:* Reuters.

Merrill bond trader calls up a Salomon bond trader and says, 'I got a $20 million lot of Treasury bonds I need to sell to you today.' And the Salomon guy responds, 'Oh yeah? I got $30 million I need to sell *you*.' They're like two lonely kids on the street corner trading marbles back and forth. No one else in the game!"

"OK. But how did that affect the Treasury, the U.S. government?"

"Don't you get it? If dealers can't sell to the public—can't even sell to each other—how the heck is the U.S. government going to sell *its* new bonds? Typically, a dealer can move hundreds of millions of dollars in U.S. government bonds almost instantly. But on February 11, 1980, they can't find a buyer for a relatively small lot of just $5 million. There are quite a few astute traders working that lot practically all day long, and they still can't place it. There are no buyers. The entire government bond market is dead or dying."

"So what do they do about it?"

"They get together and run down to Washington to talk to Carter and his advisers. I don't know what they say exactly, but let me translate the basic message down to its bare-bones essentials. They say, in effect, 'Either you do something drastic to end this bond market nightmare or it's all over. If we can't sell your bonds, the government won't be able to finance the deficit. You've got to do whatever it takes to kill the inflation scare, even if that means sinking the economy.' "

"What's Carter's response?"

"Of course, Carter doesn't like that. He's a Democrat and he's up for reelection that year. The last thing he wants is a recession in an election year. But the bond dealers insist. 'Look here,' they say, 'if you can't raise the money, you can't pay your bills. You can't meet government payroll. The paychecks of all the senators and congressmen are gonna bounce. *Your* paycheck is gonna bounce!' Carter likes that even less. He decides to do something to kill the inflation scare *then and there* . . . and take his chances with the election *later*. He gets Fed Chairman Volcker to slap strict controls on credit cards and other forms of credit—something that's never been done before in American history. They virtually crush the economy, and Carter loses the election. But they save the bond market."

Johnston had no idea that bond investors and bond dealers could wield so much power over the destiny of the country. But it made sense. They were America's creditors. And just like common stock investors could make or break corporate management, government bond investors could ultimately sway Washington's economic policy, even make or break the administration.

The bond dealer broke into his thoughts: "If something like that ever comes again, the end result will be the same. The precise circumstances may be different. But the president will sacrifice everything—the economy, corporate earnings, jobs, even the next election—for the sake of protecting his ability to continue borrowing freely in the open market. He'll have no choice. That's what happened in 1980, and that's what will happen next time too."

"So what you're saying is that . . ."

"That . . ." The bond dealer paused for a moment, then turned to a broader issue. "Most people think the government is all powerful and can bail out companies in trouble, pump up the economy, hold up the markets. 'Don't worry,' they say, 'Uncle Sam will save you.' Not true; Uncle Sam will be too busy saving himself!"

CHAPTER 10

THE REAL ESTATE BUBBLE

In the year 2000, tech stocks collapsed, ending the economic boom of the 1990s.

In response, the Federal Reserve pumped large sums of fresh money into the economy, pushing interest rates down a record 11 times in 2001.

Then, in 2002, the low interest rates prompted millions of Americans to rush to refinance their home mortgages, helping to drive home prices higher.

Was it a bubble? If it was, it would not become apparent until *after* it burst. Nor would consumers get warnings from their real estate brokers and agents.

So it should come as no surprise that when Gabriel Dedini began talking to real estate professionals about buying a home for his parents, he encountered absolutely unanimous, unflinching, bullish advice.

The woman who recently helped Gabriel and his wife sell their summer home was a perfect example. She had been a Virginia-licensed real estate agent for over 20 years, throughout which she never *once* had a client who lost money buying and holding residential real estate. In her experience, middle-class homes in a suburb of a major metropolitan area like Washington, D.C., were as close to a sure bet as you could get.

Gabriel called the agent at her office. She proposed a home in a quiet neighborhood in Fairfax County. He wanted something even further away from the hubbub of city traffic, with more isolation and better security.

At first, she tried to nudge him, using subtle hints, toward the bigger, better-located properties. Finally, she threw down the gauntlet, pulled out a fact sheet she had extracted from various industry newsletters, and poured on the hype with no punches pulled. "See how home prices are spurting upward again all over the country?" she asked excitedly.

"Where?"

"Right here in Arlington, for example!"

"That's just one community in one state," Gabriel remarked.

"No, no. All over the country, everywhere. Look at Long Island! Up 13 percent in 2002. Look at Fort Lauderdale. Check out Providence, Rhode Island. Same thing! Homes are up 13, 14, even 15 percent! And all of that is just in *one* year!"

"Yeah, but . . ."

"Virginia is not California, but consider what's happening over a longer period of time! San Francisco—up more than 70 percent. San Jose—80 percent. San Diego, Santa Cruz, Santa Barbara, Santa Rosa—also 80 percent. A while back, you could have bought a three-bedroom ranch house for $60,000 or $70,000. Care to guess what they're going for now?"

"About $300,000?"

"Hah! Guess again. Those same $60,000 homes are now going for $840,000 in Malibu, $790,000 in Burlingame, $742,000 in Beverly Hills, $727,000 in La Jolla, $882,000 in Carmel, and—"

"How does that connect to me?"

"It's going to happen here too. Even if you adjust for inflation, the price of the average American home has risen more quickly in the last seven years than in any previous period since 1945. That's when the GIs came home from World War II and drove housing prices through the roof. Now we don't have returning GIs. But we have gobs of money coming out of new mortgages, all going into homes. We have gobs of money coming out of the stock market, also going into homes . . ."

He coughed nervously, but she continued. "Even if the homes in this area go up only half as much, tell me, where can you go—

what investment can you buy—that goes up anywhere *near* this fast? Not stocks! Not bonds! I challenge you to come up with one—just one—that can give you this kind of performance, plus this kind of security, all at the same time. Look at this beautiful four-bedroom. Golf course, clubhouse, high-tech security guardhouse . . . do your parents drive?"

"Yeah."

"Good. Only a half-mile from the highway exit, 100 percent secured parking, and—"

It seemed that she would go on forever, but then the doorbell rang. Gabriel excused himself for a moment, leaving the receiver dangling off the hook. When he returned, however, he excused himself again, promising to call the agent back later.

He was skeptical. He was among the few people in the Western world who had recently witnessed plunging real estate values first-hand—in the outskirts of Buenos Aires, Argentina, where his parents now lived. Because of a banking holiday, no one had any cash money. So there were no buyers for anything—let alone homes. Desperate sellers were everywhere, and middle-class home values had plunged dramatically, especially when measured in U.S. dollars. Declines of 60, 70, even 80 percent were not uncommon—and all within a matter of months.

But that was Argentina. What about the United States? What were the chances of it happening here? A 10 percent chance? More? He tried calling Linda's adviser, but the man confessed that he was not an expert in real estate. "Whatever you do, don't rely on agents. When's the last time you were in the market for a house and an agent told you, 'No, don't buy now. It's a bad time to buy'? They never say that. If the market is soft, they'll say, 'It's the perfect time to buy 'cause the market is soft.' If the market is booming, they' say, 'See—the market is booming. Jump in now while you can!' "

"Yeah, I've noticed."

"Wait—I just remembered something." Gabriel could hear the clicking coming from the adviser's computer keyboard. "Here it is," the adviser said. "Call this man." He read Gabriel the number.

Gabriel reached the man later that evening, apparently somewhere on Florida's west coast. While the phone was ringing, he reflected on what the adviser had said about him. "This man's an

85-year-old retired-but-still-workaholic type of person. He's a no-nonsense real estate analyst. He's one of the few in the whole country who's been around long enough to have seen big price declines in the real estate market. The first thing he'll tell you is that property prices don't *always* go up forever and ever."

After six rings, the man finally answered in a lazy voice. For the first few minutes, he said very little, trying to stay noncommittal. As soon as Gabriel mentioned his experiences in South America, however, the man opened up like a gusher. "Oh, good. I can talk to you then."

"Why's that?"

"You don't know what I go through around here. If you say to someone 'the stock market is going to hell in a handbasket,' well . . . maybe you don't make many friends, but at least you're still considered human. If you start telling people 'watch out—*home values* are going to tank,' forget it; you're a rat spreading the bubonic plague. So I just mind my own business. I do my research. I write my column for the paper. I go to sleep. I wake up. I do more research. Write another column. That's my life."

"Tank?" Gabriel's command of English vocabulary was superb, but he did not understand the word "tank" in this context.

"Right. Not just go down a percent or two—you could see 'em tank 20, 30, 40 percent, maybe more, depending on a = host of factors."

"I see. But here in the United States of America? I mean—is that common? Has that *ever* happened?"

"Not common, no, but—"

"When, then?"

"In any region, at any time there's been a real estate bubble followed by a local or national economic setback."

"For example?"

"We had a real estate bust in Hawaii in 1990. We had the California housing bust—also in 1990. There was a Texas real estate bust in 1987. Here in Florida, we got hit the hardest in 1975. May I go back further in time? There was the real estate crash in San Diego in 1962. Let me see. This is going way back now—the Florida land bust of 1926, probably the worst in American history. Also, the Los Angeles bust of 1889. Chicago got smacked in 1842, 1877, and 1932."

"But most of the time, in most of the country, doesn't real estate just keep going up and up and up?"

"Yes, yes. That's very true. But home prices have also fallen *nationally*—in any period when there is a prolonged, speculative stock market boom followed by a deep stock market bust. Just like we've seen right now."

"How bad was it though, really?"

"Devastating. After the 1929 fiasco, real estate prices were smashed for a full decade. After the 1974 bear market, we witnessed *the* most severe real estate depression of the second half of the twentieth century. Now, stocks are down worse than in 1974. The only saving grace today is low interest rates. But if interest rates go back up, even a bit . . . good night shirt! This is a bubble—just like the stock market is a bubble."

The voice of a woman could be heard from across the room, apparently complaining about something. The analyst muffled the phone with his hand as he responded to her, but he spoke loudly and was still plainly audible. "Quiet! I finally got a live person who doesn't think I'm just a crazy ol' fart like you do!"

Gabriel smiled to himself and then asked, "Where's the bubble? I don't see the bubble."

"Of course you don't. Hardly anyone does. But *I* see it. Plain as day."

"Where?"

"In the mortgages. In the huge debts. I've been around for a long time. Even back in the 1940s, I was still not much younger than most first-home buyers today. Guess how much equity an average American family had in their home back then?"

"I don't know—50 percent?"

"No, 85 percent! For every, say, $10,000 in home value, a family had $8,500 in equity and only $1,500 in debt, on average. Now, it's different: For a $100,000 home, an average family's got only $55,000 in equity and a whopping $45,000 in debt. The average debt on a house has tripled."

"Hmm. $55,000 in equity on a $100,000 home? That still doesn't sound so bad. A lot of people would kill for that much equity."

"Exactly. That's the problem. This number is just an average. Meanwhile, millions of people have practically no equity at all. A lot of them took all the cash out with second mortgages, with equity loans, with refinancing. Yeah, they got a nice wad of cash. But now most of that money is gone. Where did it go? They spent it! They spent it on vacations, luxury cars, boats, and other toys. Many people even used the cash to play the tech stocks."

Gabriel swallowed hard. Playing the stock market with the proceeds from a real estate sale was exactly what he and his wife had done too.

"You have a fax machine handy?" asked the real estate analyst.

"Yup."

The analyst ran to his fax machine, sent a fax to Gabriel, and came back in less than two minutes. "It's on its way now. You can pick it up later. When you do, look at the graph. It's the equity on homes in America. Look at how it's been going down, down, down. The lowest in over half a century—just when the stock market is telling us to expect some real tough times ahead."

"Still, 55 percent equity in the average home sounds pretty darn good to me. What's so bad about that?"

"You still don't get it. When you look at that chart, I want you to remember this one all-important, earth-shattering fact: *The equity has been going down for all these years even though home values have been going up!*

He paused for a moment and then asked, "If you start with a home valued at, say, $100,000, with a mortgage for about $70,000, how much equity do you have in it?"

"$30,000—30 percent."

"Right. Now let's say your home doubles in value to $200,000. How much equity do you have now?"

Gabriel paused for a moment to figure the math in his head. "That's $130,000 in equity—60 percent. No, excuse me, 65 percent!"

"See? Your equity *more* than doubled. That's what should have happened all over the country all these years. But it didn't. The more home values went up, the more people accelerated their borrowing. So even while values were rising, their equity was plunging. That is dangerous—very, *very* dangerous."

"Why?"

"Because when home values decline, it could wipe out the remaining equity in a heartbeat. Then everyone's over their heads in debt. Then, there's no more source of equity loans. People stop investing more money in real estate. When they lose their income, they walk away from their homes. They leave their keys with the realtor and move out of town, or worse."

Gabriel temporarily ended the conversation, saying that he needed a moment to get the material from the fax machine, look it over, and try to digest it all. He called back a half hour later; an elderly woman picked up, sighed, and called the analyst to the phone right away.

"Did you see my stuff?" asked the analyst.

"Yes, thank you. Let's say I accept the fact that real estate is a bubble. What I want to know is: When is it going to go pop?"

"It already has! Right now, as we speak. But you don't see it yet, because it's first hitting commercial and industrial real estate. Then it's going to spread out from there."

The analyst went on to describe, in vivid detail, three distinct phases in a real estate bust.

He said that in the first phase, a stock market decline would make it impossible for many companies to raise money, so they would slash their expansion projects. Soon, they'd be cutting down on the space they occupied in offices, factories, and stores, as well as canceling new construction projects, leaving billions of square feet empty. If they went bankrupt, even more space would be dumped on the market.

"That's exactly what happened last time," the analyst explained. "New completions of office space plummeted from more than 100 million square feet in the second half of the 1980s to just 28 million square feet in the first half of the '90s. Occupancy rates, rents, sales, and prices all fell. That's what seems to be happening now too."

He said that in the second phase of a real estate bust, ailing companies would lay off hundreds of thousands of workers and that those laid-off workers would default on their mortgages.

"How much longer before this starts happens, do you figure?" Gabriel asked.

"You're not serious, are you? Haven't you been following the news? Nearly 10 million U.S. citizens and residents are now without jobs, struggling to keep a roof over their heads. We now have the worst mortgage delinquency rate in 30 years! We have the worst foreclosure rate on home mortgages in 52 years! We have the largest *number* of foreclosures of all time—640,000 in just one quarter alone! It's starting to happen right now, and the economy is still supposedly in a recovery."

"OK. What's the third phase?"

"The third phase will make the 1975 real estate recessions look like a Sunday picnic. Residential real estate is going to collapse like a house of cards."

"But what about all that money that's going to pour out of the stock market and into the real estate market? Where else are people going to put that money? Where else can the money go?"

"What money? Most people are frozen in the stock market like a deer in headlights. But look at what's going on even with the people who are pulling out! Right now, when they pull their money out of the New York Stock Exchange, how much do you figure they're going to get out of it? I know, because I'm an investor myself, and I can tell you how much I can get. I can get only 63 cents for every dollar I invested at the peak. If I invested in an S&P 500 stock, it's much worse: I'm not going to get much more than 50 cents on the dollar. And $1 invested in the Nasdaq at its peak? It's a joke. It's worth only about a quarter today! Do you seriously believe that with those kinds of losses, people are going to be anxious to rush into real estate?"

"I guess not."

"Keep your eyes open. Watch the vacation homes. Those will be the first to go. In the roaring '90s, affluent Americans bought second or even third homes. They bought vacation retreats in the mountains. They bought beach houses. That was in good times. But now, we've got bad times acomin'. Now, they see their stock portfolios plunging. They're worried about their job security. So what do they do? They sell their mountain retreats. They sell their beach houses. Prices plunge.

"Next," continued the analyst, "watch the mortgage rates. If they start rising, you've got all the ingredients for a first-class, all-out panic in the housing market. That's what would hit the underbelly of this market, the weakest link."

"Which is—"

"Which is, all those people with adjustable-rate mortgages–especially people who used the lower rates on the ARMs to buy a more expensive house than they could afford to otherwise. If rates go up, a lot of those people are going to fall behind on their payments. If they lose income, even more of those people are going to fall behind. A lot of them are going to want an immediate sale. They're going to list their homes at ridiculously low prices. Prices will plunge in a big splash, and then the splash will ripple outward from there."

"I see."

"One last word: This is not the stock market. You can't just call your real estate agent one day and say, "Sell this property at the market–today!" It takes time to move your property. It takes time for price trends to spread from coast to coast. So the storm may not descend on your neighborhood next week or even next month. Still, you've got to start the process sooner rather than later. You picked up my stuff from your faxer, right?"

"Yeah. I got two extra pages here. What's this other material?"

The analyst explained that he recently wrote a story for the local Sunday real estate section, but it never got published. His original headline was "What to Do before Real Estate Values Get Trashed." His editor had insisted that it be changed to "What to Do if the Real Estate Market Turns Soft." So the analyst sent it back as "What to Do when Real Estate Is Falling." But after all that back-and-forth, the story wound up on the editing room floor anyhow. "The very first thing you've got to do," he said, "is make up your mind that you're not going to do it–that you're not going to buy that new place. The rest is all there. Just read it. Call me again anytime."

WHAT TO DO WHEN REAL ESTATE IS FALLING

Step 1: Wait–don't rush to buy! As long as the stock market is falling and the economy is weakening, it's likely that you'll get a much better deal on a similar property later on. Even if mortgage rates are higher by then, the amount you can save in the price could be several times greater than any extra interest you may have to pay.

If you must buy now, however, do not assume more debt than you can comfortably afford. Low interest rates may tempt you, but never forget that the total debt you assume today will be with you for years.

Step 2: Seriously consider selling commercial properties. Their values are typically the first to fall in the wake of a stock market crash. Seek to price the properties aggressively to move quickly, without giving away the store. Forget about what you think the property *should* be worth. Get a good, realistic fix on the market and stay below it. If you try to squeeze out above- or even at-market prices, you could find yourself continually one step behind, missing your target buyers and getting stuck with an asset that just keeps on falling.

Step 3: Seriously consider selling a second home. A second home could be among the first residential properties to go down. Move swiftly, following the same instructions as given in in Step 2.

Step 4: Rental property could be the next to go. Don't assume your tenants—regardless of their income level or apparent job security—will renew their leases or even continue paying their rent on a timely basis. Seriously consider selling.

Step 5: Your primary residence—house or home? Ponder carefully and discuss with your family the following three questions:
(a) Is your house primarily a home with no other available place to live where you'd be happy? If so, selling is not even an issue for you. Whether the home's market value goes up or down, you have decided to stay put.
(b) Have you already been talking about moving anyway? If so, the best time to sell is when you have good
(Continued)

reason to believe that prices may be going lower—such as after a major stock market decline—but prices are still not far from peak levels.

If this accurately describes the current situation in your area, do your utmost to take advantage of this time window to close a sale. If prices have already begun to decline, price it below market to move it quickly.

(c) Are you near or past retirement age? And are you counting on your real estate to finance a substantial portion of your retirement or long-term care? If so, consider selling now. It's a difficult and painful decision, but it could be more prudent than risking an event that could upset your plans.

Step 6: Find out whether you're in a "bubble zone." If you are on the fence, struggling to weigh the pros and cons of staying versus selling, one extra piece of information that may help you reach a decision is whether or not you live in an area that has enjoyed a real estate boom. Other factors aside, the sharper the recent rise, the sharper the decline when values do fall. To find out, log on to the Office of Federal Housing Enterprise Oversight Web site at www.ofheo.gov. Go to the House Price Index and find the table that lists the percent change in house prices. This is a list of major U.S. metropolitan areas, with statistics on national house-price increases for the most recent quarter, one-year, and 5-year period. If homes in your area have appreciated by 25 percent or more in the last five years, it's likely that you live in the midst of a housing bubble and your home value may be at greater-than-average risk.

CHAPTER 11

THE WINNING MINORITY

In the world of politics, the majority wins and the minority loses. In the world of investments, it's often the opposite, especially at major turning points in history.

The many who join stock market booms can get crushed as crowds break down the exit doors in a crash. Conversely, the few who learn the secrets of crash profits can sometimes make more money in the decline than many people made during the preceding boom.

Linda Dedini came from a family that knew more about business and finance than most. Yet no one ever talked about crashes—let alone about crash profits.

Crashes were things that existed strictly in an ill-defined historical past and that modern society had long-ago learned to prevent. At the very worst, a crash was an aberration that could not last, an opportunity to snatch up bargains before the market resumed its semieternal rise. The entire concept of actually *making money* in a decline was totally foreign to most people, including Linda Dedini.

The classic way to make crash profits is to sell short. However, the term "selling short" was not even something she ever thought about, except in its colloquial meaning. "Never sell yourself short," her mother used to say, or "always respect your family; never sell them short." Selling short was obviously an inappropriate behavior.

Until recently, she had left investment decisions primarily in the hands of others, such as her broker. Now, however, devastating losses in the stock market left her no choice but to dig in and finally learn more about investing. The living room TV, which used to always drone in the background with Disney Channel, Nickelodeon, or MTV, now droned with talking heads on CNBC. The family's cocker spaniel, whose morning job was to mangle the *Washington Post,* now had to work double time–to mangle *both* the *Post* and the *Wall Street Journal.*

One evening, while Linda was poring through a stack of tests on elementary mechanics, two words uttered on a CNBC talk show caught her attention: "crash" and "profits."

She knew all about the crash. She had been through it herself. She knew all about profits too–that's what the broker had promised but never delivered. But crash and profits in the same sentence? It seemed totally incongruous.

She brushed it aside, stared for a moment at the still-uncorrected stack of tests, sighed, and picked up another to grade: *Physics 101. Unit 1–Mechanics. Question 1. Levers are tools that transmit and modify force applied at two points and turned about a third. Give three examples in your daily life, and explain how they fit the definition.*

The question was a giveaway. Any student who didn't get this one would likely run aground on the tougher questions requiring serious problem-solving skills. She read some of the answers. *Crowbar, car jack, catapult, spoon in cafeteria food fight, elbow of teacher smacking student for dumb test answers.* "Yes!" or "Witty!" were her comments in the margins, as the chit-chat on CNBC continued in the background.

Then, suddenly, there they were again! Those same two words, coming from the same Surround Sound speakers that habitually blasted Backstreet Boys or Britney Spears: "crash" and "profits," plus one more word–"leverage."

Leverage? In the stock market? In a crash? Generating profits? *Stop!* she said to herself. *Stop grading these tests and pay attention for a change!*

As she put down the tests and listened more intently, however, instead of the clarification she sought she got a new torrent of jargon: "shorts" ... "reverse index funds" ... "puts" ... and then, suddenly, for a third time, "crash! ... profits"!

Needless to say, it was the very *first* topic in her very *next* conversation with her adviser.

"I'm absolutely amazed at what I just heard about crash profits," she said during an earlier-than-usual morning phone call to his home. "It was on TV. I wasn't even paying attention, but the words just leaped out and grabbed me while I was engrossed in school work."

At first he seemed as perplexed as she was. " 'Crash profits?' What are you talking about?"

"No, not exactly crash profits. First it was the crash-word, *then* they said something else, *then* came the profits-word. But it was practically in the same breath. I think the Dow was down something like 300 points the day before yesterday, right? So at first I thought they were talking about some unique stock that had gone up in spite of the market decline. I assumed they meant profits *despite* the crash. Then, though, it seemed like they were talking about profits *because of* the crash itself. That's why I called you right now. Sorry for bothering you so early."

The adviser waved off the apology, explaining that he was an early riser and that he had indeed given her the OK to call him at home. "What particular investment were they referring to?" he asked.

"I haven't the faintest idea. All I know is that some of them had jumped by as much five times. Can you believe that? 500 percent profit!"

"Well, no, not exactly. If an investment jumps by five times, that's actually a 400 percent profit. For example, if it goes from, say, $100 to $500, your profit will be $400, or 400 percent of your original investment."

"That's it!" she said conclusively. "That's exactly what they said, or very close. There was one they talked about that had gone from about $100 to $250. Another had surged from $150 to nearly $800. All in one day! I urgently need to know more about these investments. Please, can you tell me what they are?"

The adviser thought for a moment before responding. "There's only one investment I know of that could go from $150 to $800 on a crash day. They're among the most powerfully leveraged investments in the world. In other words, like a big lever, they provide potentially very large gains with a very small investment. They're usually cheap. They're volatile and speculative, but they can be fun, provided you don't overplay them. But before I tell you more, I need to know: What are you trying to accomplish? What's your goal?"

She sighed. "I really don't know. All I know is, we're scared. We should never have sold our mountain retreat. We should never have put that money in the stock market. We took a huge beating. Then every time we tried to make up for it, we got killed even more. We have to recoup those losses quickly, but how?"

She hesitated for a moment and bit her lip. "Plus, now, I have more bad news. Remember my grandfather and his portfolio?"

"Uh-huh."

"We never sold it. It wasn't Grandpa so much as it was my brothers. They're both doctors. They don't know any more about the market than I do, but they *think* they know more. In their mind, selling after the market has already gone down is like closing the barn door after the horse has escaped. If anything, they said, we should *buy more*."

"What about the list I gave you?"

"List? Oh, you mean the most vulnerable stocks? Sure, we looked through that very carefully, but he's got stocks like Exxon, General Motors, Phillip Morris, IBM, and a whole bunch of blue chips he bought decades ago. Only a couple of the stocks in his portfolio were on your list."

"Then why didn't you check the stocks with one of the independent rating agencies I told you about?" the adviser asked.

"Huh? Hmm, I don't remember. I guess no one volunteered to do the work. Besides, I didn't want to fight them on it, and they didn't want to fight me on it. So we dropped it, and the whole thing fell through the cracks. My concern is that maybe now it's too late."

"No, no, it's not too late. Not at all. Most of the blue chips are still vulnerable in many ways. The portfolio is overinvested in common stocks. Better late than never."

"The other bad news," she said sorrowfully, "is that the doctors say Grandpa has only weeks to live."

"So what does the family want to do?"

"They—we—don't know. If we sold the shares now, the capital gains taxes would be huge. But it's a moot point. Although we have some influence, we don't have control over the portfolio. I figure it'll be months before it's out of probate. My mother tells me the portfolio's down over 10 percent just in the past few weeks. What are we going to do? Just sit there and watch it go down the tubes like our telecoms?"

The adviser responded reassuringly. "You've already liquidated all the stocks in your personal portfolio, right? You've already put that money into Treasury bills or something equivalent, right? Yes? Very good. That takes a lot of pressure off you right there. You've stopped the bloodletting. Now, you and your family have two remaining goals."

CRASH PROTECTION

"We do?"

"Yes. First goal—to recoup losses. Second goal—for you and the other heirs—to protect the stocks in your expected inheritance against the next market crash. The protection is your first priority. What do you know about selling short?"

"Nothing!" she said firmly, conveying a distaste for the concept.

"Don't get me wrong. I'm not going to recommend that you sell stocks short, but you need to understand how it works. Essentially, instead of buying low and selling high, you just reverse the order of the transaction. First you sell the shares high; then you buy the shares low."

"How in the world can you sell shares that you don't own?"

"You borrow them. Let's say Exxon is selling for $35 per share. You go to your broker, you borrow 1,000 shares, and you promptly sell them. That gives you a $35,000 credit in your account. Got that so far?"

"Sure. $35,000 cash in my account."

"No, not cash—*credit!*"

"Oh, OK. I have a $35,000 credit in my account. Go on."

"Then, Exxon falls to $15. You buy the 1,000 shares for $15 each to return them to the broker. How much do you to deduct from your $35,000 credit to pay for those shares?"

"One thousand at $15 per share? $15,000, I guess, but . . ."

"Just bear with me. So how much does that leave in your account?"

"$20,000?"

"Exactly. That's your net proceeds–$20,000. Naturally, if the stock goes up, you incur a loss."

"Interesting," she said unenthusiastically.

"Now, let me explain the reasons I do *not* recommend short selling to most investors. If the stock goes up and you hold on indefinitely, there's a danger that you could eventually suffer losses greater than the amount you invested. I assume–"

"No, thank you! I can't expose myself to that kind of risk. I have a family to care for. I have two kids that deserve to go to a decent college someday. In any case, I don't want to sell short the market. I'd feel like a vulture–profiting from everyone else's pain and suffering. I can't do that. It's unpatriotic, morally wrong."

The adviser, who until now had been very jovial, responded sternly. "That's pure hogwash!"

The response reminded her of her father's reaction whenever she offended him. "Why's that?" she asked apologetically.

"Let me explain. Investors who sell short–the short sellers–can be godsend in the market. They squirrel away buying power. Then, when the market is down and out, they're the first to buy. They're like the starter engine in your car that revs things back up again. Without them, the market could languish at low levels for months. Remember: Short sellers have all those credit balances in their accounts. Plus, they owe all those shares. At some point, they are going to *have* to buy the shares back, right? When the bear market is ending, who do you think is going to get us out of the hole? Who's going to get us started on the road to a real recovery? The short sellers!"

REVERSE INDEX MUTUAL FUNDS

"Fascinating, but I still can't afford to take the unlimited risk," Linda said.

"You won't and you shouldn't. Instead, you should buy only investments in which your risk is strictly limited to the amount you put up."

"Give me an example."

"You can buy a specialized mutual fund to profit from a decline. When you own shares in one of these funds, you can never lose more than you invest—just like any other kind of mutual fund. You will never get a margin call. In other words, they will never ask you to put up more money. And the more the market falls, the more your fund shares will be worth. Just visualize blue-chip stocks going down on one side and your mutual fund shares going up on the other side."

She thought about it for a moment, and the image of a seesaw came to mind. On the one side of the seesaw were her grandfather's stocks, going down with the market. On the other side was this special mutual fund, going up, to offset the losses. "What do they call that kind of fund?"

"It's called a 'reverse index mutual fund.' "

"Why are they called that?"

"Because they're the reverse of index funds. Are you familiar with index funds?"

She responded affirmatively but hesitantly.

"Let me explain them to you anyway. Index funds are matched to a major market index like the Dow 30 Industrials or the S&P 500. If you wanted to invest in a rising stock market, you'd have a hard time buying all 30 Dow stocks or all 500 S&P stocks, right? So, you could just buy shares in one of those index funds and they'd do it for you. Or, they'd use other instruments—but always seeking to keep the value of their shares in lock step with the market index. The index goes up 20 percent; the mutual fund goes up 20 percent."

He paused for a moment in case she had questions; then he proceeded. "The funds I'm talking about do the same thing, *in reverse*. They buy various investments for you that effectively sell short all of the S&P 500 or all of the Nasdaq 100 stocks, or whatever."

"How do they do that?"

"I'll give you more info on the mechanics later. For now, let's talk about the results. Consider a fund that tracks the S&P 500 in reverse, for example. If the S&P goes down 10 percent, your fund shares are designed to go *up* 10 percent. If the S&P goes down 20 percent, you should make 20 percent. The more the market falls, the more money you make."

"Any others?"

"Yes. There's also another one that does essentially the same thing for the Nasdaq 100 Index. If the Nasdaq 100 goes down 10 percent, your shares in the fund are designed to go up 10 percent."

"Sounds too good to be true."

"It's true all right but not always so good. If the market goes up, you lose. If the S&P rallies 20 percent and you have a fund that's the reverse of the S&P, then your fund goes down 20 percent. Meanwhile, though, at that point your grandfather's shares would probably be going up. Maybe not dollar for dollar, but close."

"I know what you mean," she said with complete understanding. "It won't be a perfectly balanced seesaw. The fulcrum may be off-center."

She felt very content, and the adviser promised to give her the name and phone number of some of the reverse index funds, plus a set of instructions on exactly how much, where, and when to buy.

Linda breathed more easily. Until now, she had felt naked without some kind of protection. Now that she knew how to cover herself, she could sleep nights. She vowed to act on it as soon as she got home.

"I'll send you the details in a file attached to an e-mail," he said. "I'll call it 'Crash Protection.' Check it out, and if you have any questions, let me know. Gotta run now. I have a dentist appointment—"

"But wait!" she exclaimed before he hung up. "What about the investment that can turn $150 into $800? What about helping us recoup our losses quickly?"

"First, take care of your defense—crash protection. Then, as soon as you've got that licked, call me back in a couple of days. Depending on your finances, you can go on the offense and aim for crash profits."

CRASH PROTECTION

If you cannot liquidate vulnerable stocks, consider these steps:

Step 1: Learn more about reverse index funds. If you put money in a typical stock market mutual fund, the managers will generally invest it in various stocks that they pick, depending on their research and opinion of the market.

Index mutual funds are more restricted. The managers' job is strictly to buy stocks or other instruments to match, as closely as possible, the performance of a particular stock market index, such as the Dow Jones Industrials, the S&P 500 or the Nasdaq 100. Reverse index mutual funds use the same principle—but in reverse. Instead of helping you make money when the market goes up, they are designed to help you make money when the market goes *down.*

They invest a good portion of your money in safe instruments, such as Treasury bills, to generate interest income. Plus, they allocate a portion to investments, such as futures and options, that appreciate as the market goes down, balancing the exact quantities of these instruments so that

- There is always enough cash and equivalent in the fund to cover any losses. You cannot lose more than you invest.
- The fund matches the performance of the index in reverse. If the market goes down, you will make a profit; if the market goes up, you will incur a loss.

Some examples:

Rydex Ursa (RYURX; www.rydexfunds.com, 1-800-820-0888). This fund is designed to appreciate 10 percent for every 10 percent decline in the S&P 500 Index.

Here's how it works: The Rydex Ursa fund basically maintains an open short position in the near-term S&P 500 Index using the futures markets. But these positions are fully collateralized with Treasury bills and various money market instruments, earning interest. The interest income helps cover transaction costs, operating expenses, and management fees.

Whatever income is left over gets paid out as a dividend. This dividend also helps cushion somewhat the decline in net asset value during periods when the stock

(Continued)

market is rising. During periods of market decline, it can help enhance your gains somewhat, depending on interest rate levels.

Warning: When you buy this fund, you are betting on declining stock prices. If the markets go up instead, you can lose money.

Rydex Arktos (RYAIX; www.rydexfunds.com, 1-800-820-0888). This is structured the same way as the Rydex Ursa fund, with one critical difference: Instead of tracking the S&P 500 Index, it tracks the Nasdaq 100. For every 10 percent decline in the Nasdaq 100, the fund is designed to appreciate 10 percent. Since the Nasdaq 100 Index tends to be more volatile than the S&P 500, the fluctuations in this fund's shares will also be more volatile. That means higher potential profits but also higher risks.

Profunds (www.profunds.com, 1-888-776-3637). Similar funds that are essentially clones of the Rydex funds.

Step 2: Evaluate your remaining stock portfolio. Is it almost entirely tech stocks? Or is it mostly blue-chip and other stocks, with just a small amount of techs?

If you have blue-chip or other stocks that you can't sell, consider placing a modest portion of your money into shares of the Rydex Ursa fund or equivalent. That way, if your stock portfolio is falling, your Ursa shares will be rising, helping to offset the loss.

If you have a large portfolio of tech stocks that you can't sell, you should buy shares in the Rydex Arktos fund. That way, even if your tech stocks fall still further, at least your Arktos shares will be rising, helping to offset the loss.

Step 3: Estimate your risk of loss. No one knows for sure whether the stock market is going up or down—let alone how much or how quickly. But based on recent history, it is not unreasonable to assume that a stock portfolio could fall 50 percent. If your portfolio is worth about $100,000 at one time, your risk, in this scenario, will be $50,000; If you have $50,000, your risk will be $25,000; and so on.

Step 4: Decide how much of that risk you want to protect yourself against.   If you wanted to protect yourself against the *entire* amount, you'd have to invest about dollar for dollar in one of the reverse index funds. If that is too much, consider covering half your portfolio. Then, for every $1 of current value in your stock portfolio, you would simply put 50 cents of your money into the appropriate reverse index fund (see Step 1). Assuming that your stock portfolio is worth $100,000, you'd be investing about $50,000 in the fund.

Step 5: Raise the funds for your crash protection program.   Where do you get the extra $50,000? You could take it from your cash assets. But if you did, you would in effect be moving money from a safe investment to a more aggressive investment. That may not be prudent.

Instead, a prudent alternative is to liquidate at least enough from your remaining stock portfolio to finance this program.

The formula is simple: If you want a program that will protect you against half your risk, and you don't want to take money from another source, you should liquidate one-third of your shares to generate the money.

CHAPTER 12

THE TEAM

It was a sad, tense time for economists on Wall Street and in Washington.

Until recently, they had assumed that a long-term recovery was locked in, virtually guaranteed. Not one prominent economist veered significantly from this theory, and those who did either kept silent or were told to shut up.

In public, they were touting the economy's "fundamental strength." In private, however, they were biting their nails to stubs.

One of the few vocal dissenters was Tamara Belmont. Several months earlier, while still at Harris & Jones, she had debated frequently with fellow analysts. But she had been frustrated by the rules of the game: Although it was OK to talk about a future recession in private conversations, any material for distribution was severely restricted, especially if it could fall into the hands of the public. Recession talk was considered bad for business.

Tamara had a very tough time buying into those rules. Her ancestors were related to a famous bullfighter in Spain. She was not about to back down from the infamous bulls of Wall Street.

Her fundamental argument was not radical: A recession isn't completed until it corrects its own causes, until it cleans out most of the excesses piled up during the preceding boom. Those include speculation, bad investments, bad debts, even bad people. A recession helps sweep them away, clearing the path for new ideas, new technologies, new companies waiting in the wings. It's a natural process of renewal, like a forest fire that spawns new saplings. So far, however, virtually very little of that had happened.

Her most heated debates were with Harris's Director of Research, Don Walker, who invariably toed the company line. She could always find him by the watercooler, from which he consumed liters per day.

"I think you're wrong about the economy," she had commented to him one day. While he downed another few cups, she added defiantly, "I think almost everyone around here is wrong, sleepwalking through a minefield. This recession is not over—not by a long shot. It did not cure the accounting disease or the debt illness. It has not relieved the bubble of overpriced stocks. It did not improve the horrendous finances of millions of consumers. Quite the contrary, the bad debts and fake accounting have festered. The shaky profits are still with us. Very little has changed. Instead of paving the way for a recovery, the decline you saw was merely the prelude to another big dump."

"Give me proof," he said. "Believe me, I am not married to the bullish argument. Show me the evidence, and I will bend."

Within 24 hours she had the evidence in a thoroughly documented draft report on his desk.

Walker skimmed past the opening verbiage and then read more slowly as he came to a section headlined "Postwar Twentieth-Century Recessions and the Recession of 2001, Compared." Some excerpts from the report follow.

In all postwar recessions of the last century, Americans had far less debt. In the 1973–74 recession, average families increased their debt load by only 1.5 percent and kept it below their income. Likewise, in the 1990–91 recession, the debt rose by only 1.5 percent. In stark contrast, in the early 2000s, household debt has continued to surge and has now reached levels that exceeded household income significantly: For each $100 of disposable income, consumers have $115 in debt.

After past recessions, Americans also replenished their savings. However, the most recent economic decline differs markedly in this aspect. Americans are still saving less than 2 percent of their income, near the lowest in history.

In the corporate sector, we see a similar pattern. In past recessions, corporations cut back their debts or at least did not add to them. Now, we see the opposite pattern. Corporate debt, as a share of net worth, has risen to 57 percent—a new record.

If the current recession were truly over, we should also have seen some improvement in the nation's trade deficit. Back in the 1973–74 recession, for example, we started the slump with a *deficit* of about one-half percent of GDP and ended it with a nice *surplus* of 1 percent of GDP. Likewise, during the 1978–80 period, we swung from a $3 billion trade deficit to a $4 billion surplus. And after the 1990–91 recession, we enjoyed an even more dramatic improvement. This time, however, it's not working that way. In the recent downturn, the trade gap went from bad to worse, to close to $465 billion or nearly 5 percent of GDP, twice what America spends on defense.

The report also documented a wide range of other issues—the futility of low interest rates and the accelerating declines in economies overseas, for example.

"You've read it, right?" she had asked Walker proudly during their next watercooler encounter.

He stared blankly, and she could not mask her chagrin. "You asked for proof; I've given it to you. I've given you the evidence that every past recession cleaned out excesses, paving the way for future expansions. I've given you the evidence that this recession has done nothing of the kind. At the very minimum, you now have the basis for reasonable doubt—that maybe it's *not* over yet, that maybe it has *barely begun.* Thanks to your encouragement, I now have the report ready to go—to get it out there, to the media, to the customers."

Walker, a Wharton economist, was torn. Her arguments were standard, textbook economics. Her logic was impeccable, her evidence irrefutable. Intellectually, he had no choice but to agree. In practice, however, logic and evidence had little to do with what was published by Harris.

She pressed him, and he finally consented to a limited internal distribution, provided he could edit the document. He asked for the Word file, promising to get it back to her within a couple of days. On her desk, one week later, she found hard copy accompanied by the instructions: "Review carefully but do not make any changes."

The edited version left her dumbfounded. She fully expected *some* of her conclusions would get watered down, but not *this!* Some were deleted entirely; others were twisted. Only the weakest of the arguments were still intact. Meanwhile, she had just seen an e-mail from Walker to all research staff, urging them to publish various reports under the rubric "Bullish Prospects for the Economy."

Tamara decided not to swallow her pride again. Her relatives in Pamplona, Spain, knew how to deal with bulls running wild in the street. So did she. Later that afternoon, returning from one of his frequent trips to the men's room, Walker found a copy of the original report on his chair. Across the cover were two small words and two large ones, written with a thick magic marker:

My comments: I QUIT

After this incident, no firm on Wall Street would hire her again. So she decided to move to Washington and try finding a job in government.

She applied at various federal agencies where she felt serious economic research was being done—the Treasury Department, the Department of Commerce, and the Federal Reserve—but came up empty-handed. She tried the U.S. General Accounting Office (GAO), the nonpartisan auditing arm of Congress, whose reports had uncovered waste in government, illicit activities by brokers, risks in the financial markets, and more. Still no luck.

Three tense and trying months later, she was delighted to find a voicemail message on her cell phone from an Oliver Dulles: "I have a copy of the 'We Lied' speech you gave at Columbia, and I'm impressed. Please call regarding a possible senior research position at CECAR." He left two phone numbers.

She dropped what she was doing and logged on to the Web. She tried going straight to www.cecar.com, but it was just a domain name for sale. Then, she tried an AltaVista search and immediately found www.cecar.org—the Chief Executives' Committee for Accounting Reform (CECAR), "a nongovernmental organization dedicated to unbiased, conflict-of-interest–free management, research, and reporting in private and public institutions." The more she read about it, the more she liked it.

When she reached Dulles, however, it seemed he didn't know who she was and was too busy to talk. Her heart sank. But as soon as she mentioned the "We Lied" speech, he suddenly remembered.

"Sorry, I think I left that message on your cell over a week ago. So forgive me if I forgot your name," he said matter-of-factly.

"I'm an e-mail person," she responded. She wondered how he had gotten her cell phone number but decided not to ask.

He explained that although the committee had been founded primarily to expose accounting irregularities at publicly traded corporations, over time he had personally encouraged the chairman, Paul E. Johnston, to broaden the committee's scope of research to the public sector—the federal deficit, the open market activities of the Federal Reserve, and most recently, any governmental intervention in equities markets. "At first, our focus was companies like UCBS. Now, we've expanded our horizons to also reveal hidden risks in the economy as a whole," he explained.

He offered her a relatively low-paying post but promised an incredibly attractive research environment. She would have a staff of three junior economists. She would have direct access to an illustrious list of like-minded chief executives and Wall Street professionals. She would even be able to work cooperatively with some of the same governmental agencies that she had targeted for her earlier job searches. It was a dream job, and she grabbed it practically on the spot.

The committee had recently relocated to the National Press Building, two blocks from the White House. She was given a corner office overlooking the inside of The Shops, a three-story mall that shared the same structure. Her primary focus: The Federal Reserve and the economy. *Piece of cake,* she thought.

Her first major assignment, however, caught her off guard. It came to her in the form of the following e-mail:

Tamara,

In light of the developments on Wall Street and emerging debates in various Congressional committees, it is almost inevitable that, at some time in the near future, the Administration will be looking into the consequences and policy implications of a deeper stock market decline. Our Committee intends to provide commentary on that issue, specifically with respect to unorthodox interventions.

Recently announced *kabushiki kaiage* operations by the Bank of Japan, as well as talk of common stock *Stützungskäufe* by the Bundesbank, also raise serious questions regarding the possible and probable responses of their U.S. counterparts.

Your assignment is to survey existing research on these issues, explore any hidden risks in the markets, and delineate a reasonable worst-case scenario for the future of the U.S. economy, to be delivered back to me within 90 days.

Good luck!

Oliver Dulles

P.S. Be sure not to exclude the so-called "stock market plunge protection team" from your investigations.

The e-mail blew her mind—not because of what it said, but because of what it *didn't* say. At this stage in her career, the last thing she expected to receive was a request for information that she couldn't handle. Now she had received a request for information that she couldn't even *understand*.

Finding the meanings of the Japanese and German terms was a bit time-consuming but not difficult. *Stützung* was German for "support"; *käufe* meant "purchases." Combined, they meant "support buying." *Kabushiki* was Japanese for stocks; *kaiage* meant "to buy up."

She printed out the e-mail, on which, next to each foreign word, she penciled in the English equivalents. Then she sat back in her chair and reread it.

Now she could understand. Her boss was referring to special operations by the Japanese and German central banks for actually buying common stocks to support their markets. Understanding the e-mail, however, was one thing; believing it was another. The entire concept was both shocking and naive.

Were the Japanese and the Germans actually doing it? She doubted it very much. Japan and Germany were advanced modern economies, the second and third largest, respectively, in the world. In any modern economy, such outright purchases of common stocks by the central banks would be considered a dramatic, radical departure from decades of firmly established, tried-and-tested policies.

In fact, it would be tantamount to partially nationalizing entire industries—a banana-republic-type proposition. These were the world's leading nations, the countries that so stridently urged the governments of less developed nations to get their grubby fingers the heck out of private industry—if anything, to *sell off* any remaining government-owned enterprises.

At the same time, as best she could recall, both Japan and Germany were still influenced by old-line, inflation-fearing conservatives who would undoubtedly be staunchly opposed to direct government interference in their stock markets. Wouldn't these groups make it politically impossible for their countries' central banks to embark on such dangerous missions?

She shook her head. *This memo is ridiculous! Have I made a mistake joining this group?* she asked herself. *Is this a den of conspiracy buffs?*

The P.S. was particularly disturbing. 'Plunge protection team'? "Get real!" she said to herself, barely uttering a sound. Wasn't that just the banter of Web chat rooms? If so, why did it suddenly show up in an obviously serious memo hitting her inbox soon after her first day on the job?

The worst-case scenario would have to wait. First, she would have to find adequate evidence to refute the existence or relevance of *kabushiki kaiage, Stützungskäufe,* and the plunge protection team. She soon found, however, that she was wrong on at least two out of the three.

THE BANK OF JAPAN BUYS COMMON STOCKS

She was definitely wrong about the Bank of Japan's operations. In the middle of September 2002, the BOJ announced it was going to buy common stocks to support the market. The market rallied and then promptly plunged back down to new lows. That must be the end of it, she thought. A one-time gesture that failed.

But it was not the end of it. Just a few weeks later, while conducting a Web search on Japanese banks, she ran into a shocking story from the *New York Times:*

> TOKYO, Oct. 11. Japan's central bank . . . said it would spend $16 billion of its own money in a highly unorthodox plan to buy stocks from threatened banks . . . The stock purchase plan, which calls for buying shares in investment-grade-rated companies held by 10 or so banks over the next 12 months and holding them for at least three years, has raised eyebrows at other major central banks, which studiously avoid involving themselves directly in equity markets.

She could find nothing concrete regarding *Stützungskäufe,* but there certainly was a lot of talk, including some from reliable sources. *Where there's smoke, there's at least a reasonable possibility of fire,* she thought.

Now what about the stock market plunge protection team? She was dumbfounded to discover how wrong she had been there as well.

The plunge protection team was real, all right. It was officially named the President's Working Group on Financial Markets—created by Executive Order 12631 and signed into existence by President Ronald Reagan on March 3, 1988.

The members were also real—and powerful. They included the secretary of the Treasury, the chairman of the Federal Reserve, the chairman of the SEC, and the chairman of the Commodity Futures Trading Commission (CFTC). Plus, the team had the option to call in, at a moment's notice, an even wider range of influential decision makers, including the chairman of his Council of Economic Advisors, the comptroller of the Currency, and the president of the New York Federal Reserve Bank. All the members had each other's home phone numbers, cell phone numbers, and personal e-mail addresses. Any major emergency in the markets, and they could be in touch instantly.

Tamara smiled as she thought of how she should refer to them in her final report. Washington already had "the company" (the CIA), "the bureau" (the FBI), "the commission" (the SEC), and various others. So she figured it would be fitting to call them simply "the team."

One by one, she went through the contacts Dulles had given her, leaving messages, sending e-mails, getting nowhere. Finally, a few days into the project she received a call-back from a reputable analyst at the GAO, who introduced himself as their "resident crash expert." At first, all she wanted was information on the historical background of the plunge protection team. But she soon discovered that he would also be a valuable resource for the worst-case scenario as well.

THE CRASH OF '87

"The team first emerged in the wake of the stock market crash of 1987," the analyst declared. "That may sound like a long time ago to some people, but not to me. I was there, and it's still *very* fresh in my mind. Strangely, though, most people *don't* remember—or don't want *you* to remember—what actually happened. So most of the public doesn't realize that the Crash of '87 was, in some respects, actually worse than the Crash of '29."

He proceeded to lay out several facts that supported that notion: Back in 1929, the worst single-day decline in the market was on Black Tuesday, October 29, when the Dow Jones Industrial Average plunged by 12.8 percent. In 1987, the largest single-day decline was nearly twice as severe—down a bone-chilling 22.6 percent, the deepest one-day loss in *all* history.

The crash expert also pointed out that back in 1929, most large Wall Street firms had the financial wherewithal to withstand the huge losses they suffered on Black Tuesday. In contrast, after Black Monday, 1987, some of the major Wall Street firms were hit so hard and lost so much capital that they were pushed to the edge of bankruptcy—all in just one or two days of trading.

Tamara was still in school in 1987, and she was puzzled. "I don't understand. The stock market crashes all the time. So why all the fuss?"

"When people say 'the market crashed,' they're invariably referring to a crash *in* the market. What I'm talking about is a crash *of* the market."

She did not get the point and probed further. "In terms of practical implications, what's the difference?"

"The difference is that most crashes are a sharp decline in *prices*. That's normal. But in 1987, the authorities were staring down the throat of a far more frightening monster—a crash of the market *itself*."

"OK, but . . ."

"Let's say you've got a farmer's market," he said with an air of condescension that seemed inappropriate given her credentials as an economist. "And let's say there's a glut of tomatoes. The price of tomatoes crashes, right? That's a crash *in* the market. As soon as the glut is gone, the price goes back up. No big deal, right?"

"My point entirely," she shot back defiantly.

"But now let's say some of the wholesalers default on their payments. Farmers go broke. No one shows up at the stalls. And a few weeks later, some construction outfit bulldozes them down to build a condo. That's a crash *of* the market!"

"Oh, OK. Now I understand what you're trying to say."

"Good. Because that's precisely the kind of fate the authorities faced in the Crash of '87. If the brokers went broke, who would make the trades? Who would make the market? Our entire stock market system was going into cardiac arrest."

"So what did they do about it?"

"At first, they weren't sure *what* the heck to do."

Sensing this could be a pivotal aspect of her research, she asked the GAO analyst to give her a detailed, day-by-day chronology of the events surrounding the crash. He asked her to wait for a moment while he retrieved some of his papers.

"OK," he said a moment later, "let's start from the beginning. The market for Ginnie Maes is the first to go. These are the bonds issued by the Government National Mortgage Association, a government agency. They're part of the national debt but, ironically, not part of the national budget. But that's another topic. The Ginnies crash on April 15, 1987. And when I say 'crash,' I mean *crash!* Down an earth-shattering 10 full points! Don't ask me why. One factor could be a few large failing S&Ls liquidating their portfolios. So they're dumping the Ginnie Mae bonds onto the market. It's the worst single government bond crash in history, even worse than in 1980."

"And then?"

"A couple of months later, in Japan, a similar crash hits their longest-term government bond—the 10-year *kokusai*. It goes into a tailspin. Then, the panic bounces back to the U.S. bond market and finally to the U.S. dollar. By the summer, all three of these markets—U.S. bonds, Japanese bonds, and the U.S. dollar—are in turmoil."

"I'm taking notes. For each step along the way, why don't you just give me the time reference, the event, and then your comments?"

"Okay. Wednesday, October 14, 1987: The Commerce Department announces another huge trade deficit: America has imported $16 billion more in autos, VCRs, clothes, and other products than it has exported. The Dow falls 95 points, or 3.8 percent, which is a shocker. But officials in Washington and Wall Street are calm and complacent. They go out of their way to say there are 'no signs of trouble.'

"Thursday, October 15: The market is ignoring the official words of reassurance. The Dow falls by 58 points.

"Friday, October 16: The Dow plunges 108 points, or 4.6 percent. Now, this is *big!* Triple-digit declines are very rare—the equivalent of over 400 points in today's market. Still, most people are optimistic or oblivious. In next morning's *Wall Street Journal,* reporters Tim Metz and Beatrice Garcia put it this way: 'By 8 P.M. at Harry's Bar, the Wall Street watering hole, hordes of yuppie brokers and traders clearly were preoccupied with getting dates for the evening rather than with the market collapse.' They have never experienced a really sick market before. Most of them blindly assume it will shoot back up 100 points on Monday."

"Please go on," she said.

BLACK MONDAY

"Black Monday, October 19: The morning papers give no inkling of the impending disaster. But the market plunge begins immediately, sinking steadily throughout the morning. By early afternoon, the selling is so hectic the New York Stock Exchange's new, high-speed computer falls behind by a record 85 minutes. Even without counting the backlog of sell orders, the trading volume is plowing right past its previous record of some 340 million shares, and there are still three hours of trading left to go.

"3:30 P.M.—still Black Monday: The final rally attempt has

collapsed. The market is cascading in a climactic panic finish, led by heavily indebted Wall Street firms threatened with financial ruin. No one knows where the market is or what price they'd get for their shares. Investors who punch in stock symbols on their quote machines are being given prices that are up to three hours old, the equivalent of months in a normal market. But these investors are selling anyhow, glad to get out at any price.

"Throughout the afternoon: The toll-free lines at the nation's mutual funds are overloaded and their main switchboards are jammed. By the time investors get through to a live person, most of the crash is over; by the time their sell orders are finally executed, the value of their shares has fallen still another 10 or 20 percent. The majority do not realize that when you invest in mutual funds, even if you sell early in the day, you get a 'settlement price' that reflects the overall decline during the *entire* day.

"5 P.M., still on Black Monday: The market has been officially closed for an hour now, but it will be many hours more before all the orders are sorted out. The Dow Jones Industrials has fallen 508 points, or 22.6 percent."

Tamara interrupted. "Let me see. Assuming a Dow of around 8000, in today's market that would be the equivalent of . . . No! Is something wrong with my arithmetic? One thousand, eight hundred points?"

He pulled out a calculator to confirm. "Correct. The Dow would be down exactly 1,808 points, *in one trading session.* So the 2-, even 300-point declines that you've seen in recent years are hiccups by comparison. Like I said before, it was almost *double* the decline of the 1929 crash. May I go on?"

"Yes, yes, please do."

"Crack of dawn, Tuesday, October 20: Here's what comes out in the *Wall Street Journal:* 'The reaction around Wall Street, from traders, money managers and securities analysts, was mostly of stunned disbelief . . . As stock prices collapsed, the U.S. government stood by powerless . . . Officials met at the White House, the Federal Reserve, and the Securities and Exchange Commission. But as the market continued falling, they concluded that there was little they could do other than stay calm in the face of Wall Street's panic . . . Optimistic statements rang hollow as sell orders poured in on Wall Street.'

"Tuesday morning, October 20: Trading in many major stocks–

such as IBM, Merck, plus scores of lesser issues–is frozen. Even if you own these liquid, normally actively traded stocks, you can't get out now. Stock options and futures all but stop trading for several hours. The 'specialists' on the floor of the stock exchange, who are supposed to buy or sell specific stocks in order to help maintain an orderly market, are themselves financially devastated. Nearly all their capital has vanished. Banks, frightened by the collapse, refuse to extend credit that brokers desperately need. Other banks are calling in *previous* loans.

"10 A.M., same morning: John Phelan, the head of the New York Stock Exchange, wants to shut the stock market down. He can't think of any *other* way to stop the crash dead in its tracks. Sure, the shutdown would be a desperate and dangerous measure, but he feels the alternative is even scarier. He's afraid that if they don't do *something*–immediately–the market is going to continue to plunge. And if the market continues to plunge, it will bust most of the big firms who are members of the NYSE. Then, the entire exchange itself will be in jeopardy."

"Is that what they did? Shut it down? I don't remember that."

"No, they didn't shut it down. Let's get through the chronology and you'll see.

"11 A.M.: The Dow is already down *another 10 percent* or so *beyond* the *22 percent it fell the previous day*. In just 30 hours, an amazing *one-third* of all the stock market wealth in America has been obliterated. If Wall Street firms have to value their portfolios at this moment in time, many of them are *already* broke, wiped out, kaput. People in high places, like Phelan, are panicking. But E. Gerald Corrigan, the head of the Federal Reserve of Bank in New York, is adamantly against shutting the stock market down."

"Why?" asked Tamara, almost in a whisper.

"Because he's convinced it will gum up the entire engine precisely when it needs more oil. He argues that the real, fundamental problem isn't so much the falling prices–it's the sudden shortage of cash and capital among the big Wall Street firms. He feels the most immediate danger is not necessarily more selling by investors–it's the real possibility that the big Wall Street firms will default on cash settlements."

She asked the GAO expert how he would explain this in a report for noneconomists.

"When you call your broker to buy, say, 100 shares of General Motors, he doesn't pay for those shares immediately. In fact, he doesn't have to put up the cash for five business days. So at any given period of time, there are hundreds of billions of dollars in transactions that have already taken place but have not yet been paid for. If a major firm fails to pay on time, it can set off a chain reaction of defaults. It can destroy the market just as thoroughly as the defaulting wholesalers that destroyed the farmer's market."

"Please go on."

"Still October 20: Corrigan's arguments prevail. They don't shut the market down. Instead, the authorities decide to solve the problem with money. Here's what they do: The Fed pours billions into the banking system. At the same time, they call big bankers and persuade them to lend those billions to the brokers. Wherever the authorities see a fissure that could cause a meltdown in the system, they pour in more money. The market rallies, and the immediate crisis is over."

"That's it?"

"Not quite. The shock waves of the crash continue to reverberate for months. But my point is, after this harrowing, near-death experience they decide to leave nothing to chance again, and that's what leads to the creation of the plunge protection team."

Silently, Tamara asked herself the same question that had often become a meaningless cliché: *Can it happen again?*

The crash expert from the GAO was on the same wavelength. "Now," he said, "they want you to believe that the Crash of '87 can never happen again. But the continuing existence of the plunge protection team is a tacit admission that they themselves are still afraid something like that *could* happen again."

"Has it?"

CLOSE CALLS WITH DISASTER

"No, but we've had a couple of close calls. In 1998, a company that virtually no one had ever heard of before—Long Term Capital Management—lost a fortune in esoteric, high-risk derivatives and practically set off a chain reaction of defaults that could have sunk markets and institutions worldwide. The team stepped in, and cut it off at the pass. Then, in 2001, it happened *again!* After the 9/11 attacks, the authorities feared the market crash could be even worse than the Crash of '87. And this time, they did shut down the exchange, but they had an excuse—infrastructural repairs."

"What about the trading 'curbs.' I see them on CNBC all the time."

"Hah! That's a joke, and everyone knows it. The curbs merely block a certain specialized type of selling—selling by computer-driven trading programs, directly into the stock exchange's computers. Back in the late 1980s, after much analysis and lengthy debate, they decided that program trading was a significant factor in the Crash of '87. How significant? No one knows. But that didn't stop them from developing a whole set of cockamamie rules to try to control it."

"Will they work?"

"Who the heck knows? How do you reality-test something like that? There's no way. The crux of the issue is that *none of the curbs or rules can stop the selling in the real—and far bigger—world that exists outside the limited confines of the exchange.* Suppose you get an avalanche of sell orders from U.S. institutions. From Europe. From Japan. The curbs won't amount to a hill of beans."

"What about the shutdowns? What about the rules that let them simply close down the exchange?"

The crash expert seemed flustered. "I don't think you're getting it. As long as all those sell orders are still out there, shutting down the exchange will only make things worse. Much worse. It would spread the cancer."

"Why's that?"

"Because people are selling for reasons that have nothing to do with what the exchange can or cannot handle. They're selling because of economic forces that are outside the control of the exchange authorities. When you tell those sellers you're closing down the exchange, that they *can't* sell, all it does is make them *more desperate* to sell. But it gets even hairier than that."

"Oh? In what way?"

"Once the market is closed, no one will have the faintest idea what the *real* closing price is. The closing price on any security is supposed to reflect the sum total of all the sell and buy orders that are outstanding at the time of the closing bell, right?"

"Sure."

"But if they close the exchange early—precisely because there are too *many* sell orders still outstanding—it implies, by definition, that the closing price does *not* reflect all the sell orders."

Tamara was still not grasping the significance of this. "So?"

"So, they'd be deliberately jeopardizing the entire reason for the existence of markets from time immemorial—all the way back to the earliest bazaars and the barter system."

"Can you give me a practical example?"

"Absolutely. I can give you a *very* practical example. Let's say the market crashes and is shut down early, with a big backlog of unfilled sell orders. And let's say millions of investors redeem their mutual fund shares in the early part of the day. They're supposed to get the 'net asset value' of the fund, which, in turn, is supposed to reflect the actual closing price of the day. But if that price is inflated, the funds will wind up giving away much too much cash, depleting their assets. Result: The shareholders that do *not* take their money out on that day get stuck with a disproportionate share of the losses."

"Sometimes you win, sometimes you lose," commented Tamara.

"It's more than that. There's a basic fairness principle that's violated, and once it becomes known, investor confidence will be shot."

"So what else is new?"

"No, no, this is different. Soon you'd see people saying 'the only way to get out without getting screwed is to get out before everyone else!' What do you think that would do to the market?"

"Create a stampede for the exits?"

"You better believe it! It would cause precisely the conditions that officials were trying to avoid in the first place!"

Belmont nodded. "I see, but earlier you said, 'that would spread the cancer.' What did you mean by that?"

"If investors can't sell their stocks on the New York Stock Exchange, they will rush to sell on some other exchange. They'd have to have a coordinated shutdown of all equities markets in the U.S. Then, if investors can't sell in the U.S., they'll rush to sell in London, Frankfurt, or Tokyo. Once that avenue is closed off, they'll find something else to sell—municipal bonds, even government bonds. The cancer would spread, and soon you'd have a worldwide market shutdown on your hands. How does that sound for a worst-case scenario?"

"Farfetched."

The crash analyst was not happy with her response, but he tried to be polite. "Look, I want to help you. But if your goal is to explore worst-case scenarios, you need to keep an open mind. You must not rule out any reasonable possibility. In particular, you need to explore the markets that central bankers do *not* control, that are often *beyond* the reach of buy operations, market controls, or even market shutdowns."

"What are your referring to now?"

"*Derivatives!* Follow the chain of events that can be unleashed when derivatives blow up, and you will have your worst-case scenario."

CHAPTER 13

HIDDEN RISKS

Tamara's next 60 days were chewed up strictly with information gathering.

She assigned one of her research assistants the task of digging up everything he could find about early-twentieth-century crashes, panics, and depressions. She sent another of her assistants to the Hill to confer with the staff economists of banking committees on both sides of the aisle. And she sent a third, a retired bond trader, on a field trip to Manhattan to interview specialists in key financial markets—common stocks, corporate and government bonds, foreign currencies, Japanese securities, Brazil debt, and more.

The instructions to her staff were always the same: "Meet in private. Promise anonymity and the strictest confidentiality. Encourage free-flowing discussion. Then, always ask one fundamental question: *What's the worst that can happen?*"

She saved the toughest assignment for herself—derivatives. "What do you know about derivatives?" she asked anyone and everyone at CECAR. Since the office was small and informal, it was impossible *not* to know everyone who worked there. So she asked the same question of Oliver Dulles and Paul Johnston himself. She even asked her former college roommate, who had a background in finance.

It wasn't long before a photocopied report landed on her chair from some person or persons unknown. Toward the top it had the words "GAO, United States General Accounting Office. Report to Congressional Requesters." Then toward the center it had the title and subtitle, "FINANCIAL DERIVATIVES, Actions Needed to Protect the Financial System." There followed an emblem of the GAO and, in the bottom left corner, a code number–GAO/GGD-94-133.

She read the report from cover to cover, then promptly began making some phone calls.

Long Term Capital Management

Three hours later she was in a straight-back chair, sitting face-to-face with one of the report's authors at the GAO's offices on G Street.

He seemed both surprised and pleased by her interest. "The only one who ever seems to read our reports is the single member of Congress who requests it and *maybe* the opposing member who refutes it. No, I lie; even *they* don't read it. It's usually a staffer, who then just gives the member a list of questions to ask at a hearing. We put many months of man-hours into these reports, and people don't even know they exist. How did you find the one we wrote back in 1994?"

"It just landed on my desk this morning. I have no idea who put it there."

Tamara listened intently as the coauthor of the 1994 report gave her the background. "We issued the report to warn Congress–and the world–about what could happen to the global financial system if these derivatives blow up, if there is a sudden unexpected crisis from out of the blue. No one paid one ounce of attention. Four years later, bang! Russia defaulted. Long Term Capital Management went belly-up. And those derivatives started to blow up, just as we warned, and–"

"Hold it, hold it! Long Term Capital Management? I've heard only bits and pieces. What *really* happened there?"

"It was a major private offshore hedge fund for sophisticated, wealthy investors. Uninsured but well connected. Playing the spread, the difference, between two types of bonds–on the one side, they had a position in bonds like those issued by the Russian government; on the other side, they had a position in bonds issued by the U.S. Treasury. Their theory—the spread will not exceed a certain historical maximum. Then Russia defaults. The spread goes through the roof. They get stuck with huge losses. They're about to default on their commitments to major U.S. institutions. There are fears that it could bring down the entire . . ."

"Wait, wait, wait. You're going 100 miles an hour. Slow down and give me the nitty-gritty."

The man blinked and was silent. After a few long seconds, he spoke again. "Let's say I'm Long Term Capital Management. And let's say you're—I don't know—Morgan Chase. Wait, no! Back then, it would have been Morgan Guaranty. Got that?"

"You're LTCM. I'm Morgan."

"Right. I buy foreign bonds, especially Russian bonds. At the same time—"

"Isn't that risky?"

"You don't have to tell *me* that. I'm LTCM. It's my business to *know* that. That's why I also *sell short* equivalent amounts of high-quality bonds, such as U.S. government bonds. I borrow the U.S. government bonds from banks like you, and I sell them. You understand the mechanism for selling short bonds, right?"

"If it's the same as selling short stocks, yes. You borrow them, you sell 'em at today's price, and you hope they go down. If they do, you buy 'em back at a lower price, you give 'em back to the owner, and you keep the difference."

"Exactly. It works the same with bonds. So! Back to LTCM. I own Russian bonds, right? I'm short U.S. bonds, right? So I figure my position is balanced. Like a scale. If bond prices in general go down, I lose on the Russian bonds, but that's OK, 'cause I make it up on my shorts. If bonds go up, no problem; I lose on the short position in U.S. bonds, but I make it up with profits in my Russian bonds. Either way, I don't care. I'm just betting that the price differential between the two—between the Russians and the Americans—is going to diminish. That's how I make my profit."

"Clear. Then what?"

"Then Russia defaults and my Russian bonds fall like meteorites. Now my losses in the Russian bonds are so big, I'm practically wiped out. Meanwhile, U.S. bonds fall like snowflakes. Or worse, they don't fall at all. I may have a tiny profit in my shorts, but it covers only a small fraction of my losses. Now I'm in deep doo-doo, and so are you."

"Why me?"

"Don't you remember? You're one of the banks that loaned me all those U.S. bonds. But at this point, I don't have enough money to buy them and give them back to you. I'm going to have to renege on my side of the deal with you. My losses become your losses. You're Morgan. So maybe, to you, it's a minor injury. But I have similar deals with dozens of other players in the market, and they'd be mortally wounded. What's worse, if I default on my obligations to them, they're probably going to have to default on their obligations with *their* counterparties to *their* trades. Suddenly, it's like . . ."

"The domino theory?" she suggested.

"No. A nuclear chain reaction."

"So what was the final outcome with Long Term Capital? Did the Federal Reserve bail it out?"

"Yes, but they won't admit they did, officially. They *can't* admit it. LTCM was uninsured. It was even offshore. Can you imagine the political repercussions if government officials admitted they actually put taxpayer money into an uninsured, offshore corporation? But, like I told you earlier, the principals at LTCM were *well connected*. One of them was a former Federal Reserve official. He apparently contacted the New York Fed, and the authorities immediately stepped in to engineer the rescue."

"Didn't it work?

"Yes."

"So what's the issue?"

"The issue is that there are potentially thousands of others who could need similar rescues but who are *not* so well connected. If they call the New York Fed, they won't even get past the main switchboard. Even if they did, how could the Fed engineer a coordinated rescue for so many? The authorities don't even know who's got what derivatives where and when."

The GAO staffer offered Tamara a cup of coffee, but she declined. He excused himself to get a cup for himself while Tamara again thumbed through the 1994 GAO report. When he returned a few minutes later, she asked her standard question: "What's the worst that can happen in the future?"

"You've read the report," he said. "You can see what we said. We laid out, with great care, the chain of events that could overwhelm financial markets."

Tamara sought to play devil's advocate. "You talk about derivatives as if they were a four-letter word," she said. "But you know as well as I that they can serve a very positive function. If used properly, they can help *protect* institutions from risk. Why can't you focus more on the positive?"

His response was immediate. "I can, if you wish."

"Good."

"But that's not what you said your objective was. When you called me earlier this morning, you said your objective was to paint a worst-case scenario, to ferret out the institutions that may be using derivatives *improperly,* taking excessive risks. And just a few moments ago, I didn't hear you asking me, 'What's the *best* that can happen?' I heard you asking me, 'What's the *worst* that can happen?' That's what risk analysis is all about. It's asking all the what-if questions that most people are afraid to ask. That's also the approach we took in this report. Our findings make no pretense of being 'predictions' or 'prophecies.' They are merely answers to the what-if questions, the basis for good, old-fashioned, rational contingency planning. So can we stay on that course?"

"Of course."

"First," said the GAO veteran, "we warned about an '*abrupt failure or withdrawal from trading*.' That's an exact quote from our 1994 report. Well, since then we've seen a whole series of major failures. Thailand went down in 1997. Russia defaulted in 1998, triggering the Long Term Capital collapse we just talked about. At year-end 2001, Argentina defaulted—the largest debt default in history. A few days later, Argentina devalued its currency, sending more shock waves up the spine of the financial world. Three months earlier, two hijacked jumbo aircraft crashed into the World Trade Center and one slammed into the Pentagon. Geez! If there's one thing we've learned from all this, it's that we must train ourselves to *expect* the unexpected."

The GAO veteran paused for a moment, then added, "And don't forget Enron!"

"Enron? But—"

"Yes, Enron. When Enron bit the dust, the big news was the accounting fraud. That's what Congressional committees were all shook up about. That's what *your* committee chairman made such a fuss about. But everyone seems to have forgotten about the derivatives! The real reason I think Enron went under wasn't so much because of the accounting fraud. It was mostly because so many of its trades in energy derivatives blew up. They had placed big bets on oil, gas, and electricity. The bets went bad, they lost a fortune, and the game was up."

Tamara was on the verge of desperation. On the one hand, everyone—from her bosses to her outside contacts—were telling her that derivatives were of utmost importance, that they could be pivotal to the ultimate fate of the world economy. On the other hand, almost everything on the subject was shrouded in a dark cloud of mystery. "Isn't there anything—anything at all—you can give me that is more concrete," she pleaded.

Tamara waited patiently while the GAO veteran thought of what to say. "Yes," he said at last. "Watch the big eight players—the banks that control the bulk of the derivatives business in the U.S. Last I looked, the exposure to potential losses at several of those banks was anywhere from 100 percent to 600 percent of their capital. And I'm not talking about the bloated-up face value of the derivatives. I'm talking strictly about the actual risk these banks are taking."

"From 100 to 600 percent? You mean for every dollar of their capital—of their net worth—they have up to $6 of risk exposure to derivatives?"

"Check out the data; it's on the site of the Office of the Comptroller of the Currency, or OCC," he said, giving her detailed instructions on how to find the critical information.

The meeting ended, and Tamara was about to hail a cab back to the office. But it was a pleasant day, so she decided to walk. It would give her time to think. What *really* were these mysterious derivatives, and how did they fit into the big picture? She brushed aside all the jargon and just focused on the essence of the matter: *Derivatives are obligations, just another form of debt.*

Her next question was, *What happens to institutions that have too much debt?* Her mind flashed back to the graveyard of big-name corporations that had filed for bankruptcy in recent months—Bethlehem Steel, Pharmor, Polaroid, Kmart, Global Crossing, Enron, World-Com, Adelphia Communications, US Airways, and many more.

What was the typical pattern that tied them together? First came the bubble—the companies grew too fast, borrowing too much

money and spending almost every dime of it. Then came the needle that punctured the bubble—disclosures of fraud, class action
lawsuits, or just an ordinary decline in sales.

As she walked down Pennsylvania Avenue, she began to envision a much larger bubble, but the image was still unclear.

Once back at the office, she immediately opened her Web
browser and typed in the address that the GAO veteran had given
her: www.occ.treas.gov/deriv/deriv.htm.

In the upper left-hand corner of the screen, there appeared the
words "Comptroller of the Currency, Administrator of National
Banks"; to the right, "Quarterly Derivatives Fact Sheet." She marveled that in all her years as a researcher, she had never once vis-
ited this site. Yet she recognized that it could be pivotal to any
worst-case scenario.

She noticed a list of reports toward the bottom of the screen and
clicked on the most recent one—"OCC Bank Derivatives Report,
Second Quarter 2002." It seemed as though each fact jumped out
of the screen like an electric spark.

Total derivatives in the portfolios of U.S. commercial banks—
$50.1 trillion.

Portion of these concentrated in the hands of the seven largest
banks—96%.

Portion not under the supervision of regulated exchanges—
90.1%.

Oh, my god! she thought. *Fifty trillion!* That's almost five times the
entire U.S. gross domestic product. Yes, that number overstates the
risk. But what about the fact that nearly all of it is concentrated in
the hands of just seven large commercial banks? There's no way in
the world that could be construed as prudent spreading of risk in
our economy. And what about the fact that 90 percent of the derivatives were not under the auspices of any formal exchange? If
there is a crash in the stock market, the crash protection team
could coordinate with the New York Stock Exchange. But what
central exchange would the team work with if there's a crash in the
derivatives market? There is none.

She scrolled down to page 10 of the report and stared at the
screen in a state of semishock: *Chart 5a. Percentage of Derivatives
Exposure to Risk-Based Capital. J.P. Morgan Chase—589%. Bank of
America—169%. Citibank—199%.*

This was it! This was smoking-gun evidence of a massive bubble that no sane economist could deny. In the case of J.P. Morgan Chase, for every single dollar of its net worth (adjusted for various risk factors), the bank was risking $5.89 in derivatives alone. In other words, all it would take is a 17 percent loss in this area to wipe out the bank's capital. The bank would be busted.

She closed her eyes and tried to envision that scenario. What would happen to the stock market? What would happen to millions of American households? As her mind wandered, she picked up a manila folder left on her desk by one her research assistants. Stapled to the outside was a cover memo, which she read avidly:

To: Tamara Belmont
Re: Troubles at J.P. Morgan Chase; also at largest German and Japanese banks

On May 23, 2002, the common shares of J.P. Morgan Chase were selling for $38.66 a share. By October 9, they had plunged to $15.26 per share. Precisely 60.5% of the bank's market value—$46 billion—was wiped out. That's more than the total market value of Wachovia Bank and more than the total losses investors suffered in the bankruptcy of Adelphia Communications, Kmart, and Polaroid combined. All in one bank. All in just 139 days.

Hard to believe, isn't it? J.P. Morgan Chase—the second largest bank in the United States, with $742 billion in total assets, 900 branches, over 30 million retail customers. And here it is, losing nearly two-thirds of its total market value in less than five months. One reason: In September, Morgan announced that its losses from bad loans would more than quadruple—rocketing up from $302 million in the second quarter of 2002 to $1.4 billion in the third.

But if you think Morgan's situation is bad, take a look overseas. Deutsche Bank, the largest bank in Germany, has fallen even further in the stock market. Mizuho Holdings, the largest bank in Japan, is already bankrupt, according to many analysts.

The report went on to detail the inevitability of a Japanese banking collapse, with disastrous consequences for American and European banks. The reports from her other assistants painted a similar picture in nearly every major sector of the U.S. economy. Consumers, corporations, and governments were all bogged down in debts. Every one had similar bubbles. Finally, the image that had eluded her earlier came into sharper focus: The giant bubble was the entire global economy, including some of the largest banks in the world. The needle was the unfinished recession that she had detailed two months earlier in her report to her former boss Don Walker. If the economy fell, the bubble would burst.

There was only one question that remained: Could the governments of the three largest economies in the world—the United States, Japan, and Germany—continue to prop up their economies and protect the bubbles? The answer, she concluded, would unlock the most vital secrets the future might hold.

Two Worst-Case Scenarios

Exactly 90 days after he issued his memo to Tamara Belmont, Oliver Dulles heard a ding on his computer, signaling the arrival of new e-mail. He checked his list in Outlook and found, at the top of the screen, a message from Tamara. The subject was simply "Report," and he opened it immediately.

> Attached, please find my Word file locked with our previously agreed-upon password, containing the Executive Summary. I have the full report, including graphics and tables, in hard copy. I look forward to sharing it with you in person at your next earliest convenience.

The attached file was named "Scenarios." He got up from his desk, closed the door, opened the file with the password, and began reading it on his screen. The following are excerpts.

Two Worst-Case Scenarios:
Crash Risks and Crash Benefits
Executive Summary
Tamara Belmont and staff

Due to conflicting signals regarding the current direction of monetary, fiscal, and unorthodox forms of intervention in the economy and in financial markets, it is not possible to delineate a single, unique worst-case scenario. Rather, contingent upon the decisions and actions of policy makers, two worst-case scenarios are envisioned:

Scenario A. Short but ugly.

The government follows primarily a noninterventionist policy. It does not waste precious public resources in the bailout of failed institutions of the private sector. It does not seek to artificially support the stock market. It does not flood the banking system with excess amounts of money or slash taxes indiscriminately. Nor does it impose foreign exchange controls to prevent a currency collapse and the flight of capital. Instead, it focuses almost entirely on meaningful structural reforms to restore investor and consumer confidence. Leaders provide full and honest disclosure regarding the severity of the decline and the potential pain it may cause.

Consequences: Due to massive debts, poor liquidity, and the interlocking nature of complex contractual obligations, a ripple of financial and nonfinancial corporate bankruptcies temporarily paralyzes the global economy.

U.S. stocks decline by approximately the same magnitude as they did in 1929–32. Vicious circles drive the economy into a 3- to 5-year depression. Unemployment exceeds 10 percent. Liquidity temporarily disappears in major financial markets even with many widely owned securities, such as blue-chip stocks and long-term government bonds.

In order to end the crisis, a national banking and market holiday may be needed for up to a week or two. However, a healthy recovery ensues within a reasonable time frame.

Scenario B. Long and choppy.

Fearful of a broader collapse, the government intervenes aggressively and frequently in a protracted battle against the decline. It periodically bails out banks, brokerage firms, and other corporations deemed "essential" to the fabric of the financial system. It seeks to directly and indirectly support the financial markets with massive buy operations of common stocks and corporate bonds. It floods the banking system with cash and cuts taxes wildly. It imposes stringent foreign exchange controls to prevent capital from fleeing the country and to forestall a collapse in the dollar. It delays meaningful reform and sweeps real structural problems under the rug. Leaders continually believe it is in the nation's best interest to shield the public from information that might cause them concern or fear.

Consequences: The decline is prolonged over a period of many years, with several spotty recoveries that raise false hopes and false expectations, only to be followed by further declines. After a decade or more of protracted crises, the nation's liquid resources are depleted, and its recovery powers are sapped.

U.S. stocks fall in a zigzag fashion with many long, intermediate rallies, entrapping additional investor funds and further depleting the savings of households. By the end of the decline, however, the market averages wind up at approximately the same level as in Scenario A—with percentage losses equivalent to those of 1929–32.

The decline in the economy, however, is far deeper than that of Scenario A. Its depth is apparent not only in terms of the percentage declines of real GDP but also in terms of the long-term structural damage to productivity and mass psychology.

For most citizens, the pain of the decline is less severe in the short term but far greater over the long term. Social and political repercussions are more widespread, further complicating any recovery efforts.

Many markets, as well as much of the nation and most of the world, are virtually shut down for extended periods of time by chronic financial paralysis and social malaise. Eventually, the world economy does recover, but only after a dark period lasting several decades.

Oliver Dulles read the executive summary four grueling times before he turned away from his monitor. He was the person who had helped expose accounting scams. He was the one who had helped uncover the massive federal deficits and the potential danger of a bond market bubble. So doomsday scenarios were not totally foreign to him. In addition, in his earlier career that never blossomed, he had also been an avid student of psychology. So he understood the madness of crowds. He knew how they could turn almost any economic theory inside out.

Nevertheless, he was not ready for *this*.

In both scenarios, the market would plunge by approximately the same percentage as that in 1929–32. What was that? Close to 90 percent. Where would that put the Dow? At just above 1,000? Absolutely unbelievable in our modern economy, he thought.

In both scenarios, there would also be a partial or total shutdown of banks and financial markets. When was the last time that happened? When FDR shut down all the banks in 1932? Equally unbelievable!

On his first reading, it was obvious that Scenario B was even worse than Scenario A. At least in the "short-but-ugly" version, there was hope. In the long-and-choppy version, there was far less hope, even the implication of a "dark period of decades." What did she mean by *that?*

He immediately called her into his office and prepared to question her backup. When she arrived, he bounced up from his chair and hastily moved stacks of papers from the guest chair to give her a place to sit down. Then he just stared at her, shaking his head, half grinning, half smirking.

"What is this *thing* you just sent me?" he asked finally. "Are you out of your mind?"

"You asked for a *worst*-case scenario, didn't you?"

"Sure, but if you read my instructions carefully, you would have noted that my request was for a *reasonable* worst-case scenario. What are you thinking?" He smiled. "No, what are you *smoking?*"

THE SHORT-BUT-UGLY CRASH SCENARIO

Tamara didn't notice the smile but ignored the insult anyhow. "We all seek to avoid clichés, don't we? Yet, clichés are often wellsprings of truth. Case in point: 'History repeats itself, and those who fail to learn its hard lessons are doomed to repeat them.' "

"So is that your basis for this?" Dulles asked. "Just the same old, historical arguments that gloom-and-doomers have been spouting for decades?"

"For starters, yes. Granted, each cycle adds a new dimension, a new twist, or a hidden footnote to confuse historians. But structurally and functionally, I see similar patterns. I see recurring themes. Besides, isn't historical precedent a standard mechanism for establishing parameters in worst-case-scenario testing?"

"I suppose. Go on."

Tamara had a copy of the full report on her lap. She also brought with her three expandable file folders, each submitted by one of her researchers. She placed the folders on his desk, alongside the papers he had just moved from the chair.

"Let me start with the Panic of 1901," she said.

"Must you go *that* far back?"

"Actually, I probably should have gone back even further. But from the early twentieth century, we were able to develop four detailed case studies, and given the time constraints you gave us, we felt that would be adequate for now. May I proceed?"

"Sure, sure. Do your thing."

"*Panic of 1901:* Revolved around an attempted takeover of the Northern Pacific Railroad, culminating in a battle between the Morgan-Hill and Harriman-Kuhn Loeb groups for its control. Situation today: As in 1901, powerful corporate groups have used massive amounts of debt to gain control over corporate giants through mergers and acquisitions.

"*Collapse of 1907:* Later known as the 'rich man's panic.' Followed a speculative spurt in commodities, especially copper and coffee, plus copper mining companies. Situation today: Speculation in commodities has been widespread. Except this time it is concentrated in stock indexes, foreign currencies, bonds, and a series of other financial instruments that have been transformed into virtual commodities on our modern futures exchanges.

"*Crash of 1920–21:* Resulted from the post–World War I accumulation of excess inventories. Auto and tire markers, sugar producers, and cotton farmers were among the hardest hit. Situation today: Many businesses have again been caught overloaded with inventories—such as makers of PCs, network routers, microchips, and wireless components."

Dulles interrupted. "I have always suspected these comparisons are full of holes, and you've just illustrated a perfect example. There's a vast difference between our modern 'just-in-time' inventory systems and what existed back in the 1920s. An inventory panic of that magnitude is unthinkable."

"That's what I thought too," she retorted. "But it's happening just the same. Look at the huge excess manufacturing capacity we have in the world today! Look at how easy it is for overseas producers to dump their goods everywhere! Who's controlling those inventories, or potential inventories?"

"I won't argue with you now. Go ahead."

"*Crash of 1929:* Came on the heels of a 10-year record-breaking boom, reminiscent of the 1990s. Caused by collapse of a shaky stock pyramid built by brokers, banks, tycoons, and individual investors, similar to today's. Massive debts, similar to today's. Corporate fraud and bankruptcies, similar to today's."

"And you think those old periods are relevant?"

"Yes. Granted, there is a vast technological and cultural divide separating the early twentieth century from the early twenty-first. Granted, direct comparisons are dangerous. But a couple of recurring themes are *so* self-evident that they are, by definition, directly relevant."

"And they are?"

"First, it is self-evident that the federal government was either unable or unwilling to prevent the crashes and panics of the early twentieth century."

Dulles nodded. "Obviously. Otherwise the panics and crashes would not have happened."

"Second, it's self-evident that all four were devastating panics that virtually leveled the stock market, and yet—and this is my main point—*that did not preclude healthy recoveries in subsequent years.*

"Third, it is clear that the private sector repeatedly played critical roles in those recoveries. I'm talking about high-net-worth individuals. I'm talking about cash-rich financial institutions. They stepped in. They bought up distressed assets. They got the country rolling again."

"Who, for example?"

Tamara picked up one of the manila folders and flipped through some photocopies of pages taken from an old book on panics and crashes. Then she read from areas marked with a yellow highlighter. "In 1907, it was primarily J.P. Morgan that stepped in. Then, in 1920–21, the Du Ponts and powerful banking houses supported General Motors, Goodyear, and others. In the 1930s, it was tougher but still viable. A lot of the big manufacturers, like General

Motors, had learned their lesson from the 1920 crash and had built up big reservoirs of cash. That, plus the federal programs, and finally the war, lifted the economy out of the depression."

"What's the point?"

"The point is, *panics and crashes, no matter how devastating, are not fatal.*"

"I see. But in Scenario A, you talk about drastic economic declines. What drives those declines?"

"Two vicious circles. The first is between the stock market decline and falling consumer spending. When stocks fall, consumers spend less. Then, when consumers spend less, they drive down corporate earnings—and stock prices—still lower."

She glanced down again at her full report, then looked up. "The second vicious circle is between *deflation* and *bankruptcies*. Companies are forced to discount their goods, right? So they wind up with lower prices for their products and lower revenues. Next, due to the reduced revenues, they can't pay their bills. So they go bankrupt, leading to more fire sales . . . more bankruptcies . . . and still more fire sales."

"Can you give me some more proof on that one?"

Dulles's stare was intense. Tamara could sense that she was beginning to get his attention—that his skepticism and disbelief were ebbing. She decided to hold him off on this request. "Sure. But first let me give you an overview of the long-and-choppy scenario."

THE LONG-AND-CHOPPY CRASH SCENARIO

"OK. What is the primary reference point for your long-and-choppy scenario?"

"Japan. It's the largest economic disaster to hit the world markets since the 1930s. Debt is estimated at 1.4 times its entire economy—nearly three times the relative size of Argentina's debt when it collapsed in early 2002. It's been through at least four recessions since 1990—a rolling depression. Unemployment is the highest since World War II. Its stock market has been tumbling since 1990 and is still falling—down by nearly 78 percent from its peak. Its largest banks, brokerage firms, and life insurers are so close to failure that the only thing holding them up is a thread, with a weak government holding the other end. Things got so bad recently that the governor of Tokyo threatened to pull the city's money out of the Mizuho, Japan's largest bank, for fear it would 'go up in smoke.' "

Dulles knew it was bad but didn't know it was *that* bad.

Tamara brought the point home. "Can you believe that? A decade-plus bear market! A decade-long roller-coaster depression! This is not history; this is current fact. It's here *now,* and there's no turning back the clock."

"Why do you think Japan's economy has been pummeled for so many long years?"

Tamara was gaining more confidence in her presentation, as Dulles was obviously coming around. "Because of precisely the same errors and blunders that our government must avoid. Because Japan's entrenched bureaucracy is stubbornly resisting market reforms. Because Japan's government is persistently trying to prop up its shaky banks. Because they are artificially supporting their stock market. So what are the consequences? The economy hobbles along, like the living dead. The stock market bounces down a spiraling staircase that seems to stretch as far as the eye can see. Rather than ripping off the Band-Aid from their wounds in one quick snap, Japan's leaders choose to peel it off one painful hair at a time."

Dulles held up his hand in protest. "Wait a minute. I'm not an expert on the Japanese economy. But I do know this: Japan and the United States are so different structurally that any comparison is seriously flawed."

Tamara smiled broadly but then turned serious. "Agreed. But see? That's my whole argument in Scenario B! In my Scenario B, the *United States becomes more like Japan is today*—in terms of economic policy, even structurally. We already have many of the elements. We have a huge, entrenched government bureaucracy, much like theirs. We seem to have a political mandate to prevent a financial collapse at all costs, much as they do. We have the plunge protection team and every legal mechanism in place to intervene directly in the markets, just as they do. So beware: We may already be a lot more like Japan than most people would care to believe."

LESS PAIN, MORE SUFFERING

Dulles scanned the executive summary one more time. "You talk about the bankruptcies in Japan, about the unemployment and the deflation. Why, then, do you say that Scenario B is *less* painful in the short term?"

"When was the last time you were in Japan?"

"Never."

"Go there one of these days. You won't see breadlines. You won't see urban blight or dust bowls. You will see a nation that actually looks relatively prosperous—on the surface, that is. Mickey Kantor, former U.S. secretary of commerce, recently went to Tokyo. You want to hear what he said? He said, 'The banking system is struggling, consumer spending is down, the U.S. economy is down, oil prices are near $30, there is deflation, political gridlock, reforms that have not been implemented—otherwise, things are perfect.' I think that sums it up pretty nicely. It's like winning a game of poker on the Titanic."

Dulles signed. "I have just a few more questions for you, but they're very important."

"Shoot."

"In *both* scenarios, you say 'U.S. stocks decline by approximately the same magnitude as they did in 1929–32.' I calculated that out. For the Dow Jones Industrials, it means Dow 1000 and change. Don't you think that's a wild stretch? How do you get there?"

"There was only one economic period in the last 100 years that, like today, involved a record-breaking bull market before stock prices began to collapse . . . a market decline that was wrought with corporate fraud and massive bankruptcies . . . similar patterns in stock markets around the world . . . and declining interest rates, pushed lower and lower by the Fed in a failed attempt to stymie the bear and revive the bull. That was 1929–32."

"But 90 percent?"

"Yes, you're right, in 1929–32, the Dow plunged 89 percent. Today that would take it down to about 1,300. You say that's unthinkable, impossible, and my response is *exactly* the same as yours. It can't happen. Then, I think back just a few years. And I remember: Isn't that exactly what *all* analysts on Wall Street–every single last one of them–also thought about the Nasdaq when the Nasdaq was at *its* peak? Now look! The Nasdaq has *already* plunged almost as far as the Dow did back in the early 1930s." [See Figure 13.1.]

"Some people would argue that Wall Street has learned its lesson, that they are now singing a new tune. What would your response be?"

"All they've done is change their pitch: 'Oh, yeah, the *Nasdaq* was an *obvious* bubble,' " they say. " 'But not the *Dow*. The Dow is different.' The truth is, the Nasdaq bubble was obvious to them only *after* the Nasdaq was decimated. In my two scenarios, the same would be true for the Dow. They wouldn't recognize the bubble in the Dow until after it falls."

As Tamara spoke, she sensed that someone had walked into the office behind her, but it wasn't until she heard a familiar voice that she looked up. It was Linda Dedini.

Linda excused herself for the interruption and asked Dulles permission to look through some papers she had left for him on the chair. After she retrieved what she wanted, she was about to turn back but then hesitated.

In recent months, she had been hanging around her father's office more frequently–first for investment ideas, but later just out of sheer curiosity regarding a fascinating science that, she said, seemed to ultimately conform to many of the physical principles of nature she was so familiar with.

Dulles belatedly waved away her apology. "We're just talking about future scenarios. Care to sit in?"

VALUE AND PSYCHOLOGY

Her eyes lit up. There was nothing that fascinated Linda Dedini more than future scenarios. She went into the adjoining office to get another chair, rolled it back in, and sat quietly, forming an uneven triangle with Dulles and Tamara.

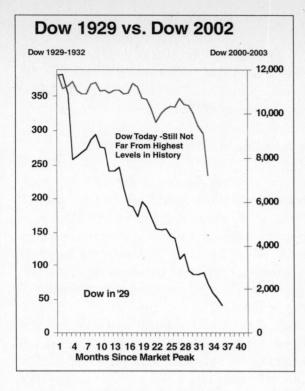

Dow 1929 vs. Dow 2002

Dow 1929-1932   Dow 2000-2003

Dow Today -Still Not Far From Highest Levels in History

Dow in '29

Months Since Market Peak

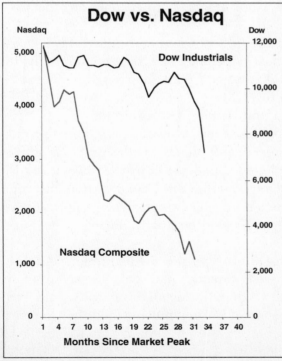

Dow vs. Nasdaq

Nasdaq   Dow

Dow Industrials

Nasdaq Composite

Months Since Market Peak

Figure 13.1 There are no fool-proof benchmarks for establishing a reasonable worst-case future scenario. However, risk analysts typically refer to either (1) the worst historical experience in the modern era or (2) the worst contemporary situation in a comparable environment.

The top graph illustrates the historical approach—it compares the Dow Jones Industrial Average of 2000–2002 to the Dow in the early 1930s. If the Dow were to suffer a decline of approximately the same magnitude as the decline in the early 1930s, it would fall to approximately the 1,000–1,500 range.

The bottom graph illustrates the contemporary approach—it compares the Dow Industrials of 2000–2002 to the Nasdaq Composite Index during the same period. If the Dow were to suffer a decline of approximately the same magnitude as the Nasdaq's decline of 2000–2002, it would fall to approximately the 2,500–3,000 level.

If these were specific forecasts, various arguments could be offered to support or refute their validity. However, as worst-case scenarios, these estimates conform to widely accepted principles of risk analysis.

Dulles turned back to Tamara and declared, "You're an economist and stock analyst. I'm a CPA. We both know that *value* is what the market is ultimately all about. Plus, I'm also a psychologist by training. So I know that *perception* of value is equally important. Have you taken that into consideration?"

"Yes. The Dow is now trading at 20 times earnings."

"Isn't that reasonable?"

Linda, remembering the 20 times earnings she had originally paid for UCBS, was about to shake her head, but she kept still.

"It depends," said Tamara. "In great bear markets like this one, the Dow can plunge to an average of six or seven times earnings before it bottoms. That alone implies that *the Dow could fall to the 2,500 level*. And that's assuming corporate earnings don't decline any further. Yet, earnings of the Dow 30 companies *are* declining."

"Where's the bottom in earnings?"

Tamara's thoughts flashed back to the bottom-fishing analysts she used to debate at Harris. "In either of my scenarios, I'm sure all of Wall Street would be asking the very same question. The fact is, there is no foolproof bottom in earnings. Even zero earnings is not a foolproof bottom. Take a look at what happened among the Nasdaq stocks!"

Tamara went back to the folders again and pulled out a chart entitled "Nasdaq Earnings Wipeout." She showed it briefly to Linda, who nodded thankfully, and then she passed it over into Dulles's hands. [See Figure 13.2.]

"I see, but what is that portraying?" Dulles replied.

"Point A is showing nearly seven years of accumulated profits at 4,200 Nasdaq companies–$160 billion in all. Point B is showing that they were completely wiped out in just 15 short months. I'm not talking about an average, nor am I talking about just one year of profits. I'm talking about every single penny of profit that was made by every single Nasdaq company during that entire period."

"Wait a minute," said Dulles. "Let me see if I understand you correctly. Let's say all these companies had socked away all their profits in one global bank account during all those years. And let's say they never spent a penny of it. How much would they have in that account?"

"Like I said, $160 billion."

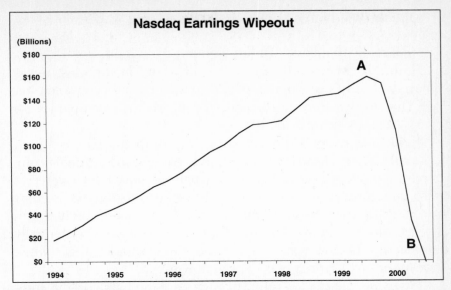

Figure 13.2 Nearly seven years of profits gone! Between April 1, 1994 and June 31, 2000 (point A in the chart), all of the companies listed on the Nasdaq earned a total of $159.8 billion. However, in just 15 months, between July 1, 2000 and September 31, 2001, the Nasdaq companies *lost* $161 billion. These losses wiped out every single penny of profits they had made in the previous seven years combined. This wipeout was due primarily to (1) accounting adjustments to correct exaggerated earnings, (2) declining sales, and (3) deflation—declining prices for their products.

"And now you're saying all that money was wiped out with losses?"

"Poof! Obliterated off the face of the earth! Every single penny."

"You're not saying this could happen to Dow stocks, are you?"

"No, but let's consider some other factors." Tamara picked up her Dow chart, pointing to the line labeled "Dow Today." "What you don't see in this chart," she declared, "is all the things going on behind these lines, in other, related markets–like corporate bonds, for example."

"Please explain."

"I have the data here from Moody's Investors Service. They say the creditworthiness of American companies is so poor that it has dropped for 18 quarters in a row. That's *four and a half years* of sinking balance sheets! That means their assets are sinking, their debts are surging. And a lot of these are blue chips, Dow companies! It's

telling you that many of the blue chips may also be a bubble waiting to burst!"

"Is it really that bad?" Dulles wondered out loud.

"Look. Right here it is in black and white! In the most recent
quarter, Moody's downgraded 124 companies and upgraded just
35. That means they've downgraded nearly *four* companies for
every one they've upgraded."

"Junk companies or investment grade companies?"

"Both! Here's how it's panning out: Among the stronger companies, it's going to get a lot more expensive—and a lot *tougher*—to
raise the money they need to expand or even to stay where they
are. Among the weaker companies, these repeated credit downgrades will make it nearly *impossible* to borrow money, potentially
threatening their very survival. When they go under, that's when
profits and stock prices really spiral downward."

"Some people say the rating agencies are too harsh on the companies. What do you think?"

"Not sure. Maybe they're just playing catch-up with past problems that they previously overlooked. And in some cases, such as
Enron, I happen to know they were clearly too soft. Overall, I'd
have to say that the actual deterioration in balance sheets could be
worse than the ratings alone might imply."

"Why do you say that?"

"Because companies are up to their eyeballs in debt. Because
some can't even pay current bills. Because corporate debt now
totals $4.9 trillion, or 57.1 percent of corporate net worth—more
than half of shareholder wealth in hock! Because of the steady
drumbeat of blue-chip companies marching into bankruptcy
court—Enron . . . WorldCom . . . Adelphia . . . US Airways . . . Global Crossing. But it's not over."

Tamara paused to glance up; then she looked back down at her
materials. "Even back in 1974," Tamara continued, "just prior to
the worst recession and deepest bear market of the second half of
twentieth century, the burden of private debt in this country was
far, far less severe than it is now. Back then, for each dollar of GDP,
there was *less* than $1 in private debts. Now, it's close to $2.00. No
wonder companies are going broke left and right! No wonder so
many companies are laying workers off like crazy! No wonder people are filing for personal bankruptcy!"

"OK. Now I see what's behind your Dow forecast," Dulles said, nodding repeatedly.

But Tamara shook her head. "You keep forgetting something."

"What's that?"

"You never asked me for a forecast—you asked me for a *worst-case scenario*."

"Sorry." He paused, then added, "I may need to present this to some important people. If there were just *one word* that could sum up the short-but-ugly scenario, what would that word be?"

" 'Deflation!' " she shot back without a moment's hesitation. "But excuse me for a moment. I have to return a phone call."

CHAPTER 14

DEFLATION!

hile Dulles waited, he recalled an old comedy routine from decades ago.

A fellow on a 1930s breadline asks his neighbor: "Which do you prefer? Inflation or deflation?" The second man responds: "Just give me flation. Plain, unvarnished flation."

Unfortunately, however, the public's longing for price stability—neither inflation nor deflation—was not satisfied in most economies of the world throughout history.

In the second half of the twentieth century, inflation was nearly everywhere. There was wage-push inflation, demand-pull inflation, and inflation-driven inflation. There was creeping inflation, galloping inflation, runaway inflation, and hyperinflation.

Then, as the century ended and a new one began, for the first time in more than 60 years, an old but powerful force reared its head and began to pound key regions or sectors of the world economy. It was *deflation*—falling prices, the opposite of inflation. Ironically, however, it was largely ignored. Most people were too deeply engrossed in their daily battles to sense the winds of change.

Commodity deflation had been around for a long time. But consumer price deflation, the kind that average people feel directly in their lives, first appeared in a big way overseas—in 2000 and 2001.

In Brazil, a brand new VW Passat, which used to cost $15,000, was going for less than $7,000. Brazil's VW Santana, another popular sedan, cost even less, with the cheapest model below $5,000. Luxury condominiums were reduced from $150,000 to under $80,000.

On the other side of the world, in Japan, the deflation was more widespread and more persistent. For much of 2000, 2001, and 2002, Japanese consumer prices tumbled virtually nonstop. A hamburger fell to half of what it cost a year earlier. Cotton polo shirts were 60 percent cheaper. Real estate was down 50, 60, even 80 percent in key areas.

In North America of 2000 to 2002, however, deflation was more spotty. Some prices, especially housing and health care, were still rising, while prices in other sectors, such as technology, were plunging. The going price for registering an Internet domain name fell from $70 to $7. You could buy almost-new computer servers made by IBM, Compaq, or Sun for 30 cents on the dollar. The price of a 128-megabyte dynamic random-access memory chip (DRAM), used in virtually all personal computers, plunged from $14 to $2 in just 10 months.

"Deflation!" Tamara repeated to Dulles, as she returned from her phone call. "Yet most people don't even know what it is. They think it's the same thing as depression. But you and I know it's not. It's falling prices, which may or may not happen as the same time as a depression. Falling grocery prices. Falling rent. Falling salaries. Everything falling."

"That's frightening," said Dulles.

"Yes. But are lower prices and cheaper goods such a bad thing in the long run? Not necessarily. Yes, deflation is part and parcel of the short-but-ugly scenario, but that same deflation is the key that makes the subsequent recovery so feasible. Why? Because the purchasing power of the currency—the dollar—would be restored. Because average people who work hard to save a relatively small amount of money would be able to buy a lot more with that money, and would reap the fruits of their labor. The crux of the problem is . . ."

"Yes?"

"The crux of the problem is that deflation also happens to be the one thing that nearly everyone in government and industry seems to fear the most. It's politically unacceptable."

"Agreed."

"There's no doubt that runaway inflation is far, far worse than deflation. And yet, at some point during Scenario B, inflation returns with a vengeance, and it's a killer. It erodes productivity. It corrodes the fabric of society. It jinxes the chances for recovery."

LESSER OF THE EVILS

Dulles pondered the dilemma. What Tamara was saying was so true, no economist could possibly disagree. Deflation was clearly the lesser of the evils, and for all those with savings or stable earnings, it could even bring significant advantages. Nevertheless, in the highest pinnacles of Washington, Wall Street, and Main Street, deflation also happened to be *the* most feared of economic forces. He knew why. The people in power had much more to lose. The average citizen had less to lose and possibly a lot to gain.

"How does deflation play itself out in your short-but-ugly scenario?" asked Dulles.

"The kinds of price declines you've seen sporadically in certain sectors begin to spread. I told you earlier about the vicious circle between bankruptcy and deflation. Well, as a result of that vicious circle, nothing is spared from price declines. It even impacts items that people think will *never* go down—a doctor's visit, college tuition, a New York City subway token."

"That reminds me," Dulles remarked. "I asked for more evidence on the deflation and bankruptcy thing, but you never gave it to me."

"Sorry. Here's a clipping from a while back. Let me read this short passage: 'As the number of bankruptcy filings by public companies surges to a record, companies are increasingly being forced to liquidate instead of reorganizing . . . to sell pieces of their business to the highest bidder.' "

"And that was when?

"November 11, 2001. See? Even back then, it was beginning in a few sectors. Rather than using bankruptcy as a way to fix their balance sheets, many companies were simply closing shop and selling off their assets. They were selling inventories, receivables, real estate, equipment, furniture, technology, customer lists—anything for almost any price."

"So?"

"So in Scenario A, that kind of selling produces deflation of the meanest variety—the kind of deflation that spreads with fury. The kind of deflation that takes even the savviest of economists by surprise. But it's over relatively quickly. And once it's over, the crisis is *really* over—no hidden land mines that will blow up months or years later."

Dulles thought back to his accounting days. "So it's a positive long term. I see that. But can't also be a positive short term? Let's say I run a business. Doesn't that mean I can count on lower labor costs, lower material costs?"

"Short term, negative; *long term,* positive."

Dulles closed his eyes briefly. *Tamara is right,* he thought. *For every dollar of cost reduction, the typical business would suffer $2, $3, or $4 in profit losses due to deflation.*

The CPA remembered one computer-server manufacturer that they used to consult with. He wasn't on the auditing team, but he was familiar with the numbers.

In one year, on one particular line, the manufacturer sold an average of 1,000 units per month for roughly $4,000 each. Total monthly sales: $4 million.

In the following year, it was selling only 700 units per month, a 30 percent drop from the previous year's rate. That was bad enough, but then came the deflation: The company was battered by a 50 percent decline in the average price of each unit—to about $2,000 each. Result: Revenues got slaughtered—from $4 million to a meager $1.4 million.

Sure, the cost of components also declined. But marketing and overhead costs barely budged. Before, when it was selling the servers for $4,000, the manufacturer's total expenses per unit were $3,500—a profit of $500 each. Now, although the servers were selling for $2,000, the per-unit expenses were still running at about $3,000—a $1,000 loss on each sale. The more business it did, the more it lost. "We're losing money, but we're making it up in volume," was the common PR line. Losing money but making it up in volume? What a crock of BS that was! Yet, this was typical of what went on in the tech industry of the 1990s.

Now, the short-but-ugly scenario laid out by Tamara Belmont was all about a similar pattern spreading to the entire economy. For the first time, Dulles was beginning to feel he could get completely behind this scenario. He asked Tamara for three copies of her full report, telling her he would take it to Johnston himself and go through all the points in great detail. She seemed very pleased and went back to her office.

Dulles swiveled his chair around and stared out the window to 14th Street. What was the best way to approach Johnston? It clearly had to be the *technology price deflation*. That had been Johnston's home turf. He knew all about it, and they had talked about it frequently in the past. Even before Johnston resigned from UCBS, technology price deflation had clearly begun to slice through all of the various divisions—and was probably *still* wreaking havoc in the company under the new management.

Yet most people outside of the industry—even many *inside* the industry—didn't realize how serious the technology price decline would be for the companies. They didn't realize that it had been an important factor behind the worst collapse in corporate profits since the Great Depression (every penny of the *total* profits earned by 4,200-plus Nasdaq companies after mid-1994 wiped out), the largest single losses in the history of the world (JDS Uniphase and AOL), and the greatest and fastest destruction of investor wealth ($5 trillion lost in the Nasdaq in just 11 months).

He looked again at Tamara's chart showing the total wipeout of corporate profits among the Nasdaq companies. Certainly, one reason was the accounting manipulations. The profits weren't there to begin with. So when the big accounting revelations came to light, the mirage dissolved with the sunshine. But deflation was the other big factor, the factor that few people were talking about.

Deflation was the nightmare of the tech industry. Now, in the short-but-ugly scenario, it would become the nightmare for other industries as well—autos, appliances, housing, even services. It would come as a total shock, for no one would be expecting it. Yet, in the long run, it would be one of the *crash benefits*.

Tamara had linked it to bankruptcies, and Dulles sensed intuitively that she was right on target. Indeed, thinking back, he remembered that most of the failing companies he had known as a consultant got hit by deflation in one form or another. They had big debts coming due every day. But they were living from hand to mouth. So they were counting on ever-higher prices and ever-larger revenues to acquire the cash they needed to repay those debts. Then it happened, like two colliding freight trains: debts and deflation. And the company was history.

His thoughts went back to some of his own research—loose ends that had mystified him but were now beginning to make more sense.

No wonder so many investment grade bond issuers (triple-B or better) were being downgraded to junk status (double-B or lower)— American Greetings, Providian Financial, Lucent Technologies, Royal Caribbean Cruises, AMR, Delta, plus dozens of other listed companies!

No wonder so many junk bond issuers were defaulting in record numbers! Bethlehem Steel had defaulted on $179 million in bonds, gutting the portfolios of thousands of investors. Swiss Air had defaulted on 1.5 billion, destroying the wealth of thousands more. Banana producer Chiquita had defaulted on $700 million in debt. Wireless data provider Metricom—$300 million in high-yielding 13 percent bonds that were due in 2010. Apparently 13 percent had sounded great to thousands of investors. But what good had it done them? They never got paid!

FINANCING DRIES UP

Dulles then thought about the financing problems many of his former clients were now facing. Even if they were in relatively good shape, they would now be having trouble raising money.

Where and when did that start? he asked himself. He quickly remembered: In venture capital. Everyone knew someone who had had lost fortunes on IPOs for companies that no longer existed. What people didn't know was how many supposedly "smart" venture capitalists fared even worse.

Indeed, in 2001 and 2002, venture capital firms had experienced their worst years *in history*. New investment capital put up by venture capitalists plunged by an incredible 62 percent in 2001, and by *an additional* 92 percent in 2002.

He remembered back to 1999. That's when Chase Manhattan broke into venture capital by buying up the small cap investment banking firm Hambrecht & Quist. Later, even after the Chase merger with Morgan, the company was still suffering the consequences of the H&Q disaster.

He recalled the case of Safeguard Scientifics, one of the few publicly traded venture capital firms. This was a firm that had a stellar and colorful 50-year history. But none of that made a bit of difference when the Internet bubble popped, driving Safeguard from $99 a share to $1.03 in October 2002.

Nor was this just a "dot-bomb" phenomenon. The same pattern of disappearing financing that struck down dot-coms was now beginning to hit almost every industry in America. In both worst-case scenarios, bond investors would withdraw from any company that did not have stellar ratings. Big banks would recoil in horror from the new, heightened risk of making additional loans to companies that were already overloaded with debt.

Dulles wondered whether it was, in fact, already beginning. Wasn't it Wachovia Bank that had publicly announced it would be stricter with loans to airlines, aircraft parts suppliers, hotels, and food suppliers to restaurants on the East Coast? Hadn't Bank of America shut down a crucial credit window on commercial contractors?

If this was already happening, what would happen in one of Tamara's scenarios? He could easily see nearly all banks limiting the size of offered credit lines, increasing fees, and requiring more collateral. He could see credit windows closing everywhere and the lights going out at companies that relied on that credit the way addicts rely on drugs.

Just as in the tech companies and the telecoms, nothing could sink a credit-addicted company more quickly than cold turkey—the sudden withdrawal of that credit. So far, though, the credit squeeze was primarily felt by small- and medium-sized companies. Big blue chips still had access to new credit.

ART, ANTIQUES, AND COLLECTIBLES

Dulles also thought about his own favorite assets. He wasn't wealthy. But he was a collector of some art and antiques. He remembered reading that, back in the 1930s, when wealthy families ran into a cash pinch, they'd auction off rare art and antiques for pennies on the dollar. Similarly, after the Crash of '87, art and antiques at major auctions fell as much as 30, even 50 percent. The plunge didn't last very long. But it illustrated how susceptible those items were to deflation.

If Tamara's deflation scenario came true, what would happen to the price of a Tiffany Favrile floor lamp? A 1918 U.S. airmail Curtis Jenny stamp? An autographed Jackie Robinson baseball card? A Ming Dynasty vase? They were all vulnerable to steep plunges, much like the stock market.

Would price declines be sporadic or across the board? Would the wealthy buyers in America, Japan, Hong Kong, and the Middle East be affected? When deflation struck their businesses and other assets, would it force them to sell too? It was certainly possible.

He began to envision deflation as a snowball, feeding on itself as it rolled down a mountain. It would be no different than the selling frenzies he had already seen in the stock market: Prices would fall because people were selling . . . and people would sell more because prices were falling. They would sell for all kinds of reasons—perhaps because they were driven by their inner psyche or pushed by external pressure, or simply because everyone else was doing it.

Dulles prayed neither worst-case scenario would come to pass, but if he had to choose between one or the other, he would clearly choose Scenario A, short but ugly. "Get it over with! Don't drag it out! Let's move on to better times!" he whispered to no one in particular.

THE DANGER OF HIGHER YIELDS

One reason Linda Dedini was so interested in the discussion in Dulles's office was that she had a key concern regarding money markets, bonds, CDs, and so forth. When she realized that none of these was a primary topic, she left. Besides, she had a 1 P.M. with her adviser, and traffic on the parkway to Baltimore was always uncertain.

While driving, she refocused her mind on the strategy she was seeking to develop—a strategy that would give her the higher yields she needed *without* the higher risk.

"These Treasury bills are killing me," she said to the adviser via her cell phone, after alerting him that she was running a bit late. "No, I'm not complaining. Thank God I'm not losing money any more. But look at these low interest rates! They're a rip-off! Plus, I have to pay income taxes on the interest, right? Then, I have to cover inflation. What's inflation running now?"

"Maybe 2 percent. Maybe less."

"That doesn't sound right to me. But OK, we can talk about it some more when I get there."

She parked the car in his driveway, walked to the door, and rang the bell. As they walked back to his home office, she picked up exactly where they had left off. "I don't believe those low inflation numbers that the government keeps putting out. My insurance bills are going up by a helluva lot more than that. They just jacked up the kids' school tuition again this year. It's nonstop."

"What about deflation?" asked the adviser. "Have you ever thought of that prospect? With deflation, even if you make *zero* percent, the value of your cash is growing, perhaps by leaps and bounds. You've already seen it in the stock market. For the same dollar, you can now buy *four* times the number of UCBS shares you could buy before. You've already seen it with PCs. You can buy 10 times the computer power for one-fourth the price of just a few years ago. How much deflation is that? Something like 97 percent deflation? Someday, you could see it spread to your grocery bills and even your electric bill."

Linda was not at all convinced. In practice, she simply did not see it. "That's conjecture," she said. "Right now, I absolutely have to do better than these Treasury bills. So here's my idea. I find corporate bonds rated, say, triple-B. That's still pretty secure, right?"

"Yes, that's the lowest grade of bonds that are still considered nonspeculative—'investment grade.' Anything below that, like double-B or worse, is considered speculative or 'junk.' "

"Good. Then I get the triple-B. If they're downgraded below

triple-B, I sell 'em. As long as they hold up, I hold 'em and earn those higher interest rates."

The adviser was impressed with how much she had learned about bonds, but he felt a fiduciary responsibility to make sure she understood the dangers. "That *could* work, but I want to warn you about two pitfalls," he said with genuine concern. "The first pitfall is that companies are going bankrupt left and right."

"I know that. I have experienced that myself, with Global Crossing and WorldCom. I'm willing to take that risk because of Moody's and S&P. *They* will warn me, won't they?"

The adviser felt that the bond ratings from these companies were certainly less subject to payola than the stock ratings from Wall Street investment banking firms. But "less biased" was not good enough. The bond ratings were still bought and paid for by the companies being rated. Downgrades were still delayed. In a rapidly spreading bankruptcy crisis, the downgrades could be too little, too late to be of much value to investors.

"You know all about Enron, but do you know what happened behind the scenes with the Enron bond ratings?" asked the adviser.

"No. What happened?"

"I'll tell you." As he spoke, he got up from his chair, opened a file cabinet, searched for a few moments, and then pulled out a folder marked "Enron." From the file, he extracted a newspaper clipping with a Post-it note that read "Enron bond ratings" and sat back down.

"Even when it was absolutely obvious to the rating agencies that Enron's finances were in total disarray," he said, still scanning the clipping, "the rating agencies refused to downgrade the company to 'junk' and insisted it was still 'investment grade.' Hold on; I'm looking for something in this clipping from the *New York Times*. Oh, here it is. It says, and I quote, 'Executives at big securities firms that stood to profit from the deal'–they're talking about the Dynergy deal to rescue Enron–'pressed Moody's to keep ratings at investment grade, even as Enron bonds fell to levels indicating that the debt was highly risky.' "

"Translate, please."

"In other words, it was so obvious to everyone that Enron bonds were junk, the bonds were already selling for junk bond prices in the open market. But still, Moody's and S&P failed to act."

"And then?"

"Then, in a matter of just 24 hours, the rating agencies finally announced massive downgrades. Moody's cut Enron's rating by five notches. S&P slashed its Enron rating by six notches. Fitch outdid them all, squashing Enron's rating by *10* notches. All three agencies dropped their investment grade ratings like a red-hot potato. But it was too late for bond investors. By that time, Enron's bond had plunged from over 100 to 22 cents on the dollar, a loss of 80 percent from its peak just four months earlier."

"So much for my idea of holding corporate bonds until *after* they're downgraded to junk!"

"I'm glad you're giving it up. It's fraught with dangers at this time. Maybe in the future, when we've been through the worst of the crisis and most everything is on its way back up again! By the way, does your grandfather's portfolio have any bonds in it?"

"Actually, now that you mention it, yes. But I never even thought to bring them up, because, well, we were concentrating on the stocks."

The adviser seemed a bit sad. "That's OK. Just remember we're in for some very rough times. You can't leave one stone unturned. You've got to go through everything you own that might be vulnerable and carefully review the risks. Corporate bonds, as we've discussed before, can definitely be risky in a falling economy. What about your 401(k)?"

"My 401(k)? Gee. I really dropped the ball on that one, didn't I?" she said.

"Quite to the contrary. I'm the one who should have asked you about it. Here. I have instructions for both: "What To Do With Your Bonds," and "Managing Your 401(k) In A Down Market." Refer to them as needed.

WHAT TO DO WITH YOUR BONDS

All bonds can decline in value because of a rise in prevailing interest rates. In addition, all but U.S. Treasury bonds can decline for other reasons, such as ratings downgrades and defaults. In a crisis environment, bonds can also decline because of selling by bond holders seeking to raise cash, often to pay current bills.

There are two ways you can protect yourself from falling bond prices:

- *Go for the best quality.* Naturally, the higher the bond rating, the lower the chance of a price decline from a default or bankruptcy. The highest-rated bond issuer in the world is the U.S. Treasury.
- *Favor the shortest maturities.* This advice will vary depending on the expected direction of interest rates. However, to reduce risk, seek to avoid long-term maturities and purchase mostly short-term maturities.

Here are the steps to follow:

Most urgent step. Sell all junk bonds. The official definition of junk is any bond with a rating of double-B or lower (S&P's BB; Moody's Ba). When defaults and bankruptcies are rampant, these bonds are the first to default. And even if your bonds do not default, falling confidence in the junk bond market as a whole can lower the price of all junk bonds—including yours.

Urgent step. Sell all corporate bonds that do *not* boast a rating of single-A or higher—including triple-B bonds (S&P's BBB; Moody's Baa) bonds. Triple-B bonds are often the favorites of investors because they offer the highest yields but still qualify as "investment grade" bonds. However, triple-B is only one grade level above junk. In turbulent times, when rapid downgrades are possible, you may want to have a better cushion of safety.

Less urgent step. Sell all remaining corporate bonds with a maturity of five years or more. A lot can happen to a bond even if it doesn't default. Downgrades alone can depress its value. When interest rates go up, bond prices automatically go down. And if large institutional investors

(Continued)

such as insurers or banks seek to liquidate their bonds in large enough quantities, they could cause a sharp decline in bond prices. A key point to remember: All else being equal, the longer the maturity, the more vulnerable the bond to price fluctuations; the shorter the maturity, the less vulnerable.

MANAGING YOUR 401(K) IN A DOWN MARKET

As long as the stock market remains in a long-term decline, follow these steps:

Step 1. Do not pull the money out of your 401(k) umbrella. Even if the investment options in your 401(k) plan are limited, most do offer alternatives that are safer than the stock market. And if you are unhappy with your 401(k) administrator or firm, you may be able to switch without breaking up the plan or suffering tax consequences.

Step 2. Within your 401(k) or similar retirement plan, favor safety over performance for the duration of the stock market decline. Generally, the following are safer alternatives than stock mutual funds, starting from the safest:

- *Safest.* Money market mutual fund that invests exclusively in short-term U.S. government securities. Unfortunately, few 401(k) plans offer this option.
- *Safer.* Almost any money market mutual fund. The only exception might be those that invest in nonprime securities, but these are rare.
- *Safe.* A bond fund that invests exclusively or almost exclusively in high-grade bonds and/or U.S. Treasuries. The shorter the maturity and the higher the average quality of the bonds, the safer the fund is likely to be.
- *Lesser of the evils.* An income fund investing in some mix of high-dividend common stocks, preferred shares and bonds. This would be a suitable investment

in a stable environment, but could suffer losses in a crash or prolonged market decline. Therefore, this option should be used only as a last resort when no other safer alternatives are available.

Step 3. If your 401(k) plan does not offer safe alternatives, petition your employers or benefits managers. Let them know that given the risks in the market, you feel that they are not fulfilling their fiduciary responsibility under federal law to provide plan participants with a wide enough variety of appropriate choices. If the performance of the funds in the plan has been mostly poor in the most recent year or two, use this information to support your request.

The following is suggested language that you may use in your petition, modified as needed to fit your individual circumstances. "All, or nearly all, of the funds available under the current 401(k) plan invest in the stock market to some degree. However, based on recent performance, I have decided that it is not in my best interest to allocate any portion of my retirement funds to stocks at this time. Therefore, please add, as soon as possible, at least one fund that is designed to invest exclusively in fixed instruments or money markets, always avoiding equities. Under ERISA (Employee Retirement Income Security Act) Section 404(c), retirement plans must offer at least three choices among diversified groups of investments. By effectively forcing plan participants to invest in the stock market, the current plan may be out of compliance with this requirement."

Step 4. If you are a more active investor, consider the program in *The Ultimate Safe Money Guide* (Wiley), pages 83–85.

"I have a friend who buys only mutual funds," she said as the adviser escorted her to the door. "What should she do?"

"If the mutual funds are invested in stocks, follow essentially the same instructions I gave you for stocks. If they're in bonds, follow the instructions for bonds."

Linda was not happy that her high-yield strategy was on the wrong track. But at least she was forewarned. Millions of other investors, however, would get caught, as the deflation–bankruptcy crisis spread. The trip to Baltimore had definitely been worthwhile. Now she could get virtually *all* her family's assets to a safe haven.

BAD OPTIONS

Linda and her brothers took all the protective steps necessary to shield their expected inheritance and retirement funds. So they breathed a deep sigh of relief and were now ready to do more.

Linda now clearly understood how stock prices could go inexorably lower—even down to levels that no one expects. She was anxious to start making the decline pay off for herself personally. But she didn't want to bother her adviser so soon after their last meeting. So she went online and bought some investments she had heard about on CNBC—*put options.*

She did it entirely on her own, picking the ones that seemed ridiculously cheap—$100, $50, even $25 for 100 shares. Some were so cheap, the commissions alone cost more than the investment. She waited for something to happen, and it did: The market moved sideways, and within just a few weeks every dime she had spent on the put options was gone. The put options had all turned to dust—worthless.

"I could have had more fun with a Vegas slot machine that never pays a dime than I could with those options," she said to her adviser a few days later during a phone conversation.

He laughed heartily, as usual, but this time she didn't think it was amusing. "How much did you lose?" he asked.

"Only about $2,000, but that's not the point. The point is, these things are worse than lottery tickets."

"You said it! Look. I'll be at my D.C. office tomorrow afternoon. Meet me there at around 5 P.M."

OPTIONS BASICS

When she arrived, the adviser was having lunch from a Styrofoam take-out box. He apologized for eating while talking, but said it had been a busy day. Linda smiled and wished him *bon appétit*.

"I'll walk you through each step slowly and take you through as many possibilities as I can," he said, deftly manipulating a pair of chopsticks.

Step-by-step was precisely what she felt she needed. She had purchased some books on options, but despite her scientific mind, she ran into a brick wall—butterflies, straddles, strangles. The terminology alone was baffling.

"To begin with," he said, "forget about learning a whole bunch of complex options strategies. Instead, start with the kind of options you are probably most familiar with."

"I thought I told you: I'm *not* familiar with *any* options."

He laughed. "Actually, I think you are. Let's say you're in the market for a new home. And let's say that this is a real estate office and that I'm your real estate broker. I take you out to see a beautiful house in a great neighborhood. You love the price, but you're not quite ready to buy. So we go to the owner and we say, 'How about leasing your house with an option to buy.' "

"Oh, yes, of course. I'm familiar with *those* kinds of options."

The adviser explained the terms: "The going price for similar homes is $150,000. But everyone thinks that prices in the area are going up. So the seller says that he'll give you an option to buy the house at $155,000. The term is 12 months. If you don't exercise the option within that time frame, that's it—you've lost your chance. You figure, the option is the icing on the cake. If you don't use it, you've lost nothing; if you need it, you've got it. So you accept the deal. Clear?"

"Very."

"OK. Another example. The scene changes—same desk, same props, only now we're not at the real estate office anymore; we're at a corporate recruiter's office, and I'm your agent. You say you're tired of the academic world and you want to get a job in industry. I tell you about a small upstart company with an opening for an assistant in their R&D division. They're offering a much higher salary than what you're getting now. What's your response?"

"Not interested."

"Hey, they offer great benefits—full health coverage for you, your husband, the children."

"No."

"They have a very sweet options package. You like that? Ahah! I can tell by the look on your face that now you're a bit more interested."

"Yes," she admitted.

"OK. Here's the deal," he says, feigning excitement. "This is supposedly an up-and-coming biotech company that is going to do well whether the stock market goes up or down. As a welcome-aboard bonus, this company will *give* you an option to buy 10,000 of its shares at $5 any time within the next five years. That's a pretty good strike price—$5."

"OK."

"The stock is selling for $2.75 right now. So you can't do anything with the options at this particular moment. But you just wait," he continues, still mimicking an enthusiastic recruiter. "This stock is headed for $10, $20, maybe even $50, just like those other high-tech stocks. When that happens, you can cash in—big time! No matter what the shares are selling at, you still get to buy at $5. Let's say the stock only reaches $10. In effect, you go in there and you buy the 10,000 shares for five bucks a pop. That's $50,000. Then, you turn right around and sell them for $100,000. Bingo! You've bagged a hefty $50,000 profit."

"OK, I know the pitch," she said. "You've just taken us back a few years, right? If this were for real, and if I really wanted to quit teaching, would you go for it?"

"The deal does offer distinct advantages. First, even if all their promises fall by the wayside, you've lost nothing by accepting the option. When you hold an option, it means *you* decide whether to buy. If it turns out that the company is a total flop, you throw it in the trash can.

"Second," he continued, "unlike the options you bought recently, these options don't cost you anything. The company is offering to *give* them to you—free. If you wanted to buy similar options in the stock market, you'd have to pay a pretty penny for them—many times more than what you paid for yours."

"Suppose I want to negotiate a better deal."

"OK. We can call the company and ask for ten years instead of five. Plus, we could ask for a lower strike price—at $3 instead of $5. But I doubt you'd get it."

"Why not?"

"An option to buy at $3 would be far too valuable to give away to an average staffer. If the stock goes up just 25 cents to $3, you'd already be *at* the money. If the stock goes up just 50 cents to $3.25, you'd already be 25 cents *in* the money. Plus, you'd have a full 10 years for this to happen. Heck, in 10 years this stock could be worth 100 bucks! Then you'd buy it for $3, sell it for $100, and take out a $97 profit on each share. Multiply that by 10,000 shares, and you've got close to a million. There's no way the company is going to give away that much to an assistant research person."

"Right."

While talking, the adviser put down the chopsticks and picked up a *temaki* with his hand. "OK. So let's sum up what you've learned here. First, you've learned what the 'strike price' is—the price where you can exercise the option and buy the stock. You've learned what the 'expiration' is—when the option expires, of course. You've learned concepts like 'at the money' (when the market is at the same level as the strike price) and 'in the money' (when the market has surpassed the strike price). Plus, you've learned some basic rules."

"I have?"

"You sure have! First, you've learned that the *closer* the option's strike price is to the current price of the stock, the better the chance of reaching the strike price in the allotted time—and the more valuable the option is."

"Oh, right. That's why they were willing to give me the options with a strike price of $5 but refused to give me options with a strike price of $3. The $3 option was already very close to being in the money."

He nodded. "Second, the more time you get, the more an option is worth. Third, the payoff can be large, but the risk is limited. When you purchase an option, you *can* lose every penny you invest but never a penny more."

She watched as the adviser closed the Styrofoam box and dropped it in a wastebasket beside his desk. "I'm missing something here. The dots are not connecting. On TV, they said someone made a fortune with the market going *down*—not *up!* Everything you've told me about options so far is the opposite."

PUT OPTIONS

The adviser laughed again. "Yes, of course. So far, all the options we've talked about are *call* options–to take advantage of a rising market. But the same basic principles are also valid for *put* options–to take advantage of a falling market. It's very simple: Instead of giving you the right to *buy* at a predetermined price, the put options give you the right to *sell* at a predetermined price."

"I don't get it."

"Go back to the example with the house. Make believe I'm the real estate agent again."

Linda nodded. "OK, You're the real estate agent. I'm buying a house."

"No, this time you're *selling* your house."

"Selling my house? OK, I'm selling my house. Now what?"

"Actually, you don't want to move out for another year or so. That's when your new employment contract begins."

"I see. But why don't I just wait a year and sell it then?"

"Because you're afraid your house is going to go down in value. It's been appraised for, say, $190,000, but you're worried that by this time next year, it will be down to as low as $160,000. So you come to me and you say, 'Is there any way you can help me lock in the sale price?' "

"Can you?" Linda asked.

"Actually, I can. A lot of real estate agents advertise 'if we can't sell your house, we'll buy it,' and I'll do the same for you, provided you pay me a fee of, say, $2,000. In exchange, I give you a contract that gives you the right to sell the house to me–to *put* it to me–at $190,000. That's a *put option* contract."

"Actually, I wouldn't mind doing something like that in real life. But why would you give me that option?"

"Because I don't think the price is going down. I'm pretty sure I'll be able to find you a buyer for *at least* $190,000, probably more. I figure I have nothing to lose. So I'm thinking I'll collect an extra $2,000 in easy income."

"Good for you. But what do *I* do with it?"

"If the market price goes up, you do nothing. I get you a good buyer, say, at $195,000. And you throw the put option contract in the trash. Why would you want to sell it to me for $190k if I can get you $195k from someone else? So it has cost you $2,000. So what? At least you can sleep nights. At least you know you locked in a guaranteed minimum price."

"And if the market goes down?"

"Then you *put* the house to me—you make me honor my contract to buy it from you. You get your guaranteed $190,000, and now *I'm* the one stuck with the property. I have to scramble to find a buyer, but that's not your problem. You're off to your new job with $190,000 in your pocket, minus the $2,000 you paid me for the option."

Linda smiled. She finally understood put options. But she was still having trouble connecting them to crash profits. "How does that work with stocks?"

"Same idea. I take my agent's hat off, and put my broker hat back on."

"OK, now you're the broker again," Linda said nodding.

"Let's say you've got 100 shares of Microsoft, and it's selling for $60 a share. You're unwilling or unable to sell the shares, but you're worried that in the next six months or so, Microsoft is going to crash to $40. So you come to me and you say, 'I need to lock in my sale price, just like I did on my house. I want to buy a Microsoft $55 put.' "

"I want to buy a Microsoft $55 put."

"Exactly. So I sell it to you. Now if the stock goes goes up, you rip up the put option and throw it away. If the stock plunges to $40, you *put* the 100 shares to me, and I have to pay you the $55 price you locked in. Same as I did with the $190,000 price you locked in on your house."

"Wait. Suppose I don't have any Microsoft shares? What do I do?"

"What would Microsoft be selling for at that point?"

"$40."

"And how many shares do you need?"

"One hundred."

"OK. So what are you waiting for? There are millions of Microsoft shares being offered for sale. Just go out and buy 100 for $40 a share. *Then* you can come back to me and sell them for $55."

"Can you give me another example?"

"Sure. Let's say that you expect the shares in ABC Company to drop from $100 to $50. You can buy a put option—that is, the right to sell the stock—at $90."

"If you're right and the share price drops to $50, you can buy it for $50. With the option, you have the right to sell it at $90. So, you buy it at $50 and sell it at $90. Your net is $40."

"So I'd have to buy the stock and then sell it right back?"

"No, not at all. You don't have to exercise the option to get your money out of it. You can just sell the option itself. And you don't have to wait for the option to mature. You can sell it anytime. In this case, your goal is to make a profit by buying and selling the options, not by buying or selling the stocks. This will make life a lot simpler for you. All you want to do is buy the options low and sell them high, just like anything else."

She still needed more specifics. "That's not exactly how it worked out with the ones I bought just now, is it? Can you give me some idea as to how I can make it work?"

"Sure." He pulled out a piece of paper and created what he called a 'make-believe contract,' with the following specifics:

Put Option Contract
Number of shares: 100
Underlying stock: ABC Company
Expiration: 3 months from today
Strike price: $90

She glanced at it briefly and immediately understood. The contract gave her the right to sell 100 shares of ABC Company stock. She'd have three months from today to exercise that right. Then, if she actually sold the shares, she'd get $90 per share.

"And I don't have to own the shares, right?"

"Not at all. In fact, you can forget about *ever* owning the shares. The investment you're buying is this contract—this option. Just focus your attention right now on how much this contract costs and how much you can sell it for."

"That was my question. How can I tell how much this contract costs?"

"That's easy. You can just ask your broker or check the newspaper or the Internet. Let's say the ABC Company put option is selling for $4.75 per share. This contract is for 100 shares. So that means it costs 100 times 4.75, or $475, per contract."

"And how much could I sell it for in the future?"

The adviser leaned back in his chair and thought for a few seconds. "That depends. Which do you prefer to hear about first—the losing scenarios or the winning scenarios?"

"Start with the losers. Unfortunately," she said with a thin smile, "it seems I'm pretty good at losing. I already have some real experience in that arena."

THE "OOPS" SCENARIO

"Fine. Just bear in mind that when you buy a put option on ABC Company stock, you're betting the stock will go go *down*. So when the stock price goes up—that's bad for you. When it goes down, as you planned, that's generally good for you. Got that?"

"I know, I know. That's the whole point. I want to profit from a falling market."

"OK. Let's say you just happen to buy at exactly the wrong time. Instead of falling as you expected, ABC Company shares start going up immediately to $130. The option is not exercisable at this point. You obviously would not want to sell the stock for $90 if it's worth $130. On the day the options expire, the stock is still near the $130 level."

"How much would the option be worth at that point?"

"Nothing."

"A total loss?"

"A total loss! You lose every last penny you invested in it.

"I understand," she said after a moment's reflection. "Now tell me how it works when the stock price goes down."

THE "SIDEWAYS" SCENARIO

"Later. First, let's look at a sideways market. ABC Company goes down a small fraction one day, up a bit the next day. Despite some excitement here and there, it always seems to wind up pretty much in the same spot. With every day that passes, your option goes down in value. It reminds you of an hourglass dropping grains of sand with each passing moment. Suddenly, in the last few days before your put option expires, ABC Company finally falls a few points. But it's too late. The stock doesn't fall below $90 until three weeks *after* it expires."

"No good?"

"No. The irony is that you were right about ABC Company shares. They did go *down,* just like you thought they would. But that's not good enough. You also had to be right about the timing. You bought the put option too soon. By the time the shares were about to fall, your time ran out. The end result is that the option expires worthless—same as the previous example."

"*Now* can we move on to the winning scenario?"

THE "BREAK-EVEN" SCENARIO

"We're getting closer, but we're not quite there yet. ABC Company stock falls apart right out of the starting gate. Your timing is perfect. And it continues to tumble nearly every day. The stock falls below $90, you're *in the money,* and you're delighted. But *in the money* does not necessarily mean *in the profits.* Remember, you paid $4.75 per share. Let's say your total cost is $5 with commission or $500 for each contract. So by expiration time, for you to break even, ABC Company not only has to fall to the strike price of $90, it has to fall beyond it by $5—to $85.

"And that's exactly what happens. If you exercised the option at that point, you'd sell 100 shares of ABC Company for $90 per share. And you'd be able to buy them for $85 per share. So the options are worth $5 per share. For 100 shares, that's $500—exactly what you invested in them in the first place."

"I break even. OK. But when do we get to the profit scenario?"

THE DOUBLE-YOUR-MONEY SCENARIO

"Right now. As in the previous scenario, ABC Company falls sharply right out of the box. Within a week, it reaches the strike price of $90. Within another week, it falls through the $85 level, which would be the break-even point at expiration. But the remaining life of the option is still two months, and ABC Company continues to fall. At expiration, ABC Company is trading at $80. If you exercised your option, you'd be able to buy the 100 shares of ABC Company at $80 and sell them for $90. That's a nice $10 difference, or $1,000. But you don't exercise the option; instead, you just sell it to someone else for the $1,000. You never have to exercise; you can always sell your option to close out the position."

"Now you're talking!" she exclaimed. "I go in with $500 and walk away with $1,000—double my money. Wow! That's a 100 percent profit in just three months!"

"Don't overreact. For investors used to stocks and bonds, this may sound like a fantastic result. But, with the purchase of options, a modest move in the stock can often double your money."

THE "HOME RUN" SCENARIO

"Now," he continues, "let's say ABC Company just keeps plunging, practically nonstop. It falls below the $90 level in the first few days. So almost immediately, your option is in the money. This is a very good sign. Then, a few days later, ABC Company falls below $85—your break-even point, and it just keeps crashing. Now, it's selling at $65, and there is still a lot of time remaining. You have two choices—one, you can wait until the very last day, in the expectation that ABC Company will go still lower and you'll make even more, or two, you can sell your put option now, take your profits, and run."

"How much would it be worth if I sold it now?"

"Figure it out."

"Let's see. It's worth $90 minus $65. That's $25 in the money. OK. So I figure it should be worth 25 times 100 shares. That's $2,500. If I sell it now, I can walk away with five times my original $500 investment. Not bad at all!"

"You learn fast! You call your broker and ask him to check the price. To your pleasant surprise, you discover that the put option is actually worth about $1,000 more than you estimated, close to $3,500. Why? Because the $2,500 you figured is strictly the put option's *intrinsic* value—that is, the amount that someone would profit from the sale of the stock if they exercised the option today. But in addition to the intrinsic value, this option still has *time value*. There is quite a bit of time left before it expires, and that time is worth something. In fact, investors feel that the time remaining is actually worth a lot: an additional $1,000 on top of the $2,500 intrinsic value."

"Why is the time worth so much?"

"Because ABC Company is moving down sharply and steadily every day. Like you, other investors are also assuming that this trend will continue, and they're willing to pay the $1,000 for the chance of making those extra bucks."

"Let 'em have that chance! I want to cash out. I walk away with $3,500 minus commissions. That's a profit of about $3,000. Six to one. *Now,* it's starting to be a bit more fun. Is that about the most I can reasonably expect?"

THE "GRAND SLAM" SCENARIO

"Usually, yes. But sometimes you can go even further and hit a grand slam home run. Let's go back to when you first buy the ABC Company put option. And let's say the stock is pretty quiet. In fact, the market is so quiet, you can practically hear a pin drop. With that lack of movement, few people are interested in buying options, and the few who do buy aren't willing to pay the usual price for them. Their logic is simple: 'Even if ABC Company is trading at $100, and the strike price is only 10 points away (at $90), what good is it? At this rate, it will take a month of Sundays for ABC Company to fall to $90. In this dead market, you'd be lucky if ABC Company reaches $95 in a year,' they reason.

"So I can buy the option for a lot less?"

"Yes. People already holding the ABC Company put options get discouraged. They try to find someone to take these options off their hands, but there are no takers—except you and a few others. Instead of paying close to $500 for the option, you pick it up for a song—at less than $2 per share, or just $200 for the 100-share contract, including commissions."

"Then what?"

"Then, suddenly, ABC Company announces that it missed Wall Street's earnings expectations by a mile. At the same time, the entire sector gets clobbered and comes alive with activity. Instead of moving by just a meager 10 cents or less every day, the stock plunges (and surges) in leaps and bounds, with huge gyrations of as much as $5 or even $10 per day. Within days, ABC Company is selling for $65. You hurriedly call your broker to find out how much the option is worth. You can hardly believe your ears: It has surged from the $200 you originally paid for it to $4,000."

"Why is it worth so much?"

"There are three reasons: First, the intrinsic value. You know how to figure that: It's the $90 minus $65 equals $25, or $2,500, for the contract of 100 shares. Second, the time value. With many weeks remaining, that's worth a good deal. Third, the volatility value. Remember I explained how the options lost value when the market went dead? Well, they have now *gained* tremendous value as the market has had a sudden burst of activity. ABC Company stock is not just falling in larger increments. It's also gyrating wildly all over the lot. These gyrations, even if they're sometimes in the wrong direction, make the options far more valuable, and you get the benefit."

"Good . . . and so?"

"Add them all together—one, the intrinsic value; two, the time value; and three, the volatility factor. Your ABC Company put is now worth $4,000, or a remarkable 20 times more than you paid for it—an explosive investment return."

"Is this possible in the real world?"

"Yes. It actually happens. You can't count on it . . . but your strategy has to allow for it. You've got to use options like a catapult—no, like a slingshot! The slingshot is not a gun—it can never backfire on you. But it gives you tremendous leverage. If you miss a few, you just try a few more. It can be a very powerful weapon, but you have to learn the skills."

"Such as . . ."

"The first skill is picking the stones—not expensive gems, just ordinary, well-formed, relatively inexpensive stones. The second skill is discipline—to control your greed, to recognize the bird in the hand. The third and most difficult is timing." The adviser spent another hour patiently going over the ins and outs of options

15 RULES TO GET THE MOST OUT OF PUT OPTIONS

Most investors who buy options wind up losing money—usually for the very same reasons that investors lose money in the stock market or any other investment: They let their emotions get the best of them. Plus, they don't realize that options, if abused, can be like playing the lottery or a slot machine. You can't lose more than you spend on each try, but if you play every day, month after month, your cost can add up to an unlimited amount over time.

To avoid these pitfalls and improve your chances for success, follow these rules:

Rule 1. Always limit the amount you invest in options to the amount you can afford to lose. A good rule of thumb for most investors is to keep at least 95 percent of your money in safe or conservative investments. Allocate no more than 5 percent to options. If you cannot afford to lose the 5 percent of your portfolio allocated to options, options might be too risky for you.

Rule 2. Don't invest the entire allocation at once. Spread your funds out over at least one year's time. For example, if you are planning to invest $10,000 in options, that could be $2,500 per quarter.

Rule 3. Unless it's a very special situation, try to avoid options that cost less than $50 per contract. Typically, these are options that have a very low chance of success—because they're so far out of the money or have a very short time remaining, or a combination of both. Moreover, the commissions could be as much as or more than the cost of the options itself. That's usually not a good deal!

Rule 4. By the same token, try to avoid overspending on any one option contract. Typically, if it costs much more than $500 per contract, it's too expensive. To better take advantage of the limited-risk feature of options, keep the cost down as much as possible on each option contract. That also lets you spread your funds around to a wider variety of different options.

Rule 5.   Expect losers. Indeed, with options, success can be achieved with many small losers and a few large winners—another reason why you should keep the cost of each individual option low.

Rule 6.   Among the losers, don't be surprised if there are some that wind up expiring worthless—a 100 percent loss. To help avoid total losses, try to sell them—whether at a profit or a loss—*before* the last two weeks in the life of the option.

Rule 7.   Do your best to buy put options while the market is in a rally mode. (To determine if the market is in a rally mode, see "Is the Market in Rally Mode?" on page 70.) Or, you can also use more advanced technical tools, which are beyond the realm of this book. (If you buy call options, it's the opposite—try to buy on a market correction.)

Rule 8.   Similarly, seek to sell put options you're holding while the market is still in a short-term declining mode. (Also, see "Is the Market in Rally Mode?")

Rule 9.   Seek to buy an even number of contracts of each option. This will give you more flexibility when seeking to exit the position.

Rule 10.   When you buy an option—whether a put or call—*always* specify the *maximum* price you will pay based on the last actual trade in the specific option you are buying. As an illustration, if you're buying two contracts of the XYZ option, and its last price was $2.75 per share ($275 per contract of 100 shares), you might tell your broker,

(Continued)

"Please buy two contracts of XYZ at 2.75 or better." (When you're buying, "or better" means "or less.") You may adjust the price up a bit to allow for market fluctuations. But the price you specify should not be more than about 10 percent higher than the most recent market price. Your broker can advise you on this aspect, depending on the market conditions at a time.

Rule 11. When you sell an option, *always* specify the *minimum* price you will be willing to accept. Following up with the example given in Rule 10, if the XYZ option is now selling at $5.25 per share ($525 per contract of 100 shares) and you are seeking to take a profit on both of your contracts, you would tell your broker, "Please sell two contracts of XYZ at $5.25 or better." (When you're selling, "or better" means "or more.") You may adjust the price down a bit to allow for market fluctuations. But the price you specify should not be more than about 10 percent lower than the most recent market price. Again, consult with your broker for the actual level, based on the market conditions.

Rule 12. Don't chase the market. When you specify a buy or sell price, you may not get in or out of the option as you had hoped. If this happens, it can be frustrating, but you should not bend. Instead,

- Wait at least two or three full trading days.
- If your order still has not been filled, review the situation to make sure you still want to go ahead with the trade.
- If it's still within your budget, resubmit a new order based on the most recent price.
- No matter what, do not let your broker buy or sell the options "at the market." There are two reasons at-the-market orders can hurt your performance with options:
  - Options can be very volatile, moving up and down quickly in price. If you let the broker buy at

whatever the market price may be, you may wind up spending much more than you planned, exceeding your budget and reducing your profit. Similarly, on the sell side, if you sell at the market price, you could wind up giving up much of its value. Between the two sides, what could have been a handsome winner can wind up becoming a mediocre performer or even a loser.

- Options can often be thinly traded. Too many other investors that happen to buy (or sell) at the same time you do could move the market up precisely when you're buying (or move it down precisely when you're selling) and hurt your results.

Rule 13. Do not add to winning positions. This is the opposite of what you may have heard for most other investments, so it may take some time to get used to. However, once an option is clearly in the win column, it's probably too late to get into it and too expensive to buy. There are exceptions to this rule, but they are few and far between.

Rule 14. By the same token, do not be too hasty to dump losing options. Again, this is the opposite of the advice given for most other investments. With options, it is very common for a loser to suddenly come back from behind and jump ahead into the winning column.

Rule 15. Stop-loss orders (sell stops) are usually *not* recommended. You should have already taken the steps to limit your risk by (1) budgeting your money carefully; (2) spreading it out over time; and (most important) (3) taking all the steps recommended to keep the cost of each individual option very modest. These three measures help limit your risk and largely replace the function of stops. Moreover, when you do use stop-loss orders, they typically force you to sell your options when the market is moving against you, violating Rule 8.

(Continued)

Two warnings:
- Do not sell short (or write) options. If you do so, you will open yourself up to unlimited risk, defeating the primary goals of this strategy. (There may be a practical value of writing *covered options*—a strategy for protecting your stock portfolio or for reducing the cost of other options positions. However, these strategies are beyond the scope of this guide.)
- Whenever you invest in options, you should always bear in mind the primary disadvantage: Options are wasting assets. When you buy an option, you are essentially buying time. So, if the market remains unchanged, the value of the option will naturally decline as time goes by. And to profit from options, the expected move has to happen—or at least get underway—before the option expires.

trading, summing it all up with "15 Rules to Get the Most Out of Put Options."

"The main rule is, *Never invest more than you can afford to lose.*"

"What else?"

"It's usually a good idea to buy at least two contracts of each option. Then, as soon as you can double your money, sell half of them. That covers your cost and gives you *at least* a breakeven on the entire trade. Then, let the remaining contracts ride—giving you a chance at a home run or even a grand slam."

Linda was pleased, but had one last question. "Sometimes it seems like gambling. So I'm asking myself, 'Should I be playing with options or not?' "

"I can't answer that question for you. Remember: You can effectively profit from a crash just by sitting in Treasury bills. The more the market falls, the more your money is worth. You don't have to go any further. Or you can just use reverse index funds. But I *can* tell you what some disciplined investors are doing. They put most of their money away in a safe place, as you have. They then allocate a small portion of their total portfolio—say, 5 percent—to this kind of investment. Since they can't lose more than what they invest, their keep-safe funds are always insulated from any losses, even if the entire program is a flop."

"Is that what I should do?

"Go back to your goals. Earlier, you said one of your goals was to recoup your losses quickly, right? You also said you wanted to make a lot of money in a crash, right? Now, I'm not convinced those necessarily have to be your goals. Trying to recoup losses quickly could cause you more losses—also quickly. But if you decide that's what you want, put options do offer that critical risk-limitation feature. At the worst, you will lose whatever you paid for them, plus any commissions."

15

THE FALL OF THE BLUE CHIPS

On a cold, rainy morning, the second wave of the stock market crash began. The main cause was not the regular daily revelations of corporate corruption. Nor was it a terrorist attack or any other outside threat.

The most fundamental driving force behind the decline was the unraveling of the debt pyramid and the spreading bankruptcy crisis.

Throughout history, speculative orgies swept every sector into euphoria, as individuals and institutions rushed in to grab their share of the purported benefits. It was no different in the 1990s. That's why many of the nation's brokerage firms, insurance companies and big banks, as well as the federal government itself, all participated in the great boom of the 1990s. Likewise, when the boom unraveled, all these participants were vulnerable to the decline.

The tech companies were no longer in the vanguard of the decline, but they suffered further losses as blue-chip companies—their primary customers—slashed spending on equipment.

Just months earlier, the whole notion of a sinking Dow had been ridiculed. Neither the investment guru nor the average investor could conceive of the Dow going down much further, except at independent research organizations, such as CECAR.

"The handwriting is on the wall," Dulles said to Johnston after several intense meetings about the contents and distribution strategy for Tamara's report. "It's not in some cryptic code, representing new and unforeseeable circumstances. It's right there in clear, bold letters, representing tried-and-tested, well-known, widely accepted measures of value."

"What do you mean?" asked Johnston.

"The average stock in the S&P 500 index has historically sold for 16.5 times earnings, right?"

"Right."

"But last I checked, the average S&P 500 stock was selling for 45 times what the company had made in the last 12 months and was still grossly overvalued. Now, to restore fair value, one of two things has to happen: Either these companies are going to have to start making more money in a big hurry or the S&P has got to fall."

"Agreed."

"My point is that the Wall Street gurus are still assuming the S&P cannot possibly fall any further. So, they're saying that it *has to be* the other way—that these companies will make more money in a big hurry. In fact, most of the analysts are so sure of this outcome, they've even changed the way that they estimate the company's value. Instead of using a company's proven earnings of the past 12 months, they look at future, projected earnings. They overlook the fact that such projections have consistently been wrong. 'The market is not so overvalued,' they say. 'It's selling at only 16.4 times *projected* earnings.' The decline is in the cards, but they're cheating at solitaire."

Dulles added that all this was before the impact to earnings from pension fund losses. In early 2002, he had estimated that if corporate pension funds among S&P 500 companies fell by another 5 percent in value, the shortfall in pension funding would be at least $109 billion. If they lost another 10 percent, the shortfall could be $144 billion. And if the pension funds really took a major beating of, say, 20 percent or more, the shortfall could exceed $200 billion.

Dulles warned that as the stock market fell, thousands of U.S. corporations would come under even greater financial stress for three reasons:

- Their assets and earnings, which had often been greatly over-stated by accounting manipulations, were still being adjusted downward to reflect stricter GAAP rules.
- Their actual assets and earnings, even after adjustments for previous overstatements, reflected an artificial stimulus from unbridled consumer borrowing that was no longer possible.
- The stock market decline would reduce the value of their shares in subsidiaries, joint ventures, and employee pension funds.

BANKS IN BETTER SHAPE?

Based on his review of various industry reports, however, Dulles believed that most financial corporations—especially regional banks and life insurance companies—were in relatively better shape. They had been through similar troubles a decade earlier and had learned some hard lessons from the experience.

He remembered specifically how America's depository institutions—banks and S&Ls—had suffered a devastating wave of failures in the 1980s, while some very large insurers went under in the early 1990s. Therefore, during the 1990s many built a respectable reservoir of capital, with relatively strong balance sheets. Unfortunately, after further probing, Dulles also discovered several weaknesses behind these numbers:

First, no matter how strong a bank's or insurance company's balance sheet, it was still vulnerable to losses in its profit-and-loss statement.

Second, Dulles discovered that the averages were deceiving. There were many banks and insurers that did *not* have enough capital!

Third, he recalled Tamara's report. Even some of the stronger banks might not have enough capital to withstand the pounding they would endure in a massive decline—whether short-but-ugly or long-and-choppy.

Fourth, it was obvious to Dulles that large "money center" banks, such as Morgan Chase and Citigroup, were as close as you could get to the ground zero of the crash. They were among the first hit by the tech wreck, the accounting shenanigans, the foreign-country defaults, the derivative blowups, and major corporate bankruptcies.

With these thoughts still swirling in his mind, Oliver Dulles decided to go out for some exercise. He walked down 14th Street to Pennsylvania Avenue, made a right turn, and headed in the direction of the Rotunda. It was cold but sunny.

THE NEXT DOMINO

Wall Street, 240 miles away, was also cold, but there was no sun. Rumors of another major corporate bankruptcy were sweeping through the news wires.

Selling pressure in the stock market, which had dissipated during a sharp bear market rally, cascaded into an avalanche as investors stampeded the exits. The Dow plunged 350 points by mid-morning, rallied to a negative 150, and then collapsed again, closing on its rear end, down 427.

"This is exactly like Black Monday of 1987," exclaimed an investor in Munich, Germany, watching the action from his computer screen late that evening. But it wasn't, for two reasons. First, there was not yet a "final capitulation"—the climax that market observers hoped would end the decline. Indeed, in percentage terms, even a 427-point decline was still much less than that of Black Monday. Second, unlike Black Monday, when bond markets surged, bond markets—especially corporate bonds—were plunging.

The rumors were true. One of America's great success stories of the 1990s was on the verge of default, and two of its financial backers were about to suffer a debilitating losses as a result. Its name: United Communications and Business Systems, symbol UCBS on the Nasdaq.

It didn't take a genius to figure out why. In addition to the big accounting adjustments announced a year earlier by its former CEO, UCBS had too many debts coming due. When the sales of its various subsidiaries declined, it ran out of cash to make the payments. It was that simple.

The new CEO, following in the footsteps of his predecessor,

had succeeded in instituting long-overdue accounting reforms, but he could do nothing to brake the decline in business, especially as the company's largest customers cut back sharply on their equipment orders.

The party was over, but the managers at UCBS didn't want to go home. They had underestimated how much they *needed* a strong stock market to keep them going. Some even forgot that the original rationale for many of their acquisitions had been to essentially play the stock market by buying companies low and selling them high. This was the only way they could ever expect to repay the debt and build net worth to avoid bankruptcy. In a weak market and a poor economy, that door had been shut months earlier.

UCBS's chief financial officer had planned a big bond and stock offering to raise emergency capital, but at the last minute he decided to shelve it. "Market conditions temporarily unfavorable," said UCBS's spokesperson.

The value of UCBS shares, already down 75 percent from their peak, plunged further. Their bonds, downgraded to single-B, followed suit.

Their biggest investment banking firms were also suffering acute financial stress. Their names: MetroBank and Harris & Jones. These two institutions, plus several more that had provided bridge financing to UCBS, began to press for payment. Suppliers who had granted the company trade credit were also getting nervous. Nearly everyone was demanding their money.

One day when two MetroBank employees compared notes over lunch, they made an interesting discovery. "We finally scratched up some spare change—$30 million—for UCBS," said a senior loan officer to a friend in the trading division. "It's just a drop in the bucket. But at least it'll tide them over for a couple of days until something else can be negotiated."

"I don't believe this. You just made a loan to UCBS?" retorted the trader.

"Sure! Why not? Do you have something personal against the company?"

"No, that's not it. Only this morning, I did some liquidating of our trading portfolio and dumped $20 million in long-term bonds and $30 million in 90-day paper issued by UCBS."

One of the worst-case scenarios was coming true.

THE HIDDEN DANGER OF FINANCE SUBSIDIARIES

Several decades earlier, in the 1970 money squeeze, it was Chrysler that had gone through this kind of a crisis—a surprise to most analysts, because they had forgotten to consider the debts of its captive finance subsidiary—Chrysler Financial. Chrysler made the cars; Chrysler Financial made the loans to buy the cars.

This time, analysts made the same mistake. They paid little attention to the decline of large manufacturers and even less attention to the plight of their captive finance companies.

Returning to UCBS, the finance subsidiary had borrowed heavily from investors on a very short term basis, with millions coming due each day. To stay afloat, they absolutely had to borrow—on a hand-to-mouth, day-by-day basis—$18 million a day, or nearly a million dollars an hour! Meanwhile, the parent corporation struggled under the one-two punch of plunging revenues and spreading rumors of default, shutting it out of short-term money markets, where it normally would raise emergency funds.

The bankruptcy trip wire tightened, needing only the slightest trigger. Commercial-paper owners—mostly cash-starved corporations themselves—decided not to renew. The standby credit at the banks, which was supposed to back up this commercial paper, could not be implemented.

Attempts to cut salaries across the board were blocked by the unions. Layoffs were ordered, but because of the severance pay provisions in the new labor contracts, there were no immediate savings.

UCBS's chief financial officer raced across the Atlantic on the Concorde to raise money in Europe, but the rumors, zapped instantly by e-mail, arrived first and he returned empty-handed.

An emergency meeting called between a group of bankers and some members of Congress, which was expected to result in a Chrysler-type rescue proposal, resulted instead in a collective shoulder-shrugging session.

UCBS had no choice. The lawyers were called in. The books were spread out on the boardroom table. There was a brief discussion followed by an even briefer sob session, after which the lawyers simply snapped their briefcases shut and took a last limousine ride to the bankruptcy courts.

The market for commercial paper died. "If UCBS could default," reasoned the commercial-paper buyers, "what about GMAC? Sears Acceptance? Ford Motor Credit? Citigroup?" Nearly all issuers, whether solvent or insolvent, came under suspicion.

The Nasdaq and the Dow, which had managed to stage a sharp rally, were knocked for another loop. All stocks were hit with big selling pressure—the tech stocks, the blue chips—whether "old economy" or "new economy." There were very few exceptions.

THE FLOOD OF INVESTOR LAWSUITS

This is also when the stocks of investment banking firms took some of the biggest hits. At Harris & Jones, for example, new underwriting business had virtually dried up. The company took huge losses in its own stock and bond portfolios. And, perhaps worst of all, it was drowned in wave after wave of investor lawsuits.

"How is this possible?" exclaimed Harris's CEO to Don Walker while in the men's room one afternoon. "How come we're getting smacked with all these lawsuits? I thought you told me years ago that the arbitration system would protect us from this kind of a flood!"

Don Walker wasn't sure. "I don't know. I'll have to check."

"You don't know? What do you mean, 'you don't know?' You're the director of research; it's your damn business to know."

"I'll have to check into it," Walker repeated meekly, "but it could be a combination of things—the big losses that investors are taking, the bad publicity, and now . . . this UCBS thing. I think that was the watershed: UCBS. We've got a helluva lot of pissed-off customers stuck in UCBS, most of them in at peak prices."

"Their own goddamn fault! It was obvious the company was crumbling. Didn't they know better? Why didn't they sell?"

"Well, uh, because we told them *not* to sell."

"You're kidding!" said the Harris CEO, a bit less arrogantly now. The two men walked back into the corridor.

"No, I'm dead serious. We had a 'buy' out there on the stock. We never downgraded. The company went under with a buy right up to the day it filed for Chapter 11. In fact, last I checked, Bloomberg *still* had our old buy out there."

"So it's Bloomberg's fault. The customers should sue Bloomberg!"

"No, sir. It was our responsibility to notify Bloomberg of any rating change, and the fact is, we never did change it, except maybe in private conversations with a few VIP customers."

The CEO gave Walker instructions to follow up and get to the bottom of the flood of investor lawsuits ASAP. The research director put his staff on it immediately, but he already had a pretty good idea of what was going on.

In the 2000s, once investors realized they had been duped by a corrupt system, they began to file arbitration claims in droves, driving smaller brokerage firms out of business and larger firms deep into the red.

To document this, Walker had his staff check the Web site of the NASD and pick up the latest data on the number of arbitration claims. He wanted to show his boss that investors weren't singling out Harris—it was industrywide. Sure enough, the number of claims filed against brokerage firms surged 113 percent from 1990 to 2002. No surprise there.

PENSION FUNDS FILE LAWSUIT

Then he came across a far more serious threat. Apparently, large state pension funds, especially in California, had also suffered big losses in UCBS. Plus, they had suffered big losses in WorldCom, Enron, and Global Crossing. Unlike the average investor, however, these pension funds had invested in the *bonds,* which Harris had also been involved in.

The lawyer for some of these funds was a leading corporate ambulance chaser, and he wanted blood. If anyone asked him why, say it was because his clients, the pension fund managers, wanted blood. And if anyone asked *them* why, they'd say it was because they had hundreds of thousands of public employees in California who wanted blood. The employees had lost a big chunk of their retirement because of the likes of Enron, Global Crossing, WorldCom, and now UCBS. These poor people merited fair restitution. They were angry, and they wanted their money back.

At first, the lawyer thought he'd sue the bankrupt companies, but that was hopeless. The court-appointed receivers who were running the companies in bankruptcy told him to take a hike—there was nothing left to sue for.

Next, he considered targeting the auditing firms, especially Arthur Andersen. But that was equally futile. Andersen had been found guilty of obstruction of justice, and was fading into oblivion.

Finally, he found easier targets—Harris and major banks. "Ahah!" he exclaimed. "Finally, someone with deep pockets!" He alleged that the banks were guilty of misrepresenting the bonds that they helped structure and distribute. He said the banks would have to pay through the nose to make good.

Harris, MetroBank, and many others got stung hard. The litigation costs alone tore a hole in their earnings, and major damage awards could drive them under.

With rumors flying of even larger lawsuits in the wings, banking and brokerage stocks fell sharply as investors dumped their holdings. Plus, investors continued to sell their shares of tech companies, manufacturers, and any firms suspected of accounting or financial difficulties. These, in turn, dumped their own holdings in other brokerage firms, banks, tech companies, and manufacturers.

At Harris & Jones, Don Walker was dumbfounded. In the back of his mind, he had always been aware of the dangers, but even in his wildest dreams, he never expected it to get this bad. He was equally shocked by the changes occurring in the economy.

INVENTORY BUST

Just a few months earlier, for example, he had anticipated a "soft landing"—a slowdown in growth of the economy rather than an actual or steep decline. The main reason for his relatively optimistic outlook was that interest rates were low. Yet even now, with low interest rates, money was tight.

Walker also assumed that an inventory problem would not arise. Because of just-in-time inventory systems—taking delivery of items only as needed on assembly lines—he figured inventories would always be trimmed to the bone. But it soon became obvious that he had made three big mistakes about inventories.

First, he had underestimated the extent to which sales had been artificially boosted by credit cards—and the speed at which they would sink when credit became scarce. The auto industry was a frightening example. For months, Detroit executives had marched to the tune "relax, relax, everything is under control." But when the shortage of credit hit the auto business, they were among the first to start asking for bail-outs.

Second, he had underestimated the fragility of the financing behind the inventories of many businesses. As soon as it became more difficult to finance these assets, many companies sought to sell them off on the open market, driving their prices lower.

Third, he had ignored what he was now calling "regurgitated inventories." He had assumed that once a consumer item was taken into the sanctuary of the household, it was consumed and, in essence, gone forever. He had forgotten that

- Consumers in a financial pinch could readily become sellers of autos, appliances, and furniture.
- These new sellers could find a ready marketplace for their wares.
- This market was one of the most elaborate networks of secondhand dealerships, flea markets, garage sales, and Web-based auctions in the world.

Fourth, he underestimated the impact of inventories dumped from overseas.

It was also at this stage that Walker began to notice one of the most unusual economic events of all. There was an upsurge in inventories. Simultaneously, there was a decline in revenues sharply below the level needed for meeting debts coming due. The result was a sudden *cash* shortage—what he called *illiquid demand* for *money*. What made this demand for money so unique was that it took place while the economy was contracting—not while it was expanding.

When this demand could not be met, the only alternative was bankruptcy or, as many prayed, a government bailout.

The casualty list grew daily: Not just techs and telecoms but giant manufacturers, retailers, brokerage firms, banks, life and health insurers, property and casualty insurers, and even HMOs.

CHAPTER

MOVE YOUR ACCOUNT!

Wh
en James Dubois hung up from his final conversation with Linda Dedini, he was practically in tears.

Getting tongue-lashings from irate clients was certainly not a novel experience for him—in fact, it was happening so often recently that he learned to just tune out. But this customer was different. She never raised her voice. She didn't even sound like she was scolding him. All she did was cite the facts with calm precision and cold logic. She called it the "litany of abuse," and she seemed to know about all the tricks—the sales scripts, the big bonus checks, even the Club Med vacations.

He slumped back in his chair, trying desperately to rebuild his self-esteem. It wasn't he, James Dubois, the person, who did all those things; it was some other entity. The real James Dubois, he told himself, is the guy who coaches a soccer team in Rockville Center, Long Island, who drives kids to Jones Beach every summer. The bad guy is not James Dubois, he concluded; the bad guy is the *system*.

How did he define the system? It was the world where he was first born as a broker many years ago, at a smaller Wall Street firm. He and about a dozen other salespeople in his section were required to show up for work promptly at 8 A.M. Then, just as soon as they walked through the door, they'd have to do something that one would never expect in any modern office: They had to take their shoes off!

The sales supervisor would hide all the shoes away and not return them to the brokers until they could meet their minimum sales quotas for the day. They hawked not only penny stocks but the firm's mutual funds that charged the investor huge upfront loads (commissions). They sold anything that could generate steep fees or markups.

On a typical day, a couple of top performers in the group could hit their quotas by 1 P.M., go down to one of Wall Street's most popular pubs, and have a two-beer lunch. Everyone else had to stay virtually chained to their desks all day, order lunch in, and work until midnight, making calls to the West Coast and Hawaii.

Until this day, Dubois could not shake the association between the two most memorable aspects of that experience—the stench of sweaty socks and the sheer humiliation. Nevertheless, it taught him an unforgettable lesson: *sell or die.*

When he moved to Harris & Jones, he found that their managers did not use those sales tactics, but Harris's mission and strategy were the same: sell, sell, sell. And how do you do that? By getting the customer to buy, buy, buy.

No matter what, he rationalized, Linda Dedini was wrong, wrong, wrong. She seemed to be blaming him personally. But if she had only given him half a chance, he could have told her exactly how the system worked. He would have explained that if *anyone* was to blame, then *everyone* was to blame—including, he believed, the customer. "You were making your own decisions," he muttered as if she were still on the line. "If you lost money, it was your own damn fault."

With that clarified, he felt much better. Within a few days, he was back up to his peak sales performance levels. But it was all for naught. Harris & Jones suffered an 81 percent decline in its IPO business and axed 10,000 employees, of which Dubois was among the first to go. Other Wall Street firms were doing the same thing.

Dubois was on the street. And in the bear market environment, he realized he'd need a very innovative job-search strategy. Competing directly with thousands of other laid-off salespeople would simply not cut it. Instead, he would try research or analysis. There were layoffs in that area as well, but he had once been on a career track to be an analyst, and he decided that now was the time to go back.

Who did he know who might have knowledge about that sector of the job market? Only one person came to mind: Tamara Belmont, who had also been fired recently, or so he heard. He did not know her very well, but he did have an intimate relationship with someone who did—her former college roommate, whom he had met at an office Christmas party.

"Sorry, honey, we've got another one of those urgent Saturday projects at the office," Dubois said to his wife that Friday.

It was from the roommate that Dubois learned about Belmont's "We Lied" speech at Columbia and got her cell phone number. He figured Belmont could land a great job, but he was also smart enough to realize that his own job skills were far less marketable. So his strategy, although roundabout, was not totally illogical: If he could secretly help Tamara get a job, he could later go back to her and, as a "reciprocal favor," get her to recruit him as an assistant.

That's why even as Dubois was turned down by CECAR for a job, he gave the interviewer, Oliver Dulles, a copy of the "We Lied" speech and her contact information, and it worked beautifully. He himself was surprised at how well it went. What didn't seem to work was the second part of his plan. Despite many attempts, he was unable to persuade Tamara to reciprocate. He called. He e-mailed. He became obsessed. He even went so far as to find out, again through the former roommate, what she was working on, rush to the New York Public Library main branch at midtown, and send her relevant information anonymously, calling her later to tell her about it.

Dubois was about to finally give it up when he got an unexpected call from Dulles. "I don't have a full-time job for you on-site. But I have a freelance project you can do from home. Someone we know seems to think you might be able to help us in the field of investor abuse by brokers. Is that correct?"

"Not really. No, wait! Yes, I do! I do know that stuff. What's the project?"

"Our chairman wants us to check into three issues—one, legal actions against brokers and brokerage firms; two, their advice track record; and three, their financial safety. And I'd like to give you a crack at it. Based on your findings and past experience, we want you to tell us how investors can check up on brokers on their own. You won't be responsible for the final write-up, just for the data and your personal insights. Use any sources you want, but whatever you do, don't leave out nasdr.com."

"You mean, the NASD?"

"Right; their site is www.nasdr.com. Start there. After we approve your research outline, you'll have 30 days. You get $1,000 upon delivery of a satisfactory outline and $2,000 upon completion of a first draft, with no guarantees of future projects. The offer is nonnegotiable; take it or leave it."

He took it.

INVESTOR ABUSE BY BROKERS

Dubois had no idea what he'd find on the NASD Web site. He typed in the address and pressed the Enter key.

As soon as the homepage came up, the top of the middle column caught his attention: "Check Broker/Adviser Info." He clicked on it, then selected "NASD Public Disclosure Program."

A few mouse-clicks later, he froze. Right there staring him square in the eye was a hideous thing, challenging him and haunting him. To the average person, it was just another form to fill out—last name, first name, middle name, etc. To Dubois, however, it was the most threatening Web page he had ever encountered. He got up from his chair and paced around the room, breathing deeply as if he were pumping himself up for a sprint on the soccer field. Finally, he sat back down, pressed Caps Lock on his keyboard, and began entering data into the fields with great trepidation:

Broker's Last Name: DUBOIS
Broker's First Name: JAMES
Current or Previous Employing Brokerage Firm: HARRIS & JONES

At the bottom left side of the screen was the "Begin Search for a Broker" tab, and it was *mocking* him! He tried to stare it down, but it didn't even blink; it just stared back defiantly. There was only one way to make it go away. He clicked on it.

For a minute or so, nothing happened, and he gave it up. What a relief! No reports in the database on a James Dubois. A few minutes later, however, he received an e-mail from Nasdr.com. He opened it and there, right before him, was a list of some of the regulatory and investor actions that had been taken against him. It contained a lot—but not all—of his dirty laundry—the times he had churned customer accounts, the many occasions he had put customers into inappropriate investments, and much more.

"Oh, crap!" he said out loud. Any investor could retrieve this information on him or any other named broker with a record. This material had apparently been posted on www.nasdr.com a long time ago, yet *he never knew the site even existed.*

Dubois's hands were shaking. To calm down, he began reciting his mantra anew: "It's the system. It's the system. It's the system."

It was the system that had driven him to sell so hard, and it was the sales tactics that forced him to sometimes cross the line, he reasoned. It was the sales managers from the system who pumped them up every day to make "big omelettes." Then, once in a while, the in-house compliance cops would come in and tell them not to "break any eggs." But how in the hell do you make an omelette without breaking an egg?

How bad, really, was the damage to his reputation? Dubois pondered this question. He soon breathed easy with the thought that even *he* didn't know this information existed. So how many laypeople would know? Practically none!

His second thought was to find out how unusual it was to have a record. He smiled to himself as he found the answers: There were *thousands* of brokers who had just as many—or more—infractions. In fact, according to an old 1990s GAO study he found, there were *at least* 10,000. And that didn't include the hundreds of thousands that never got caught or were disciplined informally. He was definitely not alone, and this made him very pleased.

Next, he decided to check into Harris & Jones as a whole. Sure enough, the NASD Web site also provided a similar facility with which to check up on entire brokerage firms. But this time, instead of an e-mail he got a thick package via first-class mail, containing hundreds of pages and listing case after case against Harris from as far back as the 1950s. Even as an industry insider, he could not figure it out. It didn't provide any concept of what would be a "normal" level of legal actions versus what might be abnormal. There was no way of knowing which infractions were bad and which ones were not so bad. It was even hard to tell whether the outcome for each case was a win, lose, or draw for the broker.

Dubois laughed. It was ludicrous. It was also obvious that neither he nor the firm would have anything whatsoever to worry about. Few investors would visit the NASD Web site, and even fewer would have any inkling about how to use the data. All of this was abundantly clear to him.

What was not so clear, however, was how he could now report these findings back to Dulles. He struggled with this dilemma for quite some time, then sent the following e-mail:

> Dear Mr. Dulles,
>
> The information available on nasdr.com is of little practical value to investors. If investors find a record on an individual broker or on a brokerage firm, there will be no way for them to figure out what it really means or what to do with it. If you have another project for me, I'd love to help you with it, but this one is a lost cause. I recommend you drop the idea of putting anything out on your Web site. It will just be a waste of your time and a waste of the investor's time, too.
>
> Yours truly,
>
> James Dubois

The next morning, when Dulles read the e-mail, he was flabbergasted. Officials at the NASD had assured him that their Web site provides "full disclosure" and a "major service of value to investors."

Two days later, armed with a new feasibility study of the project provided by an in-house analyst, Dulles walked into Johnston's office to give him an update on the project.

"We have a serious dilemma," he announced. "I know you want to help investors check out their brokers before doing business with them. You're right about that need, and we all agree with you. But at this time, it is *almost impossible* for individuals to get any practical value out of the data that is currently being disclosed."

Johnston was heartbroken. "You realize this is a unique and dangerous time in the history of the stock market, don't you?" he asked rhetorically.

"Of course," Dulles responded.

"You realize that the broker is the key link between the stock market and the public, right?"

"Sure."

"Then you must also realize that if that link is shaky, it could be extremely difficult to ever restore investor confidence, ever rally the market, ever see a real recovery in our country?"

"Yes, but—"

"No buts. Give me some alternatives."

Dulles told Johnston there were only three choices. They could petition the NASD to fix the problem themselves and pray they'd do something before the crash was all over and it was too late to help most investors. They could make their own CECAR staff drop everything else they were working on and do nothing but this work around the clock for the next five years. Or they could give extremely detailed instructions to investors and hope they'd be able to muddle through it themselves. Dulles felt that he had done a good job of positioning the whole project as hopeless.

Johnston sat silently in deep thought for a moment, then responded, "Great! Let's do all three!"

"But, Paul, it's not feasi—"

"Do it!

"OK," he said cynically. "What about the other two issues—the financial safety and the investor advice?"

"Do that too! You underestimate yourself. You underestimate our staff. But you know what you're underestimating most of all? The *dire and urgent nature of this project for millions of investors!* I know you'll find a way. Just *do* it!"

Dulles had no choice but to comply. In the months that followed, he hired a dedicated staff and created a separate Broker Monitoring Division. He had data specialists download the NASD's textual data by sending thousands of e-mails, one by one, and then pore through them manually. He hired two crackerjack Visual Basic programmers in a vain quest to find some automated way to extract quantitative data from the NASD's text files. He hired an outside lobbying firm to hound the NASD to fix its system. He hired a specialist who promised he could translate very complex tasks into step-by-step instructions for average investors. Then he proceeded to do the same all over again to address the other two issues—broker advice and broker safety.

Halfway through the project, the results of the analysis completed to date were posted at cecar.org and are described in the following text.

PROTECT YOURSELF FROM ABUSES BY BROKERS!

Some brokers and brokerage firms may be on your side. However, if the firm you're dealing with (1) has been the frequent target of arbitration claims for investor abuses of various kinds, (2) harbors financial weaknesses that could affect your account, or (3) has a bad-advice track record, then you should seriously consider moving your account elsewhere.

Step 1. Check to see whether your firm is among 18 largest retail firms reviewed in Table 16.1. If the frequency of legal actions against your brokerage firm is far above the average (29.28 per million accounts), it is a negative sign.

Step 2. If your firm is not among the 18 listed in the table, you can get information on the actions taken against a brokerage firm by following the instructions in the "How to Check and Evaluate the Legal Record of a Brokerage Firm" box.

Step 3. If you are interested in the legal record of an individual broker, that information is also publicly available. (See instructions in the aforementioned box.)

Step 4. If your brokerage firm (or broker) does not have a satisfactory legal record, consider moving your account to one that does.

Step 5. No matter whom you do business with, do not give a brokerage firm discretion over your account. Instead, use your broker strictly for executing buy and sell orders based on your explicit instructions. If you need advice, be sure to get it from independent third-party sources.

Table 16.1   Record of Abuses by Top Retail Brokerage Firms: 1997–2001

Brokerage Firm	Total Arbitration Cases, Regulatory, and Legal Actions	No. Per Million Accounts
Prudential Securities, Inc.	152	69.50
Ameritrade, Inc.	91	67.11
U.S. Bancorp Piper Jaffray, Inc.	47	64.46
E*Trade Securities, Inc.	118	36.92
Dulles James & Associates, Inc.	36	36.07
First Union Securities, Inc.	88	35.20
UBS Painewebber Incorporated	87	34.80
A G Edwards, Inc.	103	31.21
Salomon Smith Barney, Inc.	204	30.71
Morgan Stanley Dean Witter & Co.	151	27.96
Quick & Reilly, Inc.	34	18.89
Charles Schwab & Co., Inc.	124	16.53
Merrill Lynch Pierce Fenner & Smith	168	16.09
TD Waterhouse Investor Services, Inc.	68	15.25
American Express Financial Advisors	19	9.50
Edward D. Jones & Co. LP	38	8.09
Credit Suisse First Boston Corp.	20	4.96
Fidelity Brokerage Services LLC	43	3.74

Prudential Securities and Ameritrade ranked worst in terms of the number of legal actions taken against them by investors and regulators between 1997 and 2001, with 69.5 and 67.11 actions per million customer accounts, respectively. This was much higher than the average number of actions among the 18 firms studied, which was only 29.28 per million accounts.

Fidelity Brokerage Services, Credit Suisse First Boston, and Edward B. Jones ranked best with the fewest legal actions against them—only 3.74, 4.96 and 8.09 per million accounts, respectively.

HOW TO CHECK AND EVALUATE THE LEGAL RECORD OF A BROKERAGE FIRM

Step 1. On your Web browser, go to www.nasdr.com.

Step 2. Click on "Check Broker/Advisor Info." from the list of services in the center of the page.

Step 3. Click on "NASD Public Disclosure Program."

Step 4. Select "Perform an Online Search" from the right-hand menu.

Step 5. Scroll to bottom of the disclosure form and click on "Agree."

Step 6. From the drop-down bar entitled "*** Select Requester Type***," choose "General Public/Individual Investor."

Step 7. You will see the words "Begin a search for a." Click on "Firm."

Step 8. Enter the name of the firm and click "Begin Search for a Firm." Verify the company's exact name. Brokers often operate under abbreviated versions of their full legal name, so call the company if necessary to confirm that the broker you look up is really the one you are interested in evaluating.

Step 9. Select "Deliver Report" from the menu along the top of the screen. Fill in the information required.

Step 10. Click on "End" when you are done.

Step 11. You will receive a report, via e-mail, listing all the private and regulatory legal actions against the firm. Or if the report is very large, you will receive a hardcopy via first-class mail.

(Continued)

Step 12. Unfortunately, this does not give you a *relative* measure of broker abuses. For that information, visit www.crashprofits.net, where you will find an expanded list of brokers and their abuse records.

Step 13. The industry average among the largest firms is 29.3 per million accounts. If your firm's average is significantly higher, we believe it could indicate difficulties that you may also experience. If your firm's average is significantly lower, that could be a definite plus.

If you do not have access to the Internet, call the NASD's public disclosure hotline at (800) 289-9999. The hotline is open Monday through Friday from 8 A.M. to 8 P.M. eastern. When you call, please have as much information as possible including the name of the individual or firm, the name of the firm the individual works for, the address of the firm, and any other identifying information.

HOW TO CHECK THE LEGAL RECORD OF AN INDIVIDUAL BROKER

Step 1. On your Web browser, go to www.nasdr.com.

Step 2. Click on "Check Broker/Advisor Info." from the list of services in the center of the page.

Step 3. Click on "NASD Public Disclosure Program."

Step 4. Select "Perform an Online Search" from the right-hand menu.

Step 5. Scroll to bottom of the disclosure form and click on "Agree."

Step 6. From the drop-down bar entitled "*** Select Requester Type***," choose "General Public/Individual Investor."

Step 7. You will see the words "Begin a search for a." Click on "Broker."

Step 8. Enter the name of the broker and click "Begin Search for a Broker."

Step 9. There may be many brokers with similar names; click on the name of the broker that you are researching.

Step 10. Along the left column of the screen you will see "Broker File Contents."

Step 11. Hopefully, you will see "Disclosure Events: No." This means no actions have been filed against this broker.

Step 12. If you see "Disclosure Events: Maybe," then click on the "Deliver Report" icon at the top of your screen and fill out the appropriate information. You will receive an e-mail detailing the broker's employment history and any events that were reported to the NASD involving the broker.

Step 13. If you receive a report listing some actions against the broker, discuss the report with the broker and get his or her explanation of the actions. They may have had no merit.

Step 14. If they did have merit and there were judgments against the broker, that may be a bad sign. Seriously consider moving your account to another broker at the same firm or to another firm.

Step 15. For additional disclosures from your broker, download the questionnaires available free of charge at www.crashprofits.net or call (800) 289-9222 to request a free broker-disclosure questionnaire.

If you do not have access to the Internet, use the phone number listed in the preceding box to contact the NASD's public disclosure hotline.

PROTECT YOURSELF AGAINST BROKERAGE FIRM FAILURE!

When the stock market is falling, it can hurt a brokerage firm's revenues in several ways. It suffers declines in commission revenues. Investment banking fees dry up, especially for IPOs. To the degree that the firm holds its own securities without adequate protection from a market drop, it can suffer trading and portfolio losses itself. It could also be the target of legal actions by regulators and private investors. As long as the firm has plenty of its own capital to withstand any losses, this will not affect your brokerage account. However, if the losses begin to deplete the firm's capital, your account could be jeopardized in many ways—including market losses while your account is frozen in failure. Here's how to protect yourself.

Step 1.   Check Table 16.2 listing the 20 largest brokerage firms in the country by asset size.

Step 2.   If you find your firm on the list, and it has a rating of C–, C, or C+, it represents a yellow flag. It means that although the companies are stable based on the latest data available, many could become vulnerable if their financial performance deteriorates from current levels.

Their stability could be of particular concern if they suffer a further increase in the volume of investor legal actions, along with steeper declines in the financial markets—something that may have already taken place since the data was collected.

HOW TO CHECK THE CURRENT SAFETY OF YOUR BROKERAGE FIRM

For a free Weiss safety rating on your brokerage firm, you may check with your local public library. Ask the librarian for the Weiss Ratings' *Guide to Brokerage Firms*. (If the library does not currently carry the guide, the librarian may order a subscription by calling 1-800-289-9222.)

In the guide, look up your firm in alphabetical order. You will find not only the firm's latest safety rating (from A through F) but also critical financial information, the commission charges for sample trades, the minimum opening account size, a list of the services provided by the firm, a list of branch locations, and the number of legal actions taken against the firm.

If you wish to purchase a rating on a particular firm,

1. Go to www.weissratings.com.
2. Click on "Ratings Online" from the navigator bar on the top.
3. On the left side of the screen, click on "Purchase Ratings."
4. Click the "Brokerage Firm" tab
5. Enter the brokerage firm's name. If you've entered the exact first part of the name, click on "Starts with"; if you know part of the name but aren't sure exactly what it is, click on "Contains."
6. Click on the arrow in the "Company Type" box to choose the type of firm you are looking for—full-service, discount, online, institutional, or special. Click on "All" if you're not sure which type it is.
7. If you know where the company is headquartered, click on the arrow in the "State" box and choose the state. Otherwise, leave it at All.
8. Click on "Search"; a list of companies meeting your criteria will appear.
9. Choose the company you want from the list; then click on "Get Report."

If you don't have access to the Internet, call Weiss Ratings at (800) 289-9222.

For updated ratings, follow the instructions in the "How to Check the Current Safety of Your Brokerage Firm" box. If your firm's rating has fallen to a rating of D+ or lower, seriously consider moving your account to a safer firm.

Step 3. If your firm is not in the list, you can also get the latest rating by following the instructions as those in the preceding box.

Table 16.2 Twenty Largest Brokerage Firms Based on Asset Size

Name	Weiss Safety Rating
ABN Amro Incorporated	C+
Banc of America Securities LLC	C+
Barclays Capital Inc. and Sub.	C−
Bear Stearns & Co.	C
BNP Paribas Securities Corp.	C+
Charles Schwab & Co. Inc.	B
Credit Suisse First Boston Corp.	C−
Deutsche Bank Alex. Brown Inc.	C+
Dresdner Kleinwort Wasserstein LLC	C+
Goldman Sachs & Co. and Sub.	C
Greenwich Capital Markets Inc.	C+
J.P. Morgan Chase & Co.	C−
Lehman Brothers, Inc.	C−
Merrill Lynch Pierce Fenner & Smith	C−
Morgan Stanley & Co. Inc.	C
Nomura Securities International Inc.	B−
Salomon Smith Barney Inc.	C
SG Cowen Securities Corp.	B+
UBS Painewebber Inc.	C+
UBS Warburg LLC	C−

Weiss Safety Rating: A = Excellent; B = Good; C = Fair; D = Weak; E = Very weak.

Step 4. If you decide to move your account to a stronger brokerage firm, consider the following. They are among those that have the highest Weiss safety ratings.

- A. G. Edwards (A–)
- Edward G. Jones (B+)
- Fidelity Brokerage Services (B+)

PROTECT YOURSELF AGAINST BAD ADVICE

There were 50 Wall Street firms that issued stock ratings on companies that later failed in 2002. Among these firms, 47 recommended that investors buy or hold the shares in the troubled companies right up to the very day these companies filed for Chapter 11 bankruptcy. On the date the companies filed for Chapter 11, the following ratings were still displayed at major public outlets (Bloomberg, Yahoo!, Zacks, and First Call):

- Six buy ratings from Lehman Brothers
- Eight hold ratings from Salomon Smith Barney
- At least one buy rating from Bank of America Securities, Bear Stearns, CIBC World Markets, Dresdner Kleinwort Wasserstein, Goldman Sachs, Prudential Securities, and many other firms

This data alone should dissuade you from action on advice, reports, or ratings provided by most brokers or brokerage firms. If you must use their reports, however, do the following:

- Check whether your firm has recommended bankrupt companies at www.crashprofits.net.
- To help avoid firms with conflicts of interest, seek to rely on those that have no business relationship with the companies they cover.

Among the retail firms reviewed, Salomon Smith Barney had one of the worst advice track records. The firm failed to issue sell warnings on eight companies that went bankrupt in 2002, while its hold ratings on these companies remained at major public sources right up to the day the companies filed for Chapter 11.

In contrast, Edward D. Jones was one of the few firms that did not recommend shares in failing companies and took the initiative to warn its customers of impending troubles.

Considering all factors, Fidelity Brokers and Edward D. Jones currently enjoy the best scores overall.

CHAPTER 17

AN APPEAL
TO ACTION

As his former company was falling, Paul E. Johnston was attending his father-in-law's funeral, which was followed by a private reception at home. As is often the case, despite the somber nature of the occasion, it became an opportunity for family and relatives to chat quietly—even cheerfully—about current events or future hopes.

In the far corner of the living room, the CEO listened intently as his two sons raved about their sister's "incredibly prudent and prescient strategy" to protect their inheritance from the stock market crash.

On the other side of a large glass door, Linda Dedini's husband, Gabriel, could be seen standing by a round glass table at the pool deck, gesturing excitedly about something of obviously intense interest to him. Other family members lined up by a salad buffet, while Linda bounced a two-year-old niece on her lap.

She was putting the child down and about to amble over to the buffet when her father intercepted her. "I'm proud of you, Linda," he said fondly.

She beamed as she turned to respond. "Oh really? Why's that?"

"The boys just told me about your financial exploits, how you're hedging the family's wealth. Everyone else in the world—myself included—is losing their shirt and shorts in this market, and here you are making money for yourself and your siblings. How do you do it?"

"It's not me, Dad. It's the fee-only financial planner-slash-adviser I'm working with. He knows his stuff. He helps me to understand it deeply, almost as well as I understand mechanics or astronomy. He empowers me to make my own decisions. You've got to meet him."

They glanced out to the pool deck and smiled knowingly at each other as they watched Gabriel, still talking with animation. They had often joked how his English was eloquent and almost accent-free but his body always spoke *porteño* no matter what the language. "I'll have my advisor give you a call," she said. "He's a lot like you. If you get together for sushi or something, I guarantee you won't regret it."

MORE CRASH PROFITS

As soon as Linda gained decision-making authority over the stock portfolio in the estate, she began the process of selling to reduce their exposure to further market declines.

When her brothers questioned the strategy, she persuaded them with a simple argument: "The Nasdaq is down 80 percent from its peak, but our stocks are down only 30 to 40 percent on average. So we must ask ourselves, What is the risk that our stocks are going down to join the Nasdaq? How do you know the Nasdaq is not exerting some gravitational force on the rest of the market, pulling it down? Can we afford that risk? I don't think so. Yes, we bought the reverse index funds as a protection, as a hedge, but that was never intended to be a permanent solution. It was just a transitional measure to keep us on even keel. I think we should aim higher than just staying even, don't you? I think we should aim for growth, and those stocks are chaining us down."

They consented. They also agreed to give her the green light to make decisions on their behalf without necessarily checking back with them at every turn. They were both medical professionals, often too busy attending patients to be preoccupied with investment decisions.

Linda's adviser was not as easy to reach at his office as he used to be, but she finally caught up with him late on a Friday afternoon.

She explained her desire to liquidate the estate's stock portfolio but also expressed doubts about how and when.

"Now that we're selling off my grandfather's portfolio, should we still hold the reverse index fund or should we just get rid of that too?" she asked her adviser a few days later.

"If you want to profit from the decline, you can use the very same fund."

"Isn't that risky?"

"No riskier than investing in a regular index fund in a bull market. The key point I want to make, though, is this: Earlier when you were using the reverse index fund as a hedge, I recommended you just buy it and hold it, remember?"

"Of course. For the seesaw."

"Huh? Oh, right! Now, though, a buy-and-hold strategy could get you into trouble. To help control the risk, you will need a more flexible approach. You're going to need an exit strategy to get out of the investment when the market turns up—whether it's a bear market rally or the real turn. In fact, the more flexible approach is actually recommended for a hedge strategy. For a speculative strategy, it's a *must*."

"Why can't I just hold it as long as we're in a bear market and then sell it when the bear market is over?"

"Two reasons: First, nobody will know for sure when the bear market is over until long after the fact. Second, there are bound to be sharp or long bear market rallies that could cause you bigger losses than you would be comfortable with. Remember, with the reverse index funds you're betting on the stock market going *down*. When the market rallies, your investment goes south."

She seemed disappointed. "But you've been *so* right about the market while everyone else was *so* wrong! When you think there's going to be a big rally or when you believe we've hit bottom, can't you just give me a call and let me know?"

Rather than answering the question, the adviser leaned forward with his elbows on the desk and his hand to his chin. His eyes looked directly at Linda, but his mind was deep in thought. After a seemingly long pause, he pulled his hand away from his chin by a few inches and pointed his index finger to a bookcase immediately behind her. "See that thin book right next to the Spanish dictionary?" he asked.

"Yes."

"Why don't you pull it out for a sec?"

She twisted halfway around in her chair, nudged the dictionary to the side, and slid the book out. She examined the cover, then turned back to face the adviser. "This one? 'Innumeracy?' "

"That's it! The author, John Allen Paulos, shows how our society may be very literate when it comes to letters but 'innumerate' when it comes to understanding statistics and numbers. He teaches the average person how *not* to be deceived by deliberate distortions or lazy imprecisions in numerical proof."

"Such as?"

"It could be a CEO lying about his books. Or it could be a person making prophecies. Why do you suppose so many people were so easily deceived by the cherry-picked 'data' and sugar-coated 'conclusions' of Wall Street analysts? It was largely because of innumeracy! That's also why too many investors sometimes worship stock market gurus, believing they are somehow infallible, like demigods."

Linda frowned in self-reprimand. "Yeah. Darn, I guess I'm one of those people," she said, her thoughts flashing back to all the times she was duped by her former broker.

The adviser shook his head. "No, no. You misunderstood my point. What I was leading to is that the person seated right here before you—yours truly—is sometimes guilty of loose, undefined forecasting . . . and that *you* are doing a great job of seeking precision."

She was genuinely surprised. "You are? I am? How do you know?"

SEEK PRECISION; EXPECT ERRORS

"You proved it to me a few months ago, remember? The 'short-term bounce' thing? Remember how you made me give you a much more precise definition? You caught me, and then you pinned me down! Touché! That was *great!* That's what you've got to do with any stock market guru or adviser."

"For example?"

"For example, let's say a guru predicts that the market will fall after a rally. People see the market go up, then they see the market go down. So they say, 'Wow! That guy's a genius!' But the market *always* goes up and down, doesn't it? Even if it first goes down, *then* rallies and falls, this guru can claim that he predicted it. He gets away with it because he never tells you how much or when. The point is, you can't just follow anyone blindly—me or anyone else. Moral of the story: Seek more precision! Then expect inevitable errors!"

" 'Seek precision?' 'Expect errors?' Hmm. Sounds familiar. But how do you protect yourself against those errors?"

"You use a mechanical device—a fail safe—that gets you out of the investment if you're wrong . . . and then gets you back in again if the trend resumes in your favor, so you don't miss a big opportunity. That's why I'm giving you another set of instructions—

CRASH PROFITS FROM REVERSE INDEX FUNDS

A reverse index fund—designed to go up when a stock market index goes down—is a good investment to buy and hold if you wish to hedge a stock portfolio against losses in a prolonged bear market (See Chapter 11 for instructions.)

However, if your goal is to use a reverse index fund strictly to profit from a market decline, a buy-and-hold strategy is not recommended. Reason: In a market rally, you can lose money, and bear market rallies can be particularly sharp, often starting when the news is blackest and you least expect them.

The following is a simple procedure that helps tell you when to be invested in the reverse index fund and when staying on the sidelines. The procedure is certainly not perfect; however, it should help you capture the bulk of the potential crash profits and also protect you from losses.

Step 1. Learn about the Rydex Ursa Fund, described under "Crash Protection" in Chapter 11.

Step 2. On the Internet, go to www.bigcharts.com.

Step 3.   At the top of the screen, you'll see a box that says "Enter Symbol/keyword." In that box, type in the ticker symbol for Rydex Ursa, which is RYURX.

Step 4.   You will see a 1-year price chart for Rydex Ursa. Now click on the red button titled "Interactive Charting" at the top of the screen. A new menu of options will appear on the left-hand side of your screen.

Step 5.   Expand the menu options by clicking on each of the four buttons: time frame, compare to, indicators, and chart style. Then choose the following options:
Time = 6 months
Frequency = Daily
Index = None
Moving Average = SMA and 20
Upper Indicator = None
Lower Indicator1 = MACD
Lower Indicator2 = None
Lower Indicator3 = None

Step 6.   Scroll up to the top of the screen and click the "Draw Chart" button. You will see a set of two charts, each with two lines, as follows:

Top chart
- Rydex Ursa or "RYURX Daily" (black line).
- 20-day moving average of the Rydex Ursa or "SMA (20)" (gold line) This indicates the near-term trend.

Bottom chart
- "MACD (12,26)" (blue line). This indicates the momentum in the Rydex, which can be used to help time your entry and exit into the fund.
- "MACD EMA (9)" (brown line). This indicator is similar to the foregoing one.

(Continued)

Step 7. Once each week (preferably on a weekend), return to this site and repeat Steps 5 and 6. Each time, ask the following two questions, writing down "yes" or "no" for each.

- In the top chart, is the Rydex Ursa (black line) above the 20-day moving average (gold line)?
- In the bottom chart, is the "MACD (12,26)" (blue line) above the "MACD EMA (9)" (brown line)?

Step 8. Decide what action to take.

- If the answer to both questions is "yes" and you have funds you can afford to risk for crash profits, buy the Rydex Ursa fund. Otherwise, do not buy.
- If the answer to both questions is "no" and you have shares in the Rydex Ursa fund, sell them all.
- If the answer to one of the questions is "yes" and one is "no," do not take any action at this time. If you own shares in Rydex Ursa, hold. If you are out of Rydex Ursa, stay out.

'Crash Profits from Reverse Index Funds' to help you do just that. If you decide to pursue this, be sure to follow them carefully, OK?"

"OK."

"One last word: This method is also subject to error."

"I know," she responded. "No guarantees."

A MEETING OF THE MINDS

As it turned out, after the funeral, Johnston was the one who called the adviser, inviting him to his home. Just hours later, they met by the screened pool area, exactly where Gabriel had been standing and gesturing the night before.

They talked about the economy, the markets, investment strategies. After years of shunning investors, the former CEO welcomed the opportunity to see the world from the perspective of the individual.

Johnston was amused to learn how options—used in his world for compensating executives—were being used by investors to hedge against risk or make speculative profits. Ironic, he thought. Call options were the weapon of choice used by CEOs to gouge investors. Now, put options were being used by some of those same investors to turn the tables on the big companies and get their just revenge—*plus,* the chance for crash profits.

He marveled at the fact that he had never heard of reverse index funds, yet they were already so big.

He was especially fascinated by the adviser's passion for investor empowerment, a critical dimension sorely missing in the reform proposal he was drafting for the committee—to present to the SEC, the NASD, the NYSE, and the state of New York.

As the sun's reflection in the pool was fading, he excused himself for a moment and went to his office overlooking the deck from the east. He printed out two double-spaced copies of his draft proposal and promptly returned. The two men read through it together, not noticing that they were soon squinting in the twilight.

Johnston's wife brought out ice tea and turned on the outdoor lights, while they marked up the draft in the margins. The adviser recommended inserting a clearer call to action for investors.

Days later, Johnston invited the adviser to join him on the committee as cochairman. But the adviser declined, saying he'd prefer to remain anonymous, helping Johnston and the committee from the sidelines. He'd contribute directly to Johnston's speeches and reports, as needed. But he saw no benefit to the committee of putting his name on it.

The committee, meanwhile, was running into stiff resistance from all sides. Wall Street's sole concern seemed to keep the markets from falling, and its only interest in reform was to get the regulators off their backs.

At the same time, the committee's reform proposals, when delivered to the regulatory agencies, fell mostly on deaf ears as well. The response was either "we're doing that already" (when they really were not) or "we have that on the drawing board" (which no one could verify).

In response, Johnston decided to bypass the regulators and make a direct appeal to investors. The adviser took his earlier draft and completely rewrote the speech, adding in specific instructions for individuals.

Within just a few days, they had nailed down the logistics for a seminar to be held in midtown Manhattan, to be attended by hundreds of investors and covered nationally by C-Span. For the sake of courtesy, invitations were sent to the heads of the SEC, the NASD, the NYSE, and several state attorney generals, but Johnston did not seriously expect anyone higher than middle rank to attend.

On the appointed day, however, Johnston was pleasantly surprised to see the familiar faces of some top officials sitting at a table for panelists next to the podium. He was also happy to see cameras from CNN Financial News and CNBC jockeying for position behind C-Span's.

Oliver Dulles introduced Johnston as the keynote speaker while Johnston looked out into the audience. The auditorium was packed. Dozens of people of all ages—especially the 50-plus generation—stood in the aisles or sat on the floor. Nearly a hundred more were in the halls, pressing to get in. He spoke softly at first but then with increasing energy . . .

Not long ago, four subtle but deeply disturbing changes took place in corporate America and on Wall Street.

First, at thousands of U.S. companies, huge expenses were buried . . . mock assets were concocted . . . and earnings were exaggerated.

Second, we piled debts up to our eyeballs—often without a prayer of paying.

Third, Wall Street awarded the highly-touted buy ratings to many of the most questionable companies.

Fourth, virtually every one of the brokerage firms hyping these rickety companies had collected massive investment banking and consulting fees from them . . . had loaned them millions of dollars . . . or were vying for their future business.

It was the most massive breach of trust of the modern era. Unsuspecting investors were betrayed. Trillions of dollars—the life savings and retirement plans of millions of Americans—were trashed.

I used to be a part of that world. Now I have changed. I have become one of the most annoying men on Wall Street. I have sworn that no matter how many powerful enemies I might create, I will always sound the alarm when your wealth is threatened.

But now the time has come to do more—much more.

With more startling revelations about investor swindles at Wall Street mainstays like Merrill Lynch, Morgan Stanley, Salomon Brothers . . .

With a never-ending flow of massive, newly discovered accounting lies by the likes of WorldCom, Xerox, Tyco, and even some federal agencies . . .

With the very real threat of a new wave of surprise bankruptcies like those at Kmart, Adelphia, and United . . .

The trust you once had in our financial markets is rapidly vanishing.

This is not just a crash. It's a threat to our entire future—as investors, as citizens.

Maybe, if the crooked companies and brokers who have been exposed thus far were the only ones, the shock and bewilderment in the market would eventually subside.

Or perhaps, if the companies recently filing for Chapter 11 were among the last of the "bad apples," we could see a light at the end of the tunnel. But no, *the drumbeat of shocking revelations has barely begun!*

Consider these facts:

So far, authorities have released damning evidence only against a few major brokers. But they are conducting new investigations of widespread ratings fraud at *dozens* of major Wall Street brokerages.

So far, we've only heard about accounting irregularities at a few dozen corporations. But the fact that most of the worst manipulations were deemed "legal" leads to the undeniable conclusion that *thousands* may have engaged in similar practices.

So far, we've seen bankruptcies at a few hundred publicly traded companies. But thousands more could be at risk of failure.

It will probably take many months for all the accounting crimes to be exposed and for the companies battling bankruptcy to finally throw in the towel. In the meantime, day by day, every new revelation and failure will deepen the crisis of confidence.

As investors, you are fed up, and for good reason. There's a limit to how much you can take—an invisible psychological barrier that, once breached, cannot be reversed. Unless something is done now, this generation's trust in Wall Street will have been destroyed forever.

What is going to avert this dismal future?

I wish I could tell you that *politicians* are going to make a difference, but too many are afraid of losing their campaign contributions from Wall Street or too worried about being blamed for the market decline.

I wish I could affirm that the major *Wall Street firms* will voluntarily mend themselves. Instead, even as they promised recently to never do it again, they were deploying scores of high-powered lobbyists to squash any legislation that might hold them to those promises.

I wish I could tell you that the nation's *regulators* will be successful in exposing the wrongdoers or instituting new regulations that guarantee your fair treatment. The sorry truth is that many regulators knew about the conflicts of interest for many years and did next to nothing.

I wish I could tell you that even one single, solitary *brokerage firm* would have the courage to step up to the plate and say, "You're right. We lied, cheated, and stole billions of dollars from unsuspecting investors. Now we will pay for our crimes voluntarily."

But nobody's confessing—even when they've been caught red-handed. *No one* seems to care that with each denial and obfuscation, they're convincing more investors that Wall Street is just a shell game.

Let's face it: Crooked brokers and corporate executives don't fear Congress—they think it was bought and paid for long ago. Nor do they seem to fear the SEC. Most see it as a toothless tiger. They don't fear the NASD, an association they assume is largely by the big brokers, of the big brokers, and for the big brokers.

But there is one person they do fear: Someone who, with the touch of a few buttons on a telephone or the click of a mouse, can make a serious dent in their business. Someone who can make their most feared competitors—the handful of honest firms who rarely or never yield to the temptation to cheat you—tower over them.

That someone, ladies and gentlemen, is you.

The minute you—and the thousands of other investors who care about this nation's financial future—make yourselves heard, their arrogance will melt.

Right now, the most crooked brokers and CEOs aren't too worried about you. They think you're sheep: Too timid, too complacent, too dumb to use the power you have over them. I want you to prove them wrong. I want you to take six steps with me right now.

Your first action: Sell the most vulnerable stocks *now!*

That will do more than you can ever imagine to put the fear of God into their CEOs. However, for best results, sell them intelligently as outlined in our handout.

Your second action: Get your money to safety!

Your third action: Move your account! If you have even one lonely, solitary dollar invested with any of the brokerage firms like those listed in our "Brokerage Hall of Shame," I believe you should seriously consider closing your account. You'll be doing yourself not one but *two* huge favors:

One, by getting your money out of brokerages that have the worst records, you will be avoiding the danger of investor abuses, bad advice, or even financial difficulties at the firm.

Two, you'll be sending these brokerages a clear message: "Clean up your act or else!"

Then, move your accounts to a firm like those listed in the "Brokerage Hall of Fame." By so doing, you'll be rewarding firms that have the best record of service and provide the best safety as well.

Your fourth action: Protect your assets! Make sure you have investments firmly in place that will help protect you from the decline.

Your fifth action: Position yourself now to actually profit from a further decline.

This step is not for everyone. However, if you have some money you can afford to lose and the discipline to avoid over-doing it, you have an opportunity to make substantial profits during a market decline, with risk that's strictly limited to the amount you invest. When the market does hit rock bottom, you could have more money to invest in the best companies at the lowest prices, to help support a lasting recovery.

Your sixth action: Join us in our mission to stop the cheating on Wall Street. Support our appeal: "Protect Investors and Restore Confidence!"

In addition, our committee is calling for sweeping accounting reforms to give you a much more accurate picture of a company's financial condition.

We demand that the Federal Accounting Standards Board—the FASB—cease immediately its pandering to the industry, cease backing down every time it encounters resistance to meaningful reforms.

We demand that all the parties—the corporate executives, the auditors, the investment bankers and brokers—*immediately* cease and desist any and all functions that are compromised by conflicts of interest. Among accounting firms, it means a clean and complete split between the consulting and auditing businesses. Among Wall Street firms, it means an equally clean and complete split between investment banking and research.

We demand full and specific disclosure from all firms who have not yet divorced their salesmen from their researchers. If they have a conflict of interest, they must tell you what it is, in all pertinent and specific details.

We demand full disclosure of all hidden risks. That includes

BROKERAGE HALL OF SHAME

Prudential Securities
Ameritrade
U.S. Bancorp Piper Jaffrey

Prudential—ranked worst in terms of number of legal actions against firm, compared to 17 other large retail firms in 1997–2001; failed to downgrade two failing companies to "sell" in 2002. Ameritrade—ranked second worst in terms of number of legal actions; rated C– for safety. US Bancorp Piper Jaffrey—third worst for legal actions; had two "buy" ratings and one "hold" on failing companies. Salomon Smith Barney—rated C for safety, eight "holds" on failing companies. For more background, see www.weissratings.com/crisis_of_confidence.asp.

telling all—about their debts, and about special commitments like derivatives. It also includes telling you exactly which derivatives are for protection and which are for speculation—how and how much.

We urge Congress, the Administration, and the regulators to fully support these demands. However, once the government has done its part—to establish rules of fairness and to ensure that you get all the information you need to make informed decisions—we are asking the government to let the market do its work. You are the market. Ultimately, you can do a better job than any bureaucrat.

These steps are required *now* to restore faith in the market. Unless faith is restored, this crisis of confidence will not only continue to spiral out of control but could hurt the chance for an eventual recovery.

One of the biggest profit opportunities you will have is to buy good companies at the right time for a fraction of their peak value. But how can you do that safely if the entire market is still a cesspool of corruption and deception? Those great investment opportunities may never materialize unless we combine forces and act right now.

This message reached hundreds of thousands of investors. But millions more paid no attention whatsoever. Nor did most of the nation's leaders.

BROKERAGE HALL OF FAME

Fidelity Brokerage Services (800-343-3548)
Edward D. Jones (314-515-4959)

Fidelity—ranked best in terms of fewest legal actions; rated B+ for safety; low commissions; did not recommend failing companies. Edward D. Jones—ranked third best for legal actions; rated B+ for safety; did not recommend failing companies, downgrading one from "hold" to "sell." For more background, see www.weissratings.com/crisis_of_confidence.asp.

PROTECT INVESTORS AND RESTORE CONFIDENCE!

The U.S. Congress, the SEC, the NASD, the NYSE, and the states have all begun to take steps in an attempt to restore confidence in financial markets. Unfortunately, however, their actions are lacking in three ways:

Problem 1: After the fact. For many of today's investors in the market, it's too little, too late. Investors have already suffered more than $10 trillion in losses, much of it due to Main Street and Wall Street shenanigans. This must never be allowed to happen again.

Problem 2: Easy way out. There is a continuing danger that new laws or regulations will address primarily the easy fixes and make mostly cosmetic, feel-good changes to address the more important—but tougher—problems.

Problem 3: Industry resistance. All too often, if new proposals run counter to what the industry wants, the rules are either watered down or not enforced. Consider the track record:

- In just the four years ending in 2001, there were 4,822 regulatory actions against 612 of the largest brokerage firms—by states, the SEC, and a variety of exchanges. However, despite this activity, there was no lasting decline in customer abuses. Quite the contrary, the number of arbitration filings, a reflection of the level of customer abuses, continued to surge.

- Despite concerted actions by the regulators and repeated warnings from the former chairman of the SEC, the chairman of the Federal Reserve, and others, there was no branch or agency of government in the nation with either the will or the power to moderate the excesses of the 1990s boom—let alone prevent the ensuing bust.

It is clear that the regulators *need help badly.* They don't have—and probably never *will* have—the funding or the staff to micromanage hundreds of thousands of brokers and trillions of transactions. Instead, the best defenders of investors are investors themselves, the best regulator of the markets is the marketplace, and the most efficient dispenser of financial justice is the customer.

Investors cannot exert this function without information and, unfortunately, the information available to investors is often sorely inadequate. Too many in the industry seek to erect a shroud of secrecy to "protect investors" from what they believe investors need not know.

URGENT NEED FOR THREE TYPES OF DISCLOSURES FROM BROKERS AND BROKERAGE FIRMS

When you take out a loan from a bank, the loan officer is required to provide a disclosure statement mandated by Truth in Lending legislation. When you're doing business with a broker, however, there is no equivalent "Truth in Brokerage" disclosure.

In such a statement, the broker should give you the essential information about the following three areas:

1. **The legal history of the individual broker and the firm.** When you open a brokerage account, you're given little or no information on the following:
   - Your broker's personal background or history of legal actions.
   - Your brokerage firm's overall history of legal actions.
   - Some relative measure of legal actions, such as the quantity of actions per account.
   - A comparison of these indicators with industry averages.

(Continued)

2. **How the firm creates its stock ratings, along with the track record of its research analysts.** Currently, when you get a research report or a rating from a brokerage firm (even with the recently adopted rules),

- You receive very little information about the analysts' methods—let alone about any outside influences that could bias their work.
- You get inadequate information about any loans the brokerage firm or its affiliates have made to the companies they're recommending to you.
- You get no disclosure of other investment banking relationships they may have with those companies.
- You find it difficult to put together a complete list of (a) the stock ratings issued by a particular research analyst, (b) the ratings issued by a firm, or (c) the ratings issued on a particular company.

In short, you do not receive the information you need for making an informed decision.

3. **Financial stability of the firm.** It is often next to impossible for you to get relevant information on the financial stability of your brokerage firm because of the following:

- Privately held broker-dealers do not normally disclose their financial statements directly to you.
- Publicly traded financial corporations, including brokerage divisions, do not report the critical information you need on the brokerage operations separately.
- If you want critical financial data on private or public firms, the only source is the Washington, D.C., office of the SEC, and the most you can ask for is 10 firms per request.
- The SEC gives you virtually no assistance in interpreting the reports and hardly any educational materials regarding the financial security of the brokerage firms.
- Brokers tell you little or nothing about the risks you face in the event of a failure by the firm.

STANDARDS AND PROCEDURES URGENTLY NEEDED FOR FULL DISCLOSURE

With brokers, you should insist on the following:

1. **Full information—in context and in comparison to other brokers and brokerage firms.** That includes
   - The number of legal actions per customer account.
   - The total dollar value of awards and fines against the firm as compared to the total value of securities held for customers.
   - The number of complaints settled compared to the total number of complaints filed.

2. **Clear and easy-to-understand information, presented at the time of sale.** Many so-called disclosures are theoretically available on request but are, in reality, difficult to acquire. You are not even told that the information exists—let alone where to get it. The disclosures need to be given to you *before* you open an account, with updates made available at least yearly.

3. **Consumer education programs that disclose and explain all significant points of risk and drawbacks.** Investors recognize that stocks can go down in value. What no one told you is that stocks of well-established, household-name companies can decline significantly and swiftly, often wiping out a substantial portion of your entire investment in a very short period of time as shocking revelations are made. These events prove that brokers must do a far better job of warning you about these risks ahead of time— the risk of earnings manipulations, the risk of ratings exaggerations, the risk of fraud, and the risk of failure.

4. **Disclosure based on standard questionnaires used industrywide.** Standard questions are provided at

(Continued)

www.crashprofits.net or can be acquired at no charge by calling 800-289-9222. These can be a basis for new disclosure legislation or regulations. In the interim, you can use them yourself to demand answers. If you don't get them, consider taking your business elsewhere.

5. **Complete information, including virtually everything available to regulators and self-regulatory bodies regarding the past conduct of firms or individuals.** There's a wealth of valuable information that is either not available to you or is very difficult to acquire. Prime examples include data on arbitration complaints filed and not settled or claims settled before a decision is made, plus other data held by the NASD, the SEC, the NYSE, and the regulatory bodies of all 50 states.

    The overriding principle should be that if the regulators have the information, you should have access to that information. They should not hide it or keep it out of your reach. You paid for it with your tax money. You need it to protect yourself and the market as a whole.

6. **Strictly enforced and backed up by severe penalties.** Currently, when you open a brokerage account, you have to sign away many of your legal rights by consenting to arbitration. However, the ugly secret of the arbitration system is that *even if you prevail, less than one-fourth of the money awarded is ever paid.* This must be fixed immediately by Congress. Before the award is granted, the broker must set aside the money for the award. At the very minimum, the broker should put up a fidelity bond. If the industry lobby blocks legislation to fix the arbitration system, investors should be restored their right to sue in court.

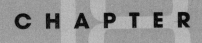

CHAPTER 18

VERTIGO

Johnston and the adviser talked endlessly about the past and the future.

They would confer over sushi at the food court or meet across the street for more elaborate dinners. They invited Dulles, who contributed insights on the "collective consciousness of America's leaders," and Tamara Belmont, who continually updated them on her scenarios, adjusting them as the actual events began to unfold.

"Why," they asked each other, "were the nation's leading decision makers so resistant to change? Why could these leaders not see the light? And even among those that did, why did they not act upon their vision?"

Their conclusion: People near the top of the world suffered from a severe case of vertigo and fear of heights. They were disoriented, afraid of falling, even afraid to look down.

These leaders, in their deepest subconscious, sensed that they had climbed too high, with onerous burdens. Too much prosperity, too fast. Too much debt, but no cash to fall back on.

However, their conscious minds rebelled against introspection just as stubbornly as they avoided peering down from steep heights.

Johnston believed it was never too late to change course. It was certainly never too late to guide the decline, minimize the long-term damage, and maximize the health of the subsequent recovery.

Even after the crisis was well underway, he felt they had many opportunities to reveal the true risks and take remedial steps.

Dulles, however, previously the optimist, was now becoming more skeptical. He was afraid that Tamara's Scenario B was the more likely. Every time the government tried to goose up the economy, he said, rather than restoring investor confidence, they revived investor complacency. Bad money was thrown after good. Distrust flushed out trust. If government continued on this path, he argued, it would lose credibility, power, and, ultimately, any semblance of meaningful control.

They debated almost endlessly. But even as they talked, the world's markets were plunging anew. More companies were going bankrupt. Unemployment surged.

WALL STREET'S APPEAL FOR HELP

Wall Street's perennial optimists turned gloomy, and its staunchest bulls turned chicken.

Nevertheless, most banking and brokerage executives still hung onto the belief that, when presented with the magnitude of the crisis, the president of the United States would approve a great, all-encompassing bailout plan. They believed that the U.S. government "had the power" and that "where there was a will, there was a way."

These Wall Street leaders felt it was their moral responsibility to send a delegation to meet with the president and convince him to wage war on falling markets—not only on behalf of America's established corporate giants, the heart and soul of our economy, but also for the sake of the entire modern world.

As long as it was just the stock market that was falling, they admitted it might be difficult to convince the president to take action. But now, in addition to stock prices, the price of bonds was also falling—not just corporate bonds but also U.S. Treasury bonds.

This was a great mystery to everyone. Yes, they could understand why some *corporate* bonds could fall—they were being downgraded, with some bond issuers on the brink of default. But they couldn't fathom why *U.S. Treasury* bond prices were falling. It was this decline in Treasury bond prices that raised some of the biggest concerns. And it was this that finally prompted two top Wall Street firms to firmly request, almost demand, a meeting with the president in the Oval Office.

The first of these firms was Harris & Jones, which had recently changed its name to HarrisJones. Unbeknownst to anyone except insiders, the firm was suffering from severe financial strains of its own because of massive lawsuits and relentless market declines.

The second of these firms was MetroBank, also under financial strains, having been caught in the middle of almost every one of the major failures and defaults of recent years.

There were no rumors, yet, of their financial difficulties, but it *was* rumored that HarrisJones and MetroBank were in the initial phases of merger talks. Indeed, each megafirm saw the other as a potential savior, a new source of capital. However, as they looked at each other's books under a magnifying glass and were able to see through each other's "complex accounting," it became evident that the only remaining powerhouse that could provide the needed capital to save them was the U.S. government.

Thus, added to their overt mission—to save the markets and the economy—there was a second, covert mission—to save themselves. Their staff contacted the White House staff to call an urgent meeting. They were among the most powerful financial institutions on the planet, and they were very concerned about the immediate future. The president would surely see them.

A SURPRISE INVITATION

The secretary of the Treasury was also concerned. Although he never spoke about it in public, he was quite aware of the financial demons that cascading stock and bond markets would inevitably awaken.

The chairman of the Federal Reserve had even deeper anxieties. He felt he had done everything in his power to avert the circumstances that were now upon them. He was worried that nearly all his power tools—lower interest rates, a rapidly increasing money supply, and more—were broken or breaking.

The two men—the secretary and the chairman—had no official reporting responsibility between them. The secretary was a part of the Administration; the chairman was not.

To help bridge that gap, these two individuals, easily the most powerful economic-policy makers in the nation, met informally each week to exchange information and ideas. They differed on many issues, but there was very little disagreement regarding one fundamental principle:

If there are no dire threats to the financial system, government bailouts are to be avoided. In the event of an emergency, however, aggressive intervention is the only option.

This implied, however, a critical dilemma: What constituted a "true financial emergency" and what did not?

The answer would hinge almost exclusively on mass investor psychology. If the public was relatively quiet, it would not be an emergency, and a few good pep talks might do the trick. If the public was in panic, however, that would leave little choice but to bring out the big guns—hundreds of billions of dollars of fresh money to be pumped into the system, or more.

Neither the secretary nor the chairman wanted that. It followed, therefore, that the key to minimizing emergencies was *confidence,* especially investor confidence. How could they restore investor confidence? How could they revitalize their own waning credibility as economic-policy makers? They didn't have an answer.

It was in this environment that, late one Friday afternoon, Oliver Dulles received a phone call from a man stating that he was an executive assistant to the secretary of the Treasury. He conveyed the secretary's personal invitation to Paul E. Johnston to join the secretary's staff in a brief weekend meeting—a meeting that, if all went well, it would lead to a meeting in the Oval Office Monday morning.

Johnston, the man noted, had earned a broad investor following. The secretary needed him, he said, to contribute his unique insights, and, at the same time, lend support to the Administration's efforts to bolster investor confidence. "All issues relating to confidence will be on the table," he said, "and future scenarios will be discussed thoroughly."

"We happen to have a new report on that," Dulles exclaimed, almost in a knee-jerk reaction. "May we bring it along?"

The assistant was hesitant, but out of courtesy he responded, "Sure, bring your report. It probably won't come up. But there's no harm if Mr. Johnston has it with him just in case."

Dulles thanked him calmly and deliberately. But as soon as he hung up, he jumped out of his chair and dashed into Johnston's office in such haste that he practically crashed into Tamara Belmont, who was walking in the opposite direction. "Meet me in my office in three minutes," he shouted. "But first I've got to talk to Paul."

Johnston was surprised but calm. He sat back and looked out his third-story window. Until now, it had never sunk in that they were just two blocks from the White House. In his mind, it had always been many miles—even light-years—away. Now, the reality of its closeness was more vivid. He told Dulles he would talk about his proposal for Wall Street reform that had been largely rejected by the securities regulators. "OK," said Dulles, "but you're missing the big one, the more urgent one, the one that's so timely it will blow their minds."

"What are you talking about?"

"The crash risks and crash benefits! The two scenarios that Belmont and her team worked up. The man I just talked to at the Treasury says they're going to talk about future scenarios. *It's a perfect fit.* Don't you see the connection? This is the opportunity we've been waiting for—a chance to start the process of overcoming the resistance, the chronic vertigo at the top."

Dulles's arguments finally prevailed, and he rushed back to his office, where Tamara had been waiting patiently.

"What's up?" she asked, trying to mask her own sense of alarm.

"Your white paper. What state is it in?"

"Almost done."

"*Almost?* Come on! What's missing?"

"Just final fact-checking, proofing, formatting. Nothing major."

"Can you have it done by Sunday morning?"

"Are you kidding? This thing is huge. I need at least a week!" she said.

He told her not to worry. He would mobilize the entire office. He'd call in outside help if needed. He'd even give her a few extra hours. In response, she divided the report into three sections and assigned tasks to each of her assistants already familiar with the project.

But it still wasn't enough manpower. So while Johnston was off to the meeting with the Treasury Department staff, Dulles called in anyone he could find. Linda's adviser found himself fact-checking the section on vicious circles. Linda herself was recruited to double-check the stats behind the charts on the Dow.

Plus, Dulles had a major task as well: To integrate the committee's two reports—the "Protect Investors and Restore Confidence" and "Crash Risks and Crash Benefits"—into one unified white paper.

At 10:30 A.M. Monday, as Johnston was getting into a limo for the two-block trip to the White House, Dulles was running down the stairs to catch up and hand off copies of the committee's white paper. Its new title: "Crash Benefits."

CHAPTER 19

THE BIG BAILOUT

*A*fter a secret closed-door meeting *of the plunge protection team—including the president, the secretary of the Treasury, the Federal Reserve chairman, and the chairman of the SEC— three former or current Wall Street executives were invited to join: The CEO of HarrisJones, the CEO of MetroBank, and Paul E. Johnston, chairman of the CECAR. The Secretary of the Treasury was presiding.*

Treasury Secretary: Gentlemen, we have come to a major crossroads. The stock market is plunging, and every single effort we have made to rally the economy is failing. We put through the tax cut, and that didn't do much good. The Federal Reserve slashed short-term interest rates to practically zero, and that, too, is failing.

Ironically, our economists have continued to tell us, all along, that most of the fundamentals point to a strong recovery. We have the lowest inflation and the lowest interest rates in decades. We have pumped more liquidity into the banking system than at any time in the last 30 years. But despite sharp rallies, the stock market continues to falter anyhow. The stock market is our Achilles' heel, and it's hurting us.

What most people don't realize, however, is that the greater threat is not the stock market. It is the bond market and, ultimately, the dollar itself. For the moment, though, let me focus your attention on the stock market's impact on the economy.

We all remember that a couple of years ago, millions of Americans would open their brokerage statements, feel suddenly flush with riches, and spend their paper profits on real estate, SUVs, high-tech gadgetry, and more. The consumer was the last pillar of strength in the economy.

Now, most are not even *opening* their brokerage statements, and we fear that despite temporary buying sprees, they may soon be pulling in their horns dramatically. We fear that the declining value of their stock portfolios could cause them to freeze up, removing that last pillar for the nation, that last ray of hope for the recovery. Already, jobs are being lost. Already, household net worth has declined $1.4 trillion in the most recent quarter. Americans are getting poorer.

Thus, we confront an urgent, unprecedented series of questions today: Do we have a true financial emergency—is it time to declare war on the turbulent stock market and the weakening economy?

If the answer is "yes," the next question is, Can we not use our traditional tools? Or must we bring out unorthodox weapons? Specifically, should we bypass our standard operating procedures and funnel public funds directly into the coffers of America's corporations through the outright purchase of their securities? *Should we buy stocks to rally the Dow?*

Fed Chairman: I am convinced that this is *not* a dire emergency. We have bankruptcies, but that is not new. We have falling stocks and bonds. That has also happened many times before. I have not talked to the board members or the members of the FOMC—the Federal Open Market Committee—in a couple of days; however, I do have a fairly good idea of what they would be saying if they were here today.

Treasury Secretary: What would that be?

Fed Chairman: There would probably be some disagreement with respect to the earlier question—is this an emergency or not? However, there would be no disagreement on the best mechanism for responding to any emergency: They would sternly urge that all funds be funneled through the Fed's standard channels—namely, through the banking system. They would sternly warn *against* any attempt to bypass the banking system, to buy common stocks. Such radical moves would be viewed as both unnecessary and dangerous.

President: Dangerous in what way?

Fed Chairman: For an illustration of the dangers, I take you to Japan and back to mid-September 2002. That's when it was announced that the Bank of Japan was going to buy shares on the Tokyo Stock Exchange to rally their market and help bolster the stock portfolios of Japanese banks on the verge of failure. The Nikkei rallied all right. But a few days later, on Friday, September 20, the market for Japanese government bonds fell apart. In fact, for the first time, they simply could not find enough bidders to cover their bond auction! *The government bond auction of the second most powerful economy in the world collapsed!*

Japanese bond investors had gone on a buyer's strike. Investors—in Japan and around the world—decided they did not want to lend money to a government that was going to use that money to buy sinking stocks.

Then, less than one week later, on September 26, 2002, all the stock market gains achieved by the government's earlier announcement were also lost.

Gentlemen, do you realize how relevant—and how ominous—that is? I repeat: The second largest economic power in the world—unable to find enough buyers for its own government bonds?!

Beware: If you ask us to do the same today—if I and the other members instruct the Federal Reserve Bank of New York to buy common stocks on behalf of the U.S. government—we shall face a very similar fate.

This is why I am fundamentally opposed to direct intervention and why I propose that we first seek to address the underlying causes of the market decline and *then* consider intervention—but only through *traditional* channels.

(The CEOs of HarrisJones and MetroBank emitted murmurs of protest and shook their heads. They felt there was no time for more research. They believed there wasn't even enough time to pump in money through regular channels. Instead, a direct and massive government intervention was precisely what they had come to ask for.)

MetroBank: With all due respect, Mr. Chairman, I question the relevance of the Japan experience that you just described to us. Japan has been through a 12-year depression; we have not. Their banks are in shambles; ours are not.

Besides, we already *know* what's causing the stock market to decline. It's falling investor confidence. What better way to shore up investor confidence than for the powerful U.S. government to put its money where its mouth is—to start buying stocks? We have the power. We have the resources. If there ever was a time—a moment— in history to wisely exercise that power, it is now.

We are confronting a $6 trillion loss in the total value of the Nasdaq-listed shares, plus another $4.5 trillion loss in the New York Stock Exchange–listed shares, for a total wealth loss of $10.5 trillion. This is what's eroding confidence in the stock market. This is what's corroding the economy!

Now consider the ultimate outcome if this continues. A much deeper recession, perhaps even a depression. An out-of-control budget deficit, plus possibly—I dare say, *probably*—meltdowns in other financial markets. Are we willing to risk all that? Are we willing to risk the resulting impact on our homeland defenses? Of course not.

In my humble opinion, we must waste no more time on a pointless search for causes. We must take action—immediate action.

Johnston: I would be interested in knowing what actions you have in mind. However, I want to make it clear from the outset that the *true* forces behind the stock market decline are not what you think they are. The stock market boom and, I would argue, the economic boom as well were largely built on a foundation of falsehoods. To bring it down, you don't need a major economic event like a recession. You don't even need an external event like a terrorist attack or war. All it takes to topple the house of cards is for one ever-present force to manifest itself: The truth—about earnings, about the budget, about the economy. The truth comes out, and down it comes. Without restoring truth, you will *never* restore confidence.

(Johnston glanced around the room to see the reaction, but it seemed that comments such as these were falling on deaf ears.)

Enron's great facade of power masked a pack of lies. As soon as the facade came down, it was gone in a flash. WorldCom's great facade of power and might masked an even greater pack of lies. As soon as it came down, its power was also gone—instantly.

Now, I ask: How much of our federal budget is masked by Enron-type accounting? How much of our economy is supported by similar props?

Secretary of the Treasury: We are all aware of WorldCom's $3 billion overstatement of earnings. We know quite well that those $3 billion represent the largest corporate fraud in the history of our country. But the regulators have taken firm steps to prevent that in the future. What's your point?

Johnston: Forgive me for making a correction of fact, but the $3 billion fraud that was initially discovered soon became $4 billion, then $7 billion, then close to $9 billion and still climbing. Each trail led to the discovery of greater and greater irregularities. My point is that this is also the pattern we are discovering on much grander scales, in government agency accounting, in the economy, and in banking and insurance. We have barely scratched the surface. There are still countless more revelations ahead.

We all know that we live in an imperfect world. We accept the fact that there will always be some bad apples that commit crimes. That's not the central issue. The central issue is all the corporate behavior that was, and is, considered "perfectly legal." And in that realm, manipulations are rampant. If it was legal, it means that almost every corporation in America had the opportunity to take advantage of it. That's one of the main reasons the stock market is going down, why over $10.5 trillion in wealth is gone.

President: What I fail to understand is, Where? Where did all that money go? Did it go into real estate? Did it go into bonds? Overseas?

Johnston: Actually, for the most part, I don't think the money went *anywhere.*

President: What? Why not?

Johnston: Because it was never there to begin with. The wealth was mostly a fantasy, a bubble. The huge pileup of riches—in Internet stocks, tech stocks, telecom stocks, and even many industrial stocks—had no substance, no real assets, profits, or, often, even sales behind it. We had stocks selling for 3- or 400 times sales. Not earnings, mind you, but *sales!* Many of these companies had no earnings whatsoever. Yet they were being touted as "the great leaders of the new economy."

Those millions of Americans the secretary talked about earlier, those people who used to look at their brokerage statements and see ever bigger numbers—what were those numbers, in essence? They were a mirage. They were strictly paper profits. Worse, those paper profits were based on papier-mâché earnings, created by layer after layer of lies.

The first layer of lies came from the CEOs who exaggerated and falsified their earnings, hid their losses, buried their debts— typically under the legal umbrella of "GAAP accounting." The second layer of lies was added by the auditors who certified the first layer with the "clean bill of health" stamp. A third layer was created by Wall Street firms that accepted those distorted earnings numbers as gospel, then hyped the companies with falsified reports under the heading "ratings." And don't forget the fourth layer added on by commission-based brokers and financial planners under the rubric of "advice," knowing all along it was just a sales pitch in disguise.

SEC: We're dealing with all that. By August 15, 2002, the CEOs of 691 large corporations in America signed the Commission Order No. 4-460, certifying the accuracy of their statements. Later, another 237 CEOs signed. This was indeed a very sad chapter in America's corporate history, but I'm happy to report that chapter is mostly closed.

Johnston: I beg to differ.

There are still widespread shenanigans associated with domestic and foreign subsidiaries. There is still widespread gimmickry associated with employee pension funds. There are immeasurable risks—and hidden losses—in various kinds of debts and derivatives. Hundreds of the CEOs who signed the certification continue to engage in these shaky practices.

I have with me today a white paper that represents the collective wisdom of some of the brightest minds in the country on the issue of crashing markets, its possible consequences, and what the government should do—or not do—in response. After we adjourn, I will provide copies to your staff. Its title: "Crash Benefits."

I implore you not to rush to judgment, not to assume a priori that all crashes must be stopped at all costs, that all deflations must be countered, regardless of the expense. Instead, I invite everyone here today to review this report to explore the crash benefits.

President: It was my understanding, Mr. Johnston, that you have joined us today to provide your input regarding how to bolster investor confidence, and that you are ready to pledge your support toward that goal. I do not understand what you mean by "crash benefits." Nor do I see how they fit in with that goal.

MetroBank: Mr. President, I think you've hit the nail on the head. We are here today to find a way to support the market, to shore up the capital of key players, to encourage investor confidence, but Mr. Johnston's goals seem to be out of synch. He speaks of "crash benefits." But the two words are themselves incongruous. What benefits could possibly accrue from a crash? Let's get back on track.

President: Yes! Are we saying that the big bubble was mostly accounting mumbo-jumbo? If that's our big problem, and the rest of the economy is fundamentally strong, what are we so worried about? Are we worried that our reforms to date are not good enough? Fine. So we pass some more reform legislation. I signed the Accounting Reform Act of 2002. I'll be glad to sign another reform act now. Every time we do that, it will restore more confidence.

Johnston: I wish it were that easy. But the accounting revelations were just the trigger—the device that burst the bubble. Over the years, we have identified a whole series of other cracks in our economy. These are fissures that few people think about in good times but which threaten to erupt volcanically in bad times.

First is the budget. If the budget were robust fundamentally, maybe we *could* get away with spending a few more bucks of taxpayer money. Unfortunately, that is absolutely *not* the case. In addition to the official deficit estimates of $150 to $200 billion, there's an off-balance-sheet deficit of at least $600 billion, according to the Fed's own Flow of Funds numbers.

Looking ahead, the OMB—the Office of Management and Budget—estimates that we face additional hundreds of billions in *future* deficit increases if corporate earnings and the economy continue to slide. All told, between the Fed's numbers and the OMB's future scenarios, you'd be talking yearly overall deficits in excess of a trillion dollars!

Separately, as you know, the OMB also reports that there could be hundreds of billions that are lost in outright accounting errors at many of the government departments and agencies.

President: Is that correct?

Treasury Secretary: I'm afraid it is.

Johnston: In this environment, it's inconceivable that you could buy stocks with federal money without shattering the already-fragile confidence of bond investors. Then, you'd certainly be facing a bond auction failure like Japan experienced in September 2002.

(The president glanced toward the Treasury secretary, who was silently nodding in agreement.)

The second risk we have identified is the government securities market, which reflects the deficits. Look back at the sequence of events: When more companies started reporting bad earnings, investors dumped their shares and rushed to corporate bonds. Then, when more companies started going bankrupt, investors dumped their corporate bonds and rushed to government bonds. Now, investors are worried we will do exactly what is being proposed here today, and they are shying away from government bonds. We tolerated the other busts. We can't tolerate a bust in government bonds.

I trust everyone remembers what happened in 1980.

Treasury Secretary: But that was an *inflationary* period, which was bad for bonds. This is a *deflationary* period, which is good for bonds.

Johnston: But if holders of government securities need the cash or fear default, they will sell regardless of inflation or deflation.

The third risk factor is the dollar. The dollar went up for years, so it was often assumed the dollar was strong, that it was not a risk. Not so. Foreign investors hold close to $1 trillion dollars in Treasury and agency securities. They hold $2.9 trillion in U.S. stocks. Plus, they hold $8 trillion in other U.S. assets. They are the single largest owner of most of our asset categories—larger than our domestic banks, insurers, or any other single domestic sector. If you do anything to shatter their confidence, if you frighten them in any way, look out below.

THE RISK OF DOLLAR DECLINE

President: Given how high the dollar is, can't we afford to let it fall for a while? Is this really a current risk?

Treasury Secretary: Mr. Johnston has a point. Think back to 2002, the last weekend in September. You remember: the International Money Fund meetings here in D.C. that we attended. What did all of their experts say? What did all *our* experts say? They all said the same thing. They said the biggest threat to the global economy is not Argentina or Brazil. It's us. It's the risk of a U.S. recession dragging down the rest of the world—a world that is already on the edge of a cliff, already tumbling *down* the cliff in some regions and sectors. It's the risk of a dollar plunge due to our record trade deficits, our record reliance on foreign capital. It's the risk that our financial markets, the fountainhead of most of the world's capital, could dry up.

Think of it this way: Here at home, vis-à-vis our own residents, there are things we've done and can do to exert some influence on their investment behavior. We've put money into their pockets with tax cuts so they could spend more, or buy more stocks and bonds. We've lowered interest rates so they could refinance their mortgages, pull cash out of their home equity, and maybe use some of that to buy *still* more stocks and bonds. If these tools aren't working even here, imagine what will happen with overseas investors who own U.S. assets! We never even had those tools of influence over them to begin with. If they start selling, there's absolutely nothing we could do about it. It could be the last nail in the coffin for our stock market and, worse, for our bond market.

Johnston: Thank you, Mr. Secretary. The fourth risk we have identified is real estate. I take you back to the earlier question: Where did all the money from the stock market go? Well, at one point a lot of people were saying most of it was going into real estate. That was only partially true. The primary source of money for real estate has always been mortgage debt, and we now have outstanding mortgage debt approaching $6 trillion. But it is not growing any more. Now, that sector is weakening, and if it continues, you can kiss the recovery goodbye. In its place, say hello to chronic recession, perhaps even depression.

There is also a *fifth* risk—derivatives. We can't tell you much about them, and therein lies the heart of the problem. It's largely an unknown risk. All we know is that in terms of their total face value, which admittedly exaggerates the problem, there are close to $50 trillion in the U.S. and perhaps another $60 trillion overseas—more than all interest-bearing debt in the world. Plus, we also know that certain large U.S. banks—Morgan Chase, Bank of America, and Citibank, for example—are at the center of the derivatives markets. The key concern is that each of these banks is risking 100 percent or more of its capital on derivatives, according to the OCC.

MetroBank: You know, I'm actually very *glad* Mr. Johnston has pointed out the risks we face, Mr. President, because in my opinion this underscores the entire reason we are here today. Our financial system may not be able to tolerate—and we therefore must not permit—a further decline in the stock and bond markets.

If we *do not* take aggressive steps, these kinds of risks, now mostly dormant, will come to the fore, making it increasingly impossible for us to control markets, to stop a chain reaction of failures. If the stock markets falls below its most recent lows, if the economy declines for just one more quarter, then we will reach the end of the fuse. One or more of these bombs will go off, with unforeseeable fallout. We *must snuff out the burning fuse now!* We must find a new way—a unique mechanism—to turn the stock market around.

President: Suppose we shut it down temporarily. We seriously considered that in 1987, didn't we? We actually did it after 9/11, didn't we? We stopped the crash then. We can stop the crash now.

SEC: We can't do that.

President: Why not?

SEC: The Crash of '87 was a 1- or 2-day event. The shock of 9/11 was an external event. That's not the nature of the beast we're dealing with here. Here, the monster we're dealing with is *a stock market plunge that has already lasted for multiple years*. What would be the rationale for closing the market now? What would be the rationale for reopening it? It's just too hazy. We must have an apocalyptic 1-day plunge to justify a shutdown, and yet it is precisely that kind of plunge that we have come here today to avert—at all costs!

President: What about dropping interest rates?

Fed Chairman: We've already dropped the Fed funds rate to the basement, and it has done us little good. The Bank of Japan dropped their rates to zero percent, and it did them no good.

President: Still more tax cuts?

Treasury Secretary: No. Deficit's already out of control. Besides, for every dollar of tax cuts we give to citizens, the state governments are going to impose a dollar or two of tax *hikes*. Even in the best-case scenario, it's a wash for the taxpayer.

President: More credit and easy money.

Fed Chairman: Done that.

President: More favorable capital gains treatment?

Treasury: Nope. We desperately need the revenue.

President: Switching Social Security funds to stocks?

Federal Reserve: That was discussed when stocks were booming. For obvious reasons, it must now be dropped, as stocks are falling.

President: OK. Knock down every single suggestion I make. I have no problem with that. But you gentlemen are the brains, the experts here. If these are no good, give me an alternative. And don't give me a wimpy, pea-gun solution that *may* have *some* trickle-down effect *someday*. The stock market is plunging *now*. All these frightening risks we've heard about are in existence *now*. So I want a cannonball solution that has big-bang impact potential—also *now*.

Federal Reserve: We all understand the urgency. But here's the dilemma in a nutshell: You have two fundamental choices—you can try to save the stock market or you can try to save the government bond market. You can't do both.

Assume choice number one—you try to save the stock market. Result: You shatter worldwide confidence in the U.S. government and you torpedo the entire government bond market.

Assume choice number two—you don't save the stock market. Result: The stock market plunges and you torpedo the entire economy.

Those are your choices: Kill the bond market or kill the economy.

President: I've had enough of this "damned if we do, damned if we don't" talk. What do you suggest we do?

Johnston: Nothing.

President: You mean you don't know?

DO-NOTHING PRESIDENT OR MARKET-NEUTRAL GOVERNMENT?

Johnston: No, sir, I know exactly what we should do in this situation: Nothing. Stand pat. Go back in history and look at the experience of the past. Every aggressive action produced an unexpected market reaction. And every action-reaction cycle has come with shorter and shorter intervals. Nixon's wage-and-price freeze bombed and led to runaway inflation and the Arab oil embargo. President Ford's budget deficits and easy money were a prelude to the first dollar collapse. Carter's bond market rescue package of 1980 resulted in a sudden recession. The 1984–86 money-pumping binge produced still another dollar collapse and the worst stock market crash in history. Clinton deregulated, and it helped open the spigots for the greatest tech stock speculation in the history of mankind.

Now, all these crises are coming to a head. We have an accounting crisis, a budget crisis, a recession crisis, a stock market crisis, a bond crisis, a bankruptcy crisis, a dollar crisis . . . a Brazil crisis, an Argentina crisis, a Japan crisis—all at the same time. Regardless of the consequences, you have only one choice, and that is to keep your hands off—not because of some invisible hand that will magically cure everything, but because at this particular juncture *the no-action choice is the wisest decision a true leader can make.*

President: Do you want a do-nothing president?

Johnston: No. But right now, we need a market-neutral government. Let the market make the decisions. We have no other choice.

President: You're proposing that we allow millions of investors to pull all the strings and, like a master puppeteer, determine not only what happens in the economy but also what the Fed and the White House can or cannot do in response. I can't allow that to happen.

Johnston: But you already have! You have *already* lost control over the markets. The more we say and do, the worse it gets.

President: No! We need action now. It's life or death for millions of people's jobs. How can we just sit back and watch the show?

MetroBank: We have a plan.

President: Yes? Tell us about it!

THE BAILOUT PLAN

MetroBank: As you know, MetroBank and HarrisJones have been seriously considering a merger. What you may not know is that we have also been conferring on these broader policy issues, debating some of the very same points that have arisen here today. To cut to the chase, we have come up with a *seven-point proposal.*

President: Please, go on.

MetroBank: The Federal Reserve of New York, acting as the broker and trader for the United States government, has the authority to buy the bonds of private corporations. The government has the authority to bring up those firms' bond values closer to the level of government bond values. It has the authority to create cash and funnel that cash anywhere it wants.

President: I agree: *We can create cash.*

MetroBank: Yes, we can create cash in virtually unlimited quantities. We have that power. And in view of the unusual new internal and external threats our country is facing, the time has now come to use that power. That's the core of our plan. But let me step back for a moment and lay it out for you, point by point.

Point one: You must reward the buyers and punish the short-sellers in the stock market. We propose that the Federal Reserve lower the margin requirements for the purchase of common stocks, making it easier for investors to borrow more directly from their brokers. At the same time, the Fed *increases* the margin requirements for short sellers, making it more *difficult* for them to borrow the money they use to sell our markets short, to sell our country short. The Federal Reserve has had this power all along, and in years past it did use this power. It varied the margin requirements as needed. Now, the time has come to revive that power.

Point two: The Federal Reserve of New York goes into the open market with the goal of supporting the stock market. However, instead of buying common stocks directly, it buys *corporate bonds.* That's the key. This is, in essence, what was done with the Reconstruction Finance Corporation in the last century. The law says you can do it too. The Fed *can* do it. The Fed can buy the bonds of hundreds of major companies. The Fed puts those bonds in its portfolio. And those companies get the cash.

Point three: We recognize this is a very unusual step, a major break with tradition. So we figured you would need a political overlay to make the plan more palatable to the public. Instead of just buying the bonds of *any* company, the government will buy the bonds strictly in those companies that can demonstrate clean accounting and/or an important role in homeland security. We figure that could be almost any company you want it to be. That gives you the excuse—sorry—the flexibility you need. Most important, it lets the government flush the private sector with cash . . . and support the stock market!

Point four: The Fed buys the corporate bonds with one simple condition: That each company must use at least 75 percent of those funds to immediately buy back its own common stock outstanding. You remember the leveraged buyouts of the 1980s—the LBOs—when companies did that on a massive scale. They borrowed the money from banks and big financiers. Then they used the borrowed money to buy back their own shares. And you remember how that boosted the stock market. Well, it's essentially the same thing we're proposing. Except this time, the funding comes mostly from the government. This time, the government orchestrates the whole thing.

Point five: You've got the problem with foreign investors. We don't want to see our billions pumped into our stock market only to watch it all leak out overseas. So you slap various currency controls on our foreign exchange markets. Make it tougher for foreigners to convert the proceeds from their stock sales back into their own currencies. That effectively closes the dollar leak.

Point six: As a temporary emergency measure, the Federal Reserve eliminates bank reserve requirements. That means the banks have more money to lend, and they can loan that money to corporations—for plugging leaky balance sheets. We don't want the government to be the sole provider of fresh, new liquidity. MetroBank and others want to help too.

Final point—seven: If the government announces it will implement all or most of our proposals, we will agree to cut our prime lending rate. That will be the icing on the cake.

Fed Chairman: No! Why must you take that unorthodox approach when we can just continue to follow our standard procedure? Why can't we add liquid funds to the banking system? The banks are then encouraged to loan those funds to corporations in need. What's wrong with that?

Metrobank: It's diluted. The stock market needs a direct shot in the vein. The traditional method—oral medication—is too slow.

Fed Chairman: Too slow? What do you mean?

Metrobank: I mean it's not working. Mr. President, it has already been said that interest rates have been dropped as far as they can be dropped. It has already been said that money is being pumped into the banking system in record amounts. Has this restored investor confidence? No. Has this stopped the stock market decline? No! Clearly, then, the traditional method has a very simple problem: *It . . . is . . . not . . . working!*

You must take a more direct approach. You must buy the corporate bonds, and if that doesn't work, we must go further. You must buy the common stocks themselves.

Fed Chairman: We must not do that! The government must not buy corporate bonds. The government must not buy common stocks. Who do you think you're going to fool? For every dollar the government uses to buy corporate bonds, it will have to borrow another dollar from the public by issuing its *own* government bonds. It just won't work. Government bond investors will see it as a subterfuge—a sneaky way for the government to indirectly buy common stocks. Foreign investors will laugh in your face. It will backfire, just as it did in Japan.

Johnston: Gentlemen, I implore you. Read our "Crash Benefits" report. It will show you that the Fed chairman is right not only for the short term but also for the long term. MetroBank and HarrisJones are clearly afraid of falling—

HarrisJones: Where did you get that impression?

Johnston: I mean we are all fearing a fall. But we must not fear a crash. We must learn to live with it, to guide it, and save our resources for the day when it can really have a great benefit. At this time, it would merely hurt government bonds, hurt the entire nation.

MetroBank: Mr. President, do we want to save millions of jobs, thousands of businesses, and the entire economy? Or do we want to pander to government bond investors and foreign investors? The choice is yours.

The President knew it was a risky venture. The Federal Reserve chairman and Treasury secretary harbored even greater fears. But

Johnston was right. All of them, especially the president, shared the same fear—the fear of a stock market fall that would plunge the entire nation into an abyss.

The president pushed hard for the MetroBank plan, and the Treasury Secretary retreated to a more neutral stance, deferring to the President.

Meanwhile, the more the Fed chairman or Johnston spoke of risks and dangers, the more convinced the president became that the Administration and the Federal Reserve needed to take *more* action—not less. If there ever was a time to go to battle, this was it, he declared with resolve and bravado.

During the week that followed, although some of MetroBank's proposals were rejected, the Administration made plans to pursue the core of the plan. Intense pressures were brought upon the Fed chairman to give this strategy a try, yet the chairman continued to resist. He was adamantly opposed to making it easier to investors to borrow from their brokers. He was even more vehement in his opposition to the corporate bond proposal.

However, in the next weekly get-together with the Fed Chairman, the Treasury Secretary conveyed this message from the president: "If the Fed does not act, *the president has the support of Congress to act without the Fed*. It will provide utterly massive financing to those same corporations to repurchase their common stocks."

The Fed chairman felt that would be even worse. He calculated that no matter how ill-conceived the Fed's operation, at least he could retain control, prevent it from getting totally out of hand, and keep it as quiet as possible. He finally relented. He would cooperate.

The Fed would pursue an indirect stock market rescue operation, using the government's outright purchase of corporate bonds as one of the primary vehicles. This way, funds could be funneled to major companies, which, in turn, would funnel the money back into the stock market, creating more demand for shares and bidding up their prices.

Thus, several days later, it was rumored that the New York Fed was planning to buy bonds issued by 14 of the 30 Dow Industrial companies, plus an even bigger list of lesser bonds—a sweeping, unprecedented rescue operation the likes of which had never been seen. It was also rumored that these companies, for their part, were about to announce gigantic stock buyback programs. Depending on the market's reaction, the programs would be greatly expanded to an even wider range of corporate bonds, including junk bonds and the bonds of companies on their deathbeds.

The first reaction came from the bond market.

CHAPTER 20

THE GREAT RALLY

The cut in the prime rate was a joke. What good was it if the banks reduced their rate but had no money to lend? The foreign exchange controls were also out of touch with reality and never pursued, except symbolically.

Nevertheless, the rumors that the Federal Reserve Bank of New York was buying corporate bonds in selected firms with "whistle-clean accounting" and rumors that it would follow up with purchases of bonds of other firms—even junk bonds—triggered the sharpest rally in the history of corporate bonds.

This rally, in turn, spilled over into the stock market. The Dow surged by over 500 points in just one day, and the rally continued, albeit at a slower pace, for weeks. Cheers reverberated through the damaged corridors of Wall Street.

Some stocks surged by nearly 50 percent in just a few trading sessions. The Dow surged by 1,400 points in just five trading sessions.

One junk bond issue selling at 62 leaped to 79 in only a few hours. Another jumped 12 points and closed the trading day with a net increase of 10 points.

Utility bonds, municipal bonds, and even the bonds of third-world nations surged by leaps and bounds.

A few days later, however, trading in the corporate bond market came to a standstill. If investors called their broker, they'd get an "indication" of the market price, way up in the stratosphere. But it was a fiction. There was virtually no trading at that high level—no buyers. This was the first sign of trouble.

The next sign of trouble came in the government bond market. In the first few days, prices went nowhere as investors tried to decipher the rumors. Then, as soon as they realized the government was buying corporate bonds with their money, they began to dump their government bond holdings.

Life insurance companies scrambled to shorten their maturities, selling long-dated government bonds and buying the shortest-term instruments. Bank trust departments unloaded. Government security dealers dumped their bond inventories or scurried to sell Treasury bond futures as a hedge. Mutual fund managers, hedge fund managers, pension fund managers—everyone was scrambling to get out of government bonds. Overseas investors were even more aggressive sellers. It didn't matter whether there was inflation or deflation. They wanted out.

Just as in early 1980, there were no buyers. Dealers were unable to sell even small lots of government bonds. Here's what came out on the news wires and on the Internet at the end of the week:

> The deeply discounted medium- and low-grade corporates have enjoyed what is said to be their sharpest rally in memory, but dealers and traders are watching quality spreads carefully for some indication of the longer-term impact of the recent Federal Reserve plan to purchase corporate paper in the hope of bringing some much needed support to the stock market, which, in recent weeks, had floundered to near collapse as a result of the rapid loss of investor confidence in the nation's accounting and financial system, all representing, however, concerns that pale in comparison to the apparent inability of government security dealers to place small lots of medium- and long-term debt issues.

Most investors who saw this run-on sentence said it left them blank. Others, tired of the constant flow of "gibberish," didn't even bother to read it.

Three days later, the Treasury secretary, who had just been in touch with the Fed chairman, called the president on the phone. "It's no good. The benefit of our plan to the stock market is a spit in the ocean. On the other hand, to the government bond market it's a potential hydrogen bomb. The quality spreads are narrowing—and in the wrong direction."

The president didn't know much about quality spreads. "What are the causes and what are the consequences of changes in quality spreads?" he asked.

"I am referring to the difference in yield between a Treasury bond and a corporate bond. A big corporation always has to pay more than the U.S. Treasury to borrow money. Typically, the difference has been about one full percentage point.

Then, several months ago, when the full threat of corporate bankruptcies was first apparent, the yield on medium-grade corporate bonds went up by 2¼ percent, but the yield on the governments went up only one-quarter percent. In other words, the spread increased by two full percentage points. It was a warning light flashing red. It revealed that confidence in all corporations—no matter how creditworthy—had collapsed. But that was before our rescue package was announced."

"And now?"

"Now the opposite is happening. Corporate bond yields are back down sharply, but government bond yields are actually up sharply. The spread between them has narrowed to practically nothing—a very bad sign." The Treasury Secretary felt satisfied that he had put forth a very clear and straightforward explanation.

"Well, isn't that what we had said we wanted—to bring up the corporate bond market, to get it back up toward the level of government bonds?"

The secretary shook his head, trying to hold his voice steady so that his feelings of frustration with the president's lack of knowledge of bond markets would not be picked up over the phone. In the past, he tried several times to explain to the president how interest rates and prices moving in opposite directions always meant the same thing, but that spreads, although moving in the same direction, could mean a variety of different things.

How does one make such things simple for a president to understand without sounding condescending? The secretary certainly didn't know how. He spent the next half hour going over the events in the marketplace until finally, after considerable effort, the president developed an image of bond markets that looked similar to the charts in Figure 20.1.

"Now I see," the president said finally. "We wanted to bring the

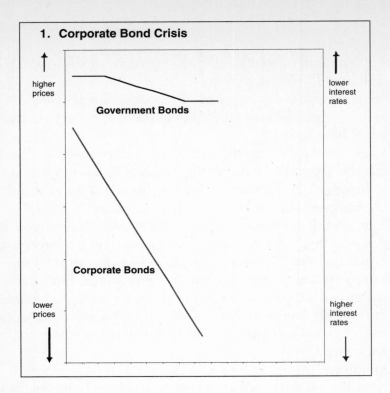

1. Corporate Bond Crisis

higher prices

lower interest rates

Government Bonds

Corporate Bonds

lower prices

higher interest rates

Figure 20.1 During any severe market decline, a critical policy issue is whether the government will intervene and how. These charts illustrate the expected outcome of any attempt by the government to support corporate bonds, in three phases.

Phase 1: Corporate bond crisis. Because of spreading failures and defaults, investors lose confidence in the ability of companies to pay the interest and principal on corporate bonds. So they sell their bonds, driving the bond prices lower (and interest rates higher). However, since investors continue to trust the government, the crisis has less negative impact on government bond prices. As corporate bond prices fall, the spread or difference between corporate and government bonds broadens sharply.

Phase 2: Government rescues corporate bonds. The government buys corporate bonds with funds that it has raised from government bond investors. This boosts the perceived and actual value of corporate bonds. But, at the same time, it lowers the value of government bonds, prompting investors to sell their government bond holdings. Corporate bond prices go up but government prices fall. As a result, the spread between them narrows.

Phase 3: Government rescue is abandoned. To prevent a collapse in its government bonds, the government is forced to abandon its rescue of corporate bonds and accept the consequences of a collapsing corporate bond market.

If the government sought to purchase common stocks instead of corporate bonds, the sequence of events described here would be very similar.

2. Government Rescues Corporate Bonds

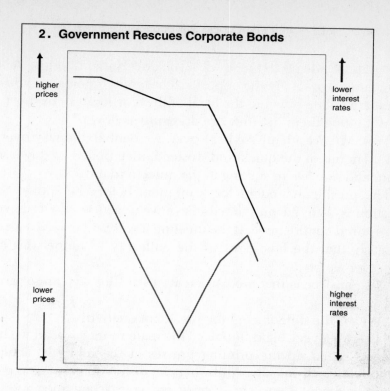

higher prices

lower interest rates

lower prices

higher interest rates

3. Government Rescue is Abandoned

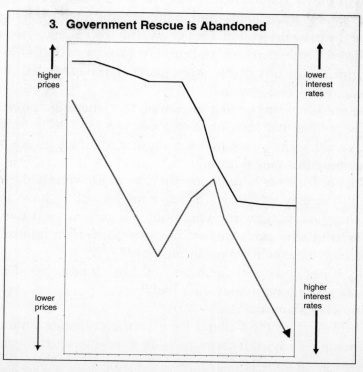

higher prices

lower interest rates

lower prices

higher interest rates

corporate bonds up to the level of the government bonds. What's happening is precisely the opposite. The 'governments,' as you call them, are falling down to the level of the 'corporates.' In short, we are not lifting them up; they are dragging us down."

"Yes, Mr. President. We bent over, we bent all the way over, to pull them out of the quicksand. Instead, they pulled us down with them, and now we're sinking in the quicksand too."

The president thought for a moment before he spoke. "The question is, Why? Don't they believe we're serious? Why haven't we restored confidence? At the meeting it was said that we can create cash, that the law gives us the authority to funnel this cash wherever we please."

"The answer is that we can create cash. But we cannot create *credit*."

"What's the difference?" the president queried.

"There's a very big difference. To create more cash, all we have to do is speed up the printing presses at the mint—or, actually, pump it in electronically. And when we dish it out, no one is going to turn us down. But to create *credit*, we have to convince investors and bankers to make loans—and in this environment of falling confidence, I can assure you that isn't easy. If it were so easy, we could have saved Bethlehem Steel or Enron or Kmart or Global Crossing or WorldCom or any of the other giants that have failed. But we didn't, and for good reason."

The president was getting impatient. "So what's the point?"

"The point is that you can create cash; you *can't create confidence*."

"It would seem to me that the more money we give 'em, the more confidence they'd have."

"No, no! It's exactly the opposite. The more we spend the government's money recklessly, the less confidence they have and the more they fear our government bonds will go down in value."

"Oh? But why can't we just buy *more* corporate bonds? That should convince them we mean business!"

"No, it just convinces them we're throwing more good money after bad—*their* good money after bad."

"But what about the law?"

"The law gives the Federal Reserve the on-paper authority to buy private securities. *It does not give them—us—the actual power to create real economic wealth.*"

"Why didn't we recognize this when we discussed the MetroBank–Harris rescue plan?"

"We did. But you overrode us, and we consented. We hoped that the marketplace might swallow it. We seriously underestimated the sophistication of U.S. and foreign investors—*very* seriously underestimated."

Still, the president sounded perplexed. "You're saying the market is sensitive. You're saying the market is smart. I see that now. But . . ."

The secretary's irritability was becoming more apparent. "Let's say I'm a foreign investor and I own U.S. Treasury bonds. This implies that I trust the U.S. government, that I loaned you my money for the purpose of running your government. Now you take my money and pass it on to a third party, a private company. So I say to you, 'What did you go and do that for? If I wanted to loan the money to that company, I would have done so myself—directly—in the first place. But I didn't. I didn't do it because I don't trust the company. I trusted you. But now I can't trust you anymore either. Now you're just one of them.' So the investor stops buying our bonds or, worse, dumps the government bonds he's holding, and then we are in trouble. Then we can't sell our government bonds anymore to pay off the old ones coming due. Then we, the United States government, default."

The president hesitated for a few seconds before responding, but it seemed like hours as the tension built.

"Then what?"

The secretary could not believe his ears. The president of the United States had treated the government's default with levity, utter levity. He could no longer control his boiling frustration—and fear. "Do you want to allow the entire market for U.S. government securities to shut down? Do you want to be the one who has to lay off hundreds of thousands of government employees because you can't raise the money to meet the government payroll? Do you want to be the last president of the United States? Do you want to risk a new republic with a new constitution? Do you want to destroy, in one fell swoop . . ."

The secretary's voice broke with emotion. Silence reigned.

"I appreciate the sincerity of your emotions, but you misunderstood me. What I said, in fact, was 'then *what*,' indicating to you my surprise and disbelief that our country could ever reach the point you've described so dramatically just now."

In the days that followed, the president thought hard about his options. He reviewed the minutes of the meeting. In the privacy of his bedroom, he even read a top-secret report on the dangers of a crash.

Finally, in a midnight call to the Treasury secretary, he asked the secretary to convey an urgent message to the Fed chairman. "Tell him one, to dispose of all corporate bond paper purchased thus far; two, to pledge that the U.S. federal government, despite its current legal authority, will not purchase securities of the private sector; and three, to promise to always discriminate between corporates and governments. For my part, I shall proceed to take those actions I deem necessary to correct this extremely dangerous situation."

"But Mr. President," the secretary murmured, "we never did get around to purchasing the corporate bonds; we only leaked our intention to do so."

"RISK, RISK, AND MORE DAMN RISK"

While the Treasury secretary was still debating with the president about the bond market, Linda Dedini faced a similar struggle with her two brothers about the stock market.

Based on the hope for a full-scale Washington bailout on all fronts, and with the impetus from a great stock market rally, the pied pipers of Wall Street were at it again. "*Now,* this is the *real* bottom," they said. "*Now,* the great bull market has *truly* returned," they chanted. "Snatch up incredible values! It's the greatest bargain-basement sale of the century!"

In this environment, the two brothers were pressing her to forget about dull Treasury bills, dump such esoteric investments as reverse index funds or put options, and immediately jump back into the market with both feet.

One hot biotech stock that caught their fancy had buy ratings from three Wall Street firms, plus two independent analysts. Another stock, this one a managed care company, was being recommended by more than 15 analysts. They trotted out forecasts by well-respected economists about the inevitable economic recovery, supported fully by the government's new plan. They spoke enviously of friends who already had close to 30 percent gains on stocks that, just weeks earlier, no one wanted to touch with a 10-foot pole.

She was adamantly opposed. "No, you still don't get it. The market is still full of risk, risk, and more damn risk. Let me recap for you: There's still the risk that the company lied to you in their statements and that the auditors looked the other way. There's still the risk that Wall Street lied to you, exaggerating the company's lie. There's the risk of excessive debt and the risk of derivatives, not to mention all the risks we've always had in the stock market—a recession, falling earnings, and outright investor panic."

"But you're the *only one* saying this," the older brother retorted.

"I may be among the few *saying* it, but there are a lot of people who *know* it. The analysts know it, the CEOs know it, even the SEC and the New York attorney general have warned you about it. You seem to forget that those analysts are the same people who supposedly didn't have a clue that the stocks they were recommending a few years ago were going down the tubes. Those are the same guys who raked in obscene salaries in return for awarding buy ratings to stocks like Priceline.com, Global Crossing, World-Com, Lucent Technologies. Those are the same ones who got rich while we were losing our shirts on a Pandora's box of other disasters—stocks their bosses needed to sell. They're also the same ones who continued to put out buy ratings even as the stocks crashed by as much as 90 percent, even as the companies were filing for bankruptcy! *Nothing has changed.* I can't believe you still believe in them."

"They're fixing all that now, aren't they?" said the younger brother.

"Where? Show me. It's still nothing more than thinly veiled sales hype. It's still bought and paid for by the very companies they're recommending. Don't you get it? The Wall Street establishment is more than happy to lie through its teeth about the stocks they rate if it will make them a buck.

"Now tell me," she continued. "What are the odds they're telling us what they honestly believe about the economy—when they say that the 'economy is going to recover' or that 'this is the beginning of a new bull market'? What's the chance they're telling us what they truly believe *now?* One in a thousand? One in a million? Nothing has changed. Honest forecasts are *still* bad for business."

She was practically out of breath but barely paused. "Look at their history, damn it. Just before each decline, they were painting a future that was so bright, you had to wear shades. Then, when things *obviously* turned sour, did they show any concern? No. They lined up on TV and forecast that the 'correction' would be over very soon, that we should 'buy *more* shares.' And now? Now, look at what they're saying. They're saying the government is our grand savior, the government will make all our troubles go away, will push the stock market higher, will guarantee that investors make profits."

"So when are we going to actually hit bottom?" they asked.

"When they finally throw in the towel and stop searching for the bottom."

Linda convinced them. And thanks to the guidelines she had gotten from her adviser, she had exited the reverse index funds before the rally took back her earlier profits.

Now, as the rally ran out of steam, she was getting ready to jump back in to profit from the *next* crash.

The next day, she also noticed that the stock market rally had significantly cheapened nearly every put option she had been interested in. She bought four puts with two months remaining on IBM for just $1.25 per share. She bought some long-term options, called LEAPS puts, on a major stock market index. She proceeded methodically to build a modest but powerful put options portfolio that had a good mix of everything—long-term puts and short-term puts, puts on individual stocks and puts on indexes, very cheap puts that were out of the money, plus a couple of puts that were closer to the money and a bit more pricey.

She even added a sprinkling of extremely cheap far-out-of-the-money put options. She knew it was a long shot—she had once lost $2,000 on these kinds of puts. But she bought them anyhow.

She knew that if the market continued to rally or go sideways for another few months, her put options would deteriorate in value and she might even lose every dime. But thanks to the inheritance, their retirement and college fund was now secure. They even had enough set aside for the long-term health care of Gabriel's parents, who were in process of moving to the States from Argentina. She limited the money she spent on options strictly to the money she could afford to lose, without jeopardizing her goals.

Moreover, the total options investment was relatively small by comparison to the money she had put into the reverse index fund. No, the fund couldn't double or triple her money in 60 days like the winning options. She hoped for "only" a 20 or 30 percent return for the year. But that was nothing to sneeze at, especially while everyone else was *losing* 20 or 30 percent.

If the market turned higher, she had an exit plan for the reverse index funds to cut her losses. She had no exit plan for the options. If they didn't work out, she'd just throw them out like outdated lottery tickets and forget about them.

Most important, the overwhelming bulk of her money was in conservative investments—mostly in the Treasury-only money market fund plus some longer-term Treasury bonds she had bought for a better yield. Her father's associate, Oliver Dulles, had warned her against buying the longer-term bonds. She had followed his advice for a while; then she had found some unique information that seemed to contradict his view.

In any case, she figured she needed some balance. Keeping *all* of the cash in short-term money markets seemed imprudent to her. She couldn't bear to keep all of her cash in such low-yielding investments. As to the longer term notes and bonds, in the worst case, she figured she would just keep them until maturity and get all of her principal back. She could live with the low yields, especially since deflation was worsening and wild inflation seemed highly unlikely.

"I'm happy," she had said to Dulles at one of her Dad's forums. "Nearly all of my cash money is still parked right outside my door. When I need it, it's there at my fingertips, rain or shine."

Linda Dedini actually had big plans for that "parked" money. That's where she would go to grab the funds she needed when the *true* bargains came. Her grandfather once told her to invest in the market like going to battle: "Invest your precious money like it was the last live ammunition to save your life—don't fire until you see the whites of their eyes."

She had ignored that advice once under the guidance of Harris

& Jones and barely survived the consequences. She would not make the same mistake again.

On his deathbed, her grandfather also had whispered a little secret in her ear; "Don't believe the family legend," he confided. "I was never a 'visionary' or an investing 'genius' like they say I was. In fact, I actually lost tons of money on stupid investments in my earlier years."

CHAPTER 21

THE GAP

Normally, in the world of markets and economics, things don't go straight down. There are usually rallies which produce a zigzag pattern. But if investors examine price charts closely, they will occasionally find what technicians call a "gap"—a hole in the chart between the point where one line ends and another begins.

The gap implies that there were no market transactions during that time, that the price suddenly jumped from one point to another. That is essentially what happened to the financial markets—and the entire world economy—when the Fed abruptly canceled its plans to purchase corporate bonds and lend support to the stock market. One moment, stocks and bonds seemed to hang in midair over the edge of a cliff; the next moment, they seemed well on their way toward a rocky bottom.

Oliver Dulles and Paul E. Johnston watched with growing anxiety as much of their crash scenarios came true. Yes, there were many differences between the scenarios and the actual reality as it unfolded. However, there was one general aspect that was unmistakably on target: Most things were going *down*.

They invited Tamara Belmont to join them for an informal dinner in Chinatown, just blocks away from the office. "We obviously have the crash," they said. "Now where are the benefits?"

She did not have an immediate answer.

Finally, after much discussion, they all agreed it was premature. The crash was not yet over. They would have to be more patient. They also agreed that, so far at least, it seemed as though the short-but-ugly scenario was predominating. The government had backed off from direct intervention.

Dulles was surprised by this. He had come to believe that politicians would never step aside—they would always want to fiddle and tinker, always seek to fool mother nature. But Johnston was not surprised. He himself had been through it before, on a much smaller scale. He had learned from experience that you can't fool the mass of investors for long. Once they rebel, you must give in. Now, it was the millions of bond holders—everyone around the world who had invested in the U.S. government—that had rebelled, saying, "Stop! Don't interfere. Don't try to plug the dike with your dirty fingers. Let it all wash out."

"I have decided we should not publish the Crash Benefits white paper at this time," Johnston said as he munched on a fortune cookie.

"Why the heck not?" asked Tamara, struggling to suppress a disturbing flashback to her old days at Harris.

"Because—"

"Paul, please, you have no idea how much effort—"

"I know, I know. I was with you and the staff the whole time. I saw the sweat and tears that went into that paper. But our mission was to send the message to our leaders that the consequences of meddling were far worse than the consequences of standing aside, correct?"

"Yes, but—"

"Now, bond investors all over the world are accomplishing that mission for us. They are already doing everything we sought to do—and more effectively than we could ever have dreamed. Their selling pressure speaks louder then reports, speeches of any other actions. Plus, there's one other reason I want to keep it out of publication right now."

"What's that?" she asked, still greatly disappointed.

"I'm afraid the paper would be misunderstood. At the Oval Office, every time I sought to give them the highlights, it merely reinforced their resolve to intervene, to stop the decline. They cannot yet see the distinction we have made between the two scenarios. All they see is the "down," "the falling." So what good will it do us to publish it now? They already realize they are falling. But they are *still* afraid to look down. My point is, If we publish it now, they will not see the hope; all they will see is the gloom, and they will just use that as another excuse to make another attempt to artificially pump things up again."

Johnston promised to publish the report at a future time "when the climate is right," and she acquiesced.

At the same time, all three began to see hope where everyone else saw nothing but dark clouds.

Where others saw only the government's failure to stem the rising tides of selling, the three of them saw a victory by investors that, in the long term, would be constructive.

Where others saw deflation as a great threat, they saw it as a democratizing process that would reverse the bloated compensation of a select few.

Where most people feared the speed of the decline, they welcomed it. They believed that the sooner they could end the crisis and put it behind them, the better the chances of only minimal social damage. They retained a fervent hope for a wholesome recovery, even if the worst-case scenario were to occur.

Tamara commented on the speed of the decline. In earlier years, she said, every critical crisis seemed to be distinctly separate from the next one. The Asia crisis struck in 1997. Russia went under in 1998. Tech stocks first got smashed in 2000. Argentina went under in 2001. Accounting disasters struck mostly in 2002. Now, however, after the government's tacit admission that it was powerless to intervene in the stock market, it seemed that nearly all the ghosts of crises past returned to haunt the markets at approximately the same time.

They talked about how the Bank of Japan's attempts to artificially support its stock market were a fiasco, and a second Asia crisis had burst onto the scene. They talked about the economic turmoil in Argentina, Brazil, and Venezuela and how it was spreading to other developing countries. They were concerned about major banks that had bet on those countries through highly leveraged derivatives. They worried about sectors, earlier believed to be safe havens that were now hurting: real estate, highest-grade corporate bonds, and mortgage bonds.

Any outsider overhearing their conversation would have thought they were hard-core gloom-and-doomers. But they saw this as a positive. The crisis would not drag out for years and years. It would soon be over.

"Look at what's happening in the corporate sector," Dulles added. "Remember all those giant corporations that were running low on cash? Remember how they were holding on by the skin of their teeth in anticipation of a government rescue? Well, now, many have suddenly rushed to file for protection under Chapter 11—I mean, Chapter 7—of the Federal Bankruptcy Act! That's liquidation! That means less burden for the courts. That means cleaning the slate for the many new, innovative companies to replace them more quickly."

TIME ACCELERATES

It was this sudden implosion in the early twenty-first century that was called the "gap"—a phenomenon that future historians would never fully understand. "The changes came so swiftly," said one observer, "and the participants were so busy salvaging their own assets or saving their own rear ends that few took the time to record the events."

Some say that the acceleration of change was so great, there actually occurred a reversal in the normal sequence of cause and effect—a "time warp" in which *reactions preceded actions*.

Investors began selling corporate bonds long before it was announced that the New York Fed was abandoning the MetroBank–HarrisJones plan. Stocks in specific companies were dumped even before many corporate insiders *themselves* got wind of impending bankruptcies. But there was no mystical reversal of time. It was strictly a hyperactive rumor mill in which top-secret insider information was routinely and promptly leaked out, and then passed around as quickly as the "love bug" computer virus.

Regardless of the cause, one thing was certain: During the gap, the economy was undergoing a rapid *structural* transformation.

Economists were not ready for this. All their computer models assumed a smooth-working economic system that did not change structurally. They had no way of plugging in catastrophic events like corporate failures or even stock market collapses. Indeed, by definition, their computer programs assumed there could be no tech wreck, no telecom crash, no defaults by major countries, no blowups in derivatives, no giant bank failures in Japan, no unusual disasters whatsoever. Yet it was obvious that these events *were* occurring, and with ever greater frequency.

Tamara Belmont explained this phenomenon to Linda Dedini at a holiday cocktail party at the Press Club. Linda thought about it for a while, then responded with this insight: "When you blow up a balloon, it expands. If you measure how much air is pumped in, you can predict how big the balloon will grow."

"Yes? And?"

"This is what I think economists do with their forecasting models. But to predict when the balloon will burst—and explain what it will look like in the following instant—is another matter entirely. You don't know how to do that. Your—our—knowledge and application of mathematics has simply not advanced that far."

Tamara nodded in agreement but began to defend the thesis of the white paper.

"Don't misunderstand; I'm with you on your report," Linda responded. "I've been with you since that hectic weekend that Dulles called me in to fact-check the tables and charts. I am not challenging you now. I am not even challenging the economics profession. All I'm saying is that we must be more humble and recognize the future is more unpredictable than we usually care to admit."

"You're usually so practical, so precise. Now you've turned philosophical."

"OK. Let me define it more precisely for you: The behavior of continuous processes—like the expanding of the balloon or of our economy—can be understood by using calculus, invented over 300 years ago. Unfortunately, no one has invented an equally effective form of mathematics for explaining and predicting discontinuous phenomena such as we're experiencing now, such as your scenarios. So we're flying by the seat of our pants. We have no way of knowing what the outcome will be."

Tamara, who was a bit on the short side, looked up defiantly to

Linda, who wore glasses and was tall and slim. "But isn't there a silver lining there as well? Doesn't that give us more freedom to steer events, more leverage to have an impact at the right time?"

CRIES FOR RELIEF

Bankruptcies swept the land like a coast-to-coast flood, and many institutions now faced their day of reckoning. Which ones were solvent, which were insolvent? Which would stay afloat, which would go under? Which would be nursed along under Chapter 11 court protection? Which would drown in Chapter 7 liquidation?

These questions were first asked about dot-com companies, other tech companies, then blue-chip companies. Now, they were also being asked about individuals, retailers, manufacturers, utilities, banks, insurers, brokerage firms, universities, foundations, city governments, state governments, and even the governments of major nations.

The answers had little to do with gross size or power. Instead, survival depended primarily upon the amount of cash and capital that the corporation or institution had built up before the most acute stages of the crisis—and the swiftness of protective action from that point forward.

"What's causing this?" asked the president in another of many emergency meetings.

"There are too many fires burning," came the response. "No one has any time anymore to deal with causes."

The U.S. economy needed a rest, a time for reflection and relief, a cease-fire from the bombardment of events.

The first to feel this need were tech companies . . . then Dow companies . . . then major Wall Street firms suffering client flight . . . then major commercial banks as large depositors yanked their uninsured CDs . . . and, finally, giant life insurers as policy holders began to pull money out of life and annuity policies with cash value.

While the stock market was plunging through its previous lows, millions of households could no longer make minimum payments on their credit cards.

Fewer still could pay their first and second mortgages, the single largest category of debt in the nation. As a result, the mortgage delinquency rate soared past what was later called the "absurdity threshold," the level at which it became physically impossible to live up to written contracts, orders, and promises of all kinds.

How could the mortgage service agencies answer all the complaints? How could they handle the legal proceedings against all those who defaulted? What new criteria would the banks use for choosing the cases to prosecute and the cases to write off as losses? The credit card statements, mortgages, repossession notices, and all the other paperwork became just that—a lot of paper and a lot of work. Most important of all: How would the banks and government agencies that issued or guaranteed mortgage bonds pay off investors? It was widely called an "absurd situation."

A grassroots movement took hold. Out of closed-door meetings held throughout the country came the word "moratorium." At first, it was only whispered. But soon it was shouted—as one of the most virulent public demands of the twenty-first century. Moratorium implied some form of global relief—a suspension of debt payments. But precisely how it would be implemented no one knew.

In Silicon Valley in California, Silicon Alley in New York, and other high-tech capitals of the world, leading companies called for special "high-tech support" legislation, harking back to support for R&D provided by the Japanese Ministry of Industry and Trade in the 1970s and 1980s. Meanwhile, they wanted debt relief—government loans or government-guaranteed bank loans.

In Hartford, Connecticut, and other insurance centers of the United States, insurers petitioned their state commissioners for a "policy-loan freeze" to prevent the "disintegration of liquidity." Meanwhile, many banks cried out for relief from withdrawals as the only way to keep their doors open.

The strongest demands for a moratorium came from some of the giant corporations. They used the term "debt freeze" with the argument that if only something could be done to stop the cash drain of debt payments, business would have a chance to improve. They also hoped this would be linked to a postponement of payments on trade credit and interest so that they wouldn't have to file for bankruptcy and further clutter the courts.

The Federal Reserve responded with vehement opposition: "Rather than face the reality of their own insolvency, what these firms are asking for is a kind of 'collective bankruptcy' with another name. They want us to somehow suspend, postpone, or even abolish—as if by magic—all the debt payments they owe. They forget, as usual, about the other side of the ledger: the creditors. For every firm that's granted relief, another—the one owed the money—is driven further into the hole. Since each has borrowed from Peter to pay Paul, any collective defaults will spread from one sector to the next in a chain reaction of bankruptcies."

According to one CEO, "The bottom didn't fall out of our market. It was the market that fell out of our bottom! And we're still trying to find it. We have a fleet of ships floundering at sea. We ran out of cash fuel weeks ago; now, we're throwing the deck furniture into big furnaces called 'debt payments.' And there's still no sign of land." The fleet he was referring to was the electric power industry.

California power companies—besieged by a lopsided deregulation and an acute energy crisis years earlier—weren't the only ones. And the nature of the crisis was also changing: Many of the power companies' big corporate customers were canceling or reducing their accounts. Some were going bankrupt. Almost all companies under financial stress were cutting corners and delaying payments.

Meanwhile, retail accounts, the same families who were delinquent on home mortgage payments, also began defaulting on their electric bills. Electric utilities, along with other utilities, found themselves in much the same position as banks and insurance companies—with a "run" on their already-thin cash resources.

The bank failure rate, which had declined to nearly zero in the late 1990s, surged again. Interest rates, which had fallen, spiked upward. All eyes turned once again to Washington for some solution to the crisis.

CHAPTER

THE BLAME
GAME

As the economy tumbled and people's outrage grew, the first item on the agenda of the Congressional leadership was neither to support nor reject their demands but to determine *who* was responsible for the crisis.

In the Senate, many staffers proposed open hearings, but the leadership, fearful that facts revealed in questioning might further alarm investors, insisted on closed-door hearings instead.

A select committee for "Crash Responsibility" was chosen, and various officials from the White House, the Treasury and Commerce Departments, the SEC, and other agencies were asked to testify. One by one, the officials were grilled—first politely, then mercilessly.

"How did you let it happen?" the senators asked. "How in the world could you have let this disaster strike our country, precisely at this juncture?"

The witnesses answered obliquely, talking freely about economic conditions in general but revealing nothing of substance. They didn't know this was going to happen, they insisted. Nobody could have known.

"Then why didn't you do something *after* it started happening?" the Senators asked. "Did you just sit there passively, eating your popcorn, while the horror show played out before your very eyes?

Have you no concept, no connection to the real world, to the suffering of millions of Americans?"

"We had no idea of what was going to happen in the future, sir. Nobody did," they all repeated, almost verbatim, one witness after another.

"Come on now!" said the committee chairwoman. "You had the best economic minds in the world. You had an economic war room. You must have had some *inkling* of what was going on, some premonition of the financial and fiscal disaster that was about to befall us! Didn't the president get status reports? Didn't he get some warning?"

"Well, yes, there were weekly 'crash status' reports, of course," said one witness finally.

"OK. *Now* we're making some headway here. Let's see those reports. Bring 'em down here."

For the next several weeks, the staff of select committee members pored through stacks of status reports, plus related memos, e-mails, and other assorted nonclassified documents that regularly came across or near the Oval Office. The White House had decided to "bury the bums" in paper and included everything from pizza delivery receipts to cash balance ledgers.

Finally, one day a staffer cried out, "Eureka! Look at this thing!"

Early the next morning, as the closed-door hearings resumed, the chairwoman tapped loudly on her microphone and held up a report so all could see. "Eureka! Look at this *thing!*" she declared. "See? Its title tells all: 'Crash Dangers.' "

"*What* is it?" she asked rhetorically. "It's apparently a lengthy report prepared for a top-ranking official at the White House, dated one month before the worst phases of the panic began. It was coordinated by the Domestic Council and was based on what appears to be submissions from various agencies. Indeed, right here on the first page, it cites, as sources, submissions from the Council of Economic Advisors, Treasury, Commerce, and the CIA. It gives the reader a detailed, point-by-point description of a single, unambiguous crash scenario, a scenario that is, ironically enough, quite reminiscent of what we appear to be experiencing today. It has charts and tables that look like they could have been either ripped out of today's newspapers . . . or Xeroxed from the script of an old horror movie. It has specific prescriptions on exactly how to combat those horrors, prescriptions that were obviously never filled. It is not clear who it was sent to. Nor are the authors' names revealed. So once again, for the third—no, the fourth—time in my long career in this body, my question is, *Who read this and when did they read it? Who knew this disaster was coming and when did they know it?*"

The next witness was a staffer at the White House who coordinated Oval Office meetings. He answered the senator's question very deliberately, perhaps *too* deliberately.

But the senator was an old hand. She had long ago learned how to sense when witnesses or politicians were thinking one thing but saying another. Invariably, they'd pause for an extra second between sentences, or they'd drop in canned phrases to fill small gaps in their response while their minds were obviously racing on some other track. All these subtle hints were dead giveaways. So the senator dug in and pursued the questioning.

"Did the secretary of the Treasury read this report?"

"It all depends on . . ."

"Just answer 'yes,' 'no,' or 'I don't know.' "

"Yes."

"Did any of his staff read this report?"

"Yes."

"What did *they* do with it?"

As the questioning proceeded, a junior staffer who felt *he* deserved to receive credit for discovering the report, left the hearing room, walked outside into the corridor and made a phone call on his cell phone.

The next morning, excerpts of the "Crash Dangers" report were on the front page of the *Washington Post,* and the following day, the full text was in the *Wall Street Journal* and the *New York Times.*

Linda Dedini opened the *Journal,* a bit mangled as usual, and read the article, feeling very surprised to see text that seemed strangely familiar to her. She turned to the inside page and was even more surprised to see a chart that was identical to Tamara's old chart comparing the Dow of 1929–32 to the Dow of the early 2000s. She called Tamara immediately to alert her.

"Yes, I saw it yesterday in the *Post,*" she said, not knowing whether to laugh or cry. "They apparently cut and pasted sections from 'Crisis Benefits' and then combined it with materials from others. Then, it seems they passed it on to the president. But they sliced out all the 'consequences' discussion of Scenario B and kept only the consequences under Scenario A. They stripped out all the hope and left in the gloom. Then they added their *own* policy recommendations, switching all the don'ts of Scenario B to do's! I know excatly how they do that type of thing! I used to see it *all* during my time at Harris."

"Ahah. I get it now," said Linda. "It was a coordinated effort to scare the president into moving forward with his war on the crash."

"No. Actually, I think it may have been something the president or the Treasury secretary requested to help them twist the arm of the Fed chairman—so he'd go along with them on their ill-fated plan to 'save' the stock market. I'm just speculating. But it doesn't matter now. The main thing is someone's going to have to get Congress on a different track before it's too late. They've got to quit playing the blame game and get focused on what they *should* be worried about—the recovery."

ALMOST ALWAYS RELATIVE

Linda was now very much in touch with economic events. Although she was a physicist, her insights on physical principles were so well received by the staff at CECAR that they invited her one day to speak to the group. They didn't specify a topic. "Just come and give us a little talk for about 15 minutes on whatever comes to mind," they said.

However, she took the invitation very seriously. As the troubles in the financial markets deepened, CECAR had grown from a small group of a half-dozen researchers into a major Washington think tank, attracting the most talented minds from the swelling ranks of Wall Street's newly unemployed. The committee had moved to larger quarters near Arlington. There would be over 60 people coming to her "little talk," so she prepared her presentation carefully. At the CECAR auditorium, she delivered it with a passion that surprised everyone.

The greatest unresolved mystery still facing us is how and why, in our post-Einsteinian era, the majority of Americans believed—and still believe—in the "absolute truths" of our time:

That the technological revolution *absolutely* guaranteed economic prosperity.

That a collapse of the magnitude of an Enron or WorldCom was *absolutely* impossible.

That a 1929-32–type stock market decline was *absolutely* unthinkable.

By this time, however, many of these absolute truths have been absolutely shattered. There is a great demand for relative truths, words of relative wisdom that can replace the old.

Yet, many still cannot shake their old habits and are still seeking the same absolute answers. . . .

Among those surprised by Linda's passion was her father. He had always known her as his "little-tall shy girl." He decided to use the same theme in his next speech.

One week later, there were new hearings–this time in the House, this time open to the public. Spectators crowded the visitors' galleries to witness the spectacle. Cable and network news cameras were everywhere. Despite the often technical verbiage, the transcripts of the hearings were the most popular downloads on the Internet, after pornography and music.

In the hearing room, solemn faces abounded. Johnston, one of the star witnesses, provided the following oral testimony:

Most Americans seek an *absolute* forgiveness of debt. Or they want an *absolute* end to the crisis. However, nothing in nature is absolute. Everything is relative.

The selling in the stock market today is a case in point. It is finally being widely admitted that we cannot stop it. It has to run its natural course. However, that raises a new, very urgent question.

Is all buying white and all selling black? Or are there different shades of each, with very different consequences? We firmly believe it is the latter and that it behooves us to look more deeply into the consequences.

Right now, irrational sellers in the United States and abroad are dumping everything, regardless of real value.

They are punishing the dishonest and manipulative companies with a vengeance . . . and they are also punishing the honest, upright companies with nearly equal wrath.

They are closing their stock brokerage accounts regardless of their broker's record. They are pulling their money out of financial institutions regardless of their safety. They are selling the good with the bad.

Tragically, in the wake of irrational selling, even companies with worthy technologies, innovative ideas, and great products are unable to raise capital. Many are hard-pressed to pay their debts. Some are even being forced into bankruptcy, despite good management.

Tragically, brokerage firms with integrity and solid finances are losing business, some falling deep into the red.

Tragically, some banks and insurance companies with an unimpeachable reputation and immaculate balance sheets are losing deposits.

Perhaps most tragically, even investors that make the right choices and buy some of the best assets in the world watch helplessly as their portfolios lose value.

In contrast, *rational* selling has the potential to be a constructive force. Investors would sell the bad but buy the good. They would punish the wayward CEOs but reward the ones that have done the right thing.

Sooner rather than later, the rational selling would open up new opportunities for companies with the best solutions and products. Investors who invested in the best—and dumped the rest—would be richly rewarded.

So, which will it be? Panic or reason? The destructive scenario . . . or the constructive scenario?

Here, too, there is no absolute answer, no black and white. We will invariably have a mix of the two. Reason and emotion will always coexist. Nor can we ever expect one without the other. But we can take concrete steps to encourage reason, whether it be to sell or to buy, and discourage the emotion, whether it be fear or greed.

It is not too late to take all those steps our committee proposed many months ago in midtown Manhattan, *before* the panic began. In my written testimony, I have included a copy of those proposals. They have not changed. Nor are they overly ambitious: Remove all the conflicts of interest from Wall Street! Align the interest of the firms with the real interests of investors! Break down the walls that block the flow of information! Disclose all aspects of risk!

It is also not too late to follow all the recommendations we made to the president's Working Group on Financial Markets one month before the panic phase of the decline began.

Indeed, there has been much ado lately about a report compiled by the Domestic Council entitled "Crash Dangers." However, I reveal now, before this august body and before the American public, the true origin of much of that report. It is this report right here, entitled "Crash Benefits."

I repeat: The original report is not "Crash *Dangers*"; it is "Crash *Benefits*," and its conclusions are exactly the opposite of the infamous report that was in the news earlier in the week.

Its subtitle is "Constructive Propo–"

Before Johnston could finish stating the name of the subtitle for the record, there was a sudden furor in the gallery. Several reporters walked hurriedly to an area near the witness table where copies of the written testimony were available. Others who had already picked up their copies walked to the back of the hall, jamming the exit doors in their haste to file their stories. Johnston waited for the din to subside and then resumed.

As I was saying, the subtitle of our report is "Constructive Proposals for a Lasting Recovery."

As good citizens, what constructive role can we play? How can we further encourage rational selling while discouraging the irrational? More importantly, now can we turn investors to an even more constructive function–rational buying.

The first step is to cease pointing fingers at others. The only appropriate place for that activity is in private, standing before a mirror. I myself have endured that experience once, and I must admit it was a very painful one. Now, we must do so on a national scale, and it will be equally painful. But I survived it, and so can others.

Our second task is to reduce debts. We knew all along that with our debts, we were borrowing from the future. Now, the

future has arrived. We knew that it would be the next generation who pays the price of our excesses. Now, we ourselves are
that generation. . . .

From that point forward, the hearings were so focused on debts
and how to resolve them, they were later dubbed "The Debt
Hearings."

Before the next witness arrived, the chairman of the House
Finance Committee gave a 10-minute speech on savings. He had
always complained, he said, that the savings rate of Americans was
far too low. So he had embarked on a secret quest of his own to
find out how to get Americans to save more.

"All we have to do is boost the savings rates somehow," he said,
"and we'll be over the hump." He asked each witness: "What
would happen if America had a much higher savings rate?"

The next witness was Donald Walker, the former Director of
Research of the now-bankrupt HarrisJones. "If we suddenly shift to
a higher savings rate, the results would be disastrous," he declared.
"The chairman of the Federal Reserve himself testified years ago to
the effect that consumers should save *less* and spend *more*. He felt
that's how we must support the economy, and I agree."

The chairman of MetroBank, also on the witness lineup and
also struggling with imminent bankruptcy, took a different
approach. "Unfortunately, senator, the question implies a great
deal of wishful thinking. Rather than improve, the U.S. savings rate
has plunged. The average American does not have enough savings, enough capital. It's fundamentally their fault our financial
institutions are now suffering a chronic capital shortage."

The congressman threw his hands up in obvious disdain and
disgust as the hearing was adjourned for the day. The following
day, he again called the one witness he hoped would be supportive, Paul E. Johnston.

The senator repeated the question: "Should we not encourage
more savings, and can it happen?"

"Yes, we should! Yes, it can!" Johnston said. "This is *precisely*
what we recommended yesterday. This is the mirror image of the
debt reduction proposals we submitted. One cannot exist without
the other. Let's face it, we were selfish; by incurring so many debts
and living high on the hog, we thought only of ourselves. Now we
need to think of our children and grandchildren."

The congressman leaned back and said, "Throughout these hearings we have heard why this or that solution won't work. Are you here to suggest how we can prevent a panic? Or are you here, just like the others, to talk in grandiose, vague terms while you find holes in the proposals of others?"

"Sir, there *is* no solution—at least not the kind you're looking for—that will solve the problem in a short period of time. You *must* let nature take its course, intervening only to avoid disorderly markets and to keep the core of the financial centers alive."

"OK, then, what is the *long-term* solution?" the congressman insisted, raising his voice.

"Here it is, sir. First, we need a period of reduced living standards and increased savings rates—hard work and sacrifice. Second, we must reorient our production priorities by retooling and recapitalizing. Third, we have to end corporate crime and, more important, redefine what we consider 'criminal' on a corporate level. Fourth, we have to end export subsidies and trade barriers. Fifth, we have to learn to live within our means, to stop sacrificing future generations on the altar of today's latest toys. Sixth, we must let our citizens have full access to *all* the accurate and *unbiased* information they could ever want or need, to be empowered, to take care of themselves, and to preventatively protect their own wealth and their own health."

Johnston leaned forward, speaking softly but deliberately into the microphone. "We thought earlier that corporate corruption and cooked books were the underlying cause of all our troubles. We now have discovered that these where merely the wrappings and trappings of a deeper problem—excessive, unpayable debts. Now, though, when you look beneath the debts, you will find that there is an even deeper layer of social issues that have been sorely neglected, that have done great damage to productivity and to the quality of life. It all ties back to integrity."

"For the economy, what is your definition of integrity?"

"It is growth, with stable populations and stable prices, over a *long* period of time—*real* wealth creation rather than false money and credit. But to achieve that, we need to have *both* good times and *tough* sacrifices occur simultaneously. That implies integrity on an individual level. It means working harder, spending less, and saving more—a fundamental change of values, habits, ethics. This is nothing new. We've done it before; we can do it again. But, clearly, this is more than just a financial shift. It requires a psychological, cultural, and political change. It's already happening, just as a natural reaction to hard times."

He paused to pick up some brochures and waved them in his hand. "Our committee has developed educational information for consumers: 'How to Reduce Debts in Bad Times!' . . . 'How to Protect Your Job in Bad Times!' . . . 'How to Save Money in Bad Times!' Now, we encourage you—Congress and the Administration—to make these available to the public for free, to do a lot more to help people in hard times, to cut debts, to protect jobs, and most important, to *save more!*"

"Aren't we doing that already?"

"No! You're doing exactly the opposite! You're saying to consumers, 'Get out there and spend, spend, spend. Support the economy by spending to your heart's content!' You say nothing about where they're supposed to get the money to spend. Nothing about how much more they're going to have to *borrow* to spend. Then, every single time we get a bit of growth in the economy, we live it up still more. We pile new debts onto our old debts. We create still newer accounting gimmicks to hide them. We launch into new speculative extravaganzas. And we set ourselves up for an even bigger fall soon thereafter."

"This is all getting too wishy-washy for my taste," said the senator. "I have just one practical, down-to-earth question: *How do we get rid of these damn debts now?*"

Johnston did not respond immediately.

"Well? Don't you know the answer to the question?"

"Yes, sir, I certainly do. Right now, a more drastic method is bound to prevail."

"Such as?"

"Chapter 7. Total shutdown of operations. Fire sales. No more Chapter 11. Chapter 11 has been used and abused. The courts are swamped with Chapter 11 cases to the point of paralysis. We don't have enough judges. We don't have enough qualified receivers that can adequately manage thousands of walking-dead enterprises. Except for very special situations, there must be only two choices: Stand up on your own two feet and pay all your bills . . . or Chapter 7 bankruptcy and liquidation. It's the only way to get rid of the deadweight and clear the path for the healthy companies."

"What about the jobs?"

"Would you prefer a good job in a dying company or a not-so-good but acceptable job in a thriving company with an opportunity for advancement?"

With rumors flying around Washington and Wall Street of many *more* major corporations and even banks going under, the talk of Chapter 7 had a ring of truth that stunned the House Committee into a momentary silence.

After a brief pause, another congressman asked, "You're saying that the best solution is to let the system collapse, and with our blessing? Who's responsible for putting this witness in the lineup?" He glanced back at the Congressional staff members. Then, turning back to Johnston, he asked, "How much longer will this crisis last?"

"The longer you try to fight it, the longer it will drag on. The sooner you recognize its inevitability—and work with it—the sooner we can put it behind us. You can slow the process down. You can make it more rational and fairer. You can streamline bankruptcy legislation to unclog the bankruptcy courts. You can do all these things—and more—to try to steer it from a purely destructive force to a more constructive force. But if you go back to bailouts, the crisis will drag the government down. You see, the earlier hearings sought to prove that the White House did not do enough to stop the crash. Our paper, and the events since, prove that it did *too* much. Fortunately, it did not pursue those failed efforts."

"But how do you propose we start the recovery."

Johnston did have a response, but he said little and was excused from the witness table. His committee had now turned its attention to a different goal. It assembled vast financial databases, hoping to begin a new, massive task: Pooling together the few remaining liquid resources around the world to spark a recovery in markets. The committee then hoped these resources could be applied, at the right time, to help bring about a recovery in key financial markets.

Those who joined its efforts would benefit by buying undervalued assets near the very bottom. At the same time, they would help the nation at its time of great need.

Johnston knew, however, that until he had something concrete to offer, any government or international agency would scoff at the committee's efforts. The International Monetary Fund would probably say that the committee suffered from an unhealthy mix of naiveté and illusion. Treasury officials would probably say something similar. He vowed to say nothing in public until he felt the time was right.

HOW TO REDUCE DEBTS IN BAD TIMES

Not all debt is bad. But it's well known that debt can be a financial drug that is highly addictive. Yet banks mail tens of millions of unsolicited credit cards to American households every year, effectively putting free samples of this potential narcotic into the hands of nearly everyone except the homeless. Mortgage companies make millions of unsolicited phone calls offering their "low-rate" mortgages. And even the Federal Reserve chairman himself, in testimony before Congress, urged Americans to spend and borrow more. The consequences are mind-boggling: The most personal bankruptcies in history. Countless divorces attributed to, or aggravated by, debt troubles. Many suicides.

And that's in relatively good times! In bad times, it's worse. If your debt is already feeling burdensome, any loss in income that you may suffer can push you over the brink. And even if you feel your debt is currently manageable, a decline in the economy can suddenly make any debts loom far larger. Deflation (falling prices and incomes) can be especially painful: It makes all debts much harder to pay.

If bad times or deflation strike your household, you may find yourself making only minimum payments on your credit card. You may notice that the balance of your checking account is running low—or running down completely—before the end of each month, and you're drawing into savings to cover the shortfall. You could find yourself filling out applications for extra loans (more debt!) or borrowing from your retirement fund or life insurance policy. Act quickly to prevent these problems. If they are *already* happening, act even more quickly!

If you have significant debts right now, *you could be sleepwalking toward bankruptcy.*

Is bankruptcy an easy way out? No. It can be a lot tougher than you think. And if bankruptcy reform laws are enacted, tougher still. So if there ever was a time to eliminate your debt, *this is it.* Follow these steps:

Step 1: Declare your own personal war on debt. If debt has the potential to disrupt your life and cause your family serious grief, we assure you it is *not* your friend. Focus your mental energy on reducing it.

Step 2: Attack your credit cards first. Get a pair of scissors. Put the scissors on your dining room table. Collect all credit cards in the household, including your own, your spouse's, and those of anyone else for whom you're financially responsible. Put them on the table too. Next, delight in that crisp "snip-snip-snip" sound as you cut them all in half. Enjoy the satisfaction of gathering them all together with one, clean sweeping motion of the hand. Watch with glee as they tumble neatly into the wastebasket.

Step 3: Attack your credit card statements next. Gather every last statement you have. If you don't have all of them, don't fret. You certainly will by the end of the month. On the statement, find the annual percentage rate (APR). At the top of each statement, write down the APR in large numbers. Then, sort the statements with the largest APR at the top, the lowest at the bottom.

Step 4: Add up your minimum monthly payments. Let's say it comes to $200. Isn't it enough to just pay the minimum? No! Credit card companies *deliberately* require very, very low minimum payments. Their agenda is to let you pile up as much debt as possible so they can earn as much interest as possible. How long would it take you to

(Continued)

pay off a credit card with minimum monthly payments alone? It's a joke. Even with all your credit cards now in the trash, if you owe $2,000 on a 17 percent card, it could take you 24 years and cost you $979 in interest alone (on top of the $1,000 principal). So minimum payments are definitely *not* the way to go.

Step 5: Figure out how much you can pay over and above the total of all the minimum payments. Try to pay at least *triple* your minimum. So if your total is $200, that means your goal should be to squeeze at least another $600 out of your budget each month.

Step 6: Pay off the worst ones first! Use 100 percent of the extra $600 to pay off the credit card with the highest interest rate. If two or more cards have the same or almost the same interest rate, send the extra $600 to the one that has the highest balance.

Step 7: Consider using your savings to get out of debt. The rate you're paying is probably close to *10* times higher than the rate you're earning! Not exactly a good deal.

Step 8: Avoid new credit cards. Period. Once you've kicked the credit card habit, don't go back. If you need the convenience of a card, get a debit card. But ask your bank to give you a *true, pure debit card*–not one that comes with a built-in credit card feature. If new ones come in the mail, trash them immediately.

Step 9: Start paying down any other personal loans you may have. If you've been able to get along with $600 less per month in spending money until now, and if your circumstances don't change, you should be able to stick with it. Use it to pay down any other personal loans you may have.

Step 10: Pay down your mortgage. Most people don't realize that all you have to do is to write a larger check than normal, put it in the business reply envelope, and send it to the mortgage company. They will automatically deduct the extra amount from your principal. So, continuing with the earlier example, if your regular mortgage payment is $1,000, write the mortgage company a check for $1,600 every month. You'd be surprised how much more quickly your mortgage will be paid off.

HOW TO PROTECT YOUR JOB IN BAD TIMES

The job cuts of 2002 were unusual for two reasons: (1) they took place when the economy was supposedly "recovering" and (2) they affected almost *everyone* in equal proportion—regardless of ethnic group, origin, gender, profession, job status, or income level. The same will probably be true in the future as well. To protect your job, follow these steps:

Step 1. Check the financial prospects of your company. If its shares are listed on a stock exchange, you can get a rating on the stock by checking with an independent rating agency cited on page 67. If you feel you can't afford to spend a few dollars for the rating, you can also get a free risk rating from Risk Metrics (212-981-7475 or www.riskgrades.com).

Step 2. If your employer does not have shares listed on an exchange, ask for the latest financial statement. If your employer says it is confidential, you can acquire an independent report from Dun & Bradstreet (www.dnb.com).

Step 3. If your company has a weak risk rating or a poor report from Dun & Bradstreet, it's not a good sign. It might do OK in good times, but your job—and possibly the entire company—may be vulnerable in bad times.

(Continued)

Step 4. Needless to say, to secure your income, there are two strategies you can follow:

Strategy A. Do your utmost to make yourself a valuable employee. Seek company-sponsored opportunities for learning new job skills. And even if none are available, allocate at least an hour per day of your spare time to learn skills of value to the firm. With the Internet, you'd be amazed at how much you can learn for free or at a very low cost. And if you do not have access to the Internet from home, free access is available at most public libraries. The librarian should be able to give you some excellent tips on the latest, best sites.

Strategy B. Do your utmost to continually stay on top of the job market. Visit www.monster.com and similar sites to take advantage of a wealth of free information on the most marketable job skills, tips on how to get a job, and updates on what's going on in various industries. Also use these sites to keep your résumé posted on the Web as much as possible.

Step 5. Use the following guidelines to decide which strategy to pursue:

- If the economy is strong and your company is low risk: Pursue Strategy A almost exclusively but continue to stay in touch with what's going on in the job market. If the economy is weak but the company seems to be low risk, pursue both strategies with equal energy.
- If the economy is strong but the company is high risk, pursue both strategies with equal energy.
- If the economy is weak *and* the risk is high, make Strategy B your first priority but do not neglect Strategy A, especially with respect to job skills. If you do change jobs, you will still need those as well.

Don't be afraid of what your employer might think or say about any job-search activities. Make it clear that you *always* stay in touch with the job market no matter what, and if you have no intention of leaving, say so.

HOW TO SAVE IN BAD TIMES

Bad times are likely to bring deflation, and deflation can make you poorer, even drive you into bankruptcy. Or it can make you significantly richer. The choice is yours.

One thing you can do that will make the biggest difference is *saving!* If you can't save, deflation could hurt you. If you *can* save, deflation will help you reap some very nice benefits:

Benefit 1. Your savings will go a long way. When you do spend, you will get more for less.

Benefit 2. At the right time, you will be able to buy great investment bargains. The investment world will be like one giant clearance sale at a major department store.

Benefit 3. Income! Right now, interest rates are low. But even low interest rates are better than a high-interest *expense*. Moreover, if you wait for a time when bond markets have fallen and their yields have risen, you could lock in a relatively high rate for many years to come.

Benefit 4. Even if there is no deflation, you will sleep better at night knowing that you have a good cushion to fall back on in case of any unexpected event. And even if inflation heats up again, you can largely keep up with the inflation by keeping your savings in a money market mutual fund—your interest income is likely to go up more or less in synch with the inflation.

To reap these benefits, follow these steps:

Step 1. Figure out how much you can *comfortably* save each month. Many people aim too high, fail, and then give up. Better to aim low and then stick with it religiously.

Step 2. If at all possible, make sure that money is saved *automatically.* Your employer, your credit union, or your bank will provide additional information on how to set it up. However, make sure it is a safe institution. For a rating on almost any bank, visit www.weissratings.com; for a rating on a credit union, visit www.veribanc.com.

(Continued)

Step 3. If you cannot set up an auto-savings program, resolve to never spend a dime until *after* your monthly savings have been set aside. There is absolutely no expenditure (except basic necessities, of course), which is more important than savings. This has always been true. In bad or deflationary times, it's not even an option. Unless you already have a substantial nest egg, you almost invariably *have* to do it.

Step 4. Let time work for you. You will be absolutely *amazed* at how much money you can accumulate just by putting the same small, comfortable amount away month after month. And that's even without any interest. Once you add the interest, plus the interest on the interest, you will be even more amazed.

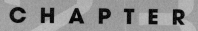

CHAPTER

ROCK BOTTOM

Not all the news was bad. In spite of the turmoil, the stock market system and many of the key financial institutions survived.

If you merely read the headlines during those panicky days, however, you'd probably think the entire brokerage and banking industry was going down the tubes. The financial press, which in previous years had understated the bad news on Wall Street, now did precisely the opposite.

The media poured out story after story of investor abuses. It slammed brokerage firms for their continuing sponsorship of bad advice and banks for their loans to dirty CEOs. It portrayed both financial industries as reckless and irresponsible. Editorials talked about the urgent need for even deeper restructuring, while news stories quoted unnamed government sources bemoaning the futility of *any* reforms in a crisis environment.

Behind the scenes, however, the reality was actually not as bad as it seemed. A lot of the investor abuse cases coming to light had been perpetrated months or even years earlier. They were old news. More importantly, while big corporate failures were making the news, there were several sound companies for every one that went under. The same was true for banks, insurance companies, and brokerage firms.

Indeed, for the investor who was willing to take some risk, this was the ideal time to buy stocks in well capitalized financial companies. But no one wanted them. The overwhelming majority of investors—and even analysts—thought "all" the brokers and banks were going broke and would "never" recover. Some even went so far as to say that the entire capitalist system was "doomed" and that democracy would soon be "dead."

Nothing could have been further from the truth. The United States was still the strongest country in the world—not just militarily but also in terms of its knowledge base. Japan and Germany still had brilliant minds. Canada, Russia, Brazil, Britain, and dozens of smaller nations were bursting with new talent.

Wall Street did not die. If anything, the crisis had taught America some very tough lessons, hardening its resolve and making it better, fairer, and stronger. Those living through it, however, could not see that far. They only saw the dark clouds, which seemed to be getting darker by the hour.

Only a handful of investors saw the light. They bought the stocks of the financial firms with the most capital and the lowest-risk investments and loan portfolios. With time, they doubled or tripled their money. The same would soon be true for investors who bought select companies in nonfinancial sectors as well.

For investors who wanted to take their money out of brokerage accounts, however, it was another story, especially if a failing firm was involved. First, they ran into delays and snags. Second, if they had unusually large accounts, beyond the insured limits, they lost the overage.

Brokerage account insurance—whether public or private—also did not cover losses caused by fraud or even the many cases of unpaid arbitration claims. Investors would walk out of arbitration court, delighted that they had won a settlement or an award from a brokerage firm, only to discover that the firm was already on its way to bankruptcy court to file for Chapter 11 to avoid paying.

But the headlines made it appear as though this was happening to all investors. It wasn't. Those who had brokerage accounts with well-capitalized firms had few such difficulties.

Unfortunately, however, neither the SEC nor the industry could prevent the *appearance* of chaos. Nor could they avoid occasional market gridlock—when trading in key stocks had to be temporarily stopped or when trading in some of the futures markets was halted due to moves beyond the daily allowable limits. These exceptional days also commanded the big headlines, while the many days when trading was normal were played down or ignored. Finally, when it was least expected and pessimism was at its peak, it happened: The stock market hit rock bottom.

BUYING THE BOTTOM

Several months earlier, Linda Dedini happened to be leaving the office of her father's committee when she bumped into her adviser and his wife, also on their way home. Since they both lived in the same D.C. suburb, they shared a cab. She didn't realize it at the time, but as it turned out, the trip was worth a lot more than half the cab fare.

"You said you can't call me when the market hits bottom," she commented to him finally, after his wife tired of twisting her neck to chat from the front passenger seat. "But can't you give me an idea of some of the conditions that will prevail at the time? I've got to know that—not just for the reverse index fund and the put options but for everything. I need to know it for my other investments, for our whole life plan. Please, can't you just give me some hints?"

The adviser was still reluctant. He said all one had to go by was history and that events were already smashing most historical records. But she insisted, and he complied.

"Dividends. Start with dividends. Remember those regular little checks you used to get from the company? Back in the good ol' days of investing?"

"Not really. My stocks never paid dividends. Anyhow, what about them?"

"They're critical. Back in the bubbling '90s, most investors paid no attention whatsoever to dividends. 'Who the hell cares if the checks they send me are ridiculously small?' they asked. 'So what if CEOs only share a few lousy crumbs of profits!' they said. 'Just make sure our stock prices go through the roof, and we're happy campers!' "

"And now?"

"Now, with the market falling apart, they *still* don't pay much attention to dividends. They're too shell-shocked from the losses. Now they're saying, 'If I have to sit around waiting for damn dividend checks, it's going to take three thousand four hundred and God knows how many years for me to recoup my losses!' Then they throw in something like, 'Wanna talk about dividends? Go walk my dog. He'll listen to whatever you have to say.' "

They laughed, and he continued. "When you get down near the bottom of the crash, it'll be the same thing. If you're paying close attention to dividends, you'll probably be one of the lonely few. You *should* pay attention, though. You'll probably see that most stock prices are so low—so, *so* low—that even the meager dividend payments are going to give you a pretty attractive yield on the stocks."

"How's that?"

"Say the company sends you a dividend check each quarter for 25 cents per share, or $1 over the course of a full year. And suppose that stock costs $100. How much is that in percentage terms?"

"One percent?"

"Right. Now suppose the stock plunges to $10 and they're still sending you $1 per share in dividend checks each year. How much would that be in percent?"

"Ten percent. Wow! I see your point. Ten percent is a great dividend yield!"

"Exactly. Even if they cut your dividend check in half, you're still getting 5 percent—quintuple what you were getting before. When you start seeing that type of thing all over the place, I figure you're going to be very near a real bottom in the market."

"What else?"

"Value, of course. Trouble is, with so many companies just struggling to stay in the black, earnings are not a very reliable measure of value. You're going to have to look at some other things too—like total revenues."

"Is that the same as 'sales'?"

"Yes. Let's say, for example, that you bought one share in an average S&P 500 company. And let's say that one share cost you $20. The question is, How much does the company have in sales to back up the value of your one share? Well, back in the fall of 2002, for example, even after the market had taken a big plunge, the average S&P 500 company was selling for 1.17 times sales."

"In other words—"

"In other words, if a stock sold for $20 per share, it would have revenues of about $17 per share."

"Is that good or bad?"

"Bad."

"Why?"

"Because if you're going to invest your hard-earned dollar in a company, you want them to be taking in a lot more than $1 in total revenues for the entire year! Remember, we're talking sales, not profits!"

"I get it now. But how much would be considered good?"

"Normally, at typical market bottoms, I'd say the stock is cheap and it's good to buy if you can get it for 0.7 times sales or less. But in a panic, when you don't know *who* is going to be dumping big blocks of the company's shares tomorrow, I'd say I'd want to wait until it's even cheaper. Perhaps 0.5 times sales, perhaps less."

"So that means—"

"It means that the price of the stock would have to be selling for *less* than the sales per share, a lot less. Maybe for *half* the sales, or lower. For example, that stock we talked about a moment ago: How much did I say it was again?"

"The $20 stock?"

"Right. Let's say we're close to a bottom now and we want to buy a stock that's selling for $20. You'd want it to have at least $40 in sales per share, maybe even more."

"But will it still be selling that high? $20?"

"No, no. I wasn't talking about the same exact stock. But you get the point. If you're buying a stock that costs $10, you should have at least $20 in sales. If your stock costs $5, then $10 in sales, etc. Clear?"

The adviser looked out the window and noticed they were just about to arrive. His wife was digging into her purse, but Linda told her not to bother. "I'll take care of it," Linda said. "I'm getting off last." Then, flustered that the conversation was about to end so soon, she turned back to Dulles and asked, "Any others?"

"Yeah, many." The cab pulled over, Dulles got out, opened the front door, and waited while his wife, ignoring Linda's offer, paid the driver. She gave him an extra $10 to cover the rest of the ride plus the tip, but Linda didn't even notice as she listened intently to the adviser's last words. "High cash level of mutual funds.

Climactic trading volume. Outrageously pessimistic sentiment. Desperate economic conditions. Major, dramatic government action. Sorry. Gotta run now. Call me later for all the details."

The next time they spoke, however, it was about other subjects, and several months later, Linda felt like kicking herself for having dropped the ball on such an important matter. She was absolutely convinced she had missed the big bottom and told her adviser how she had been a "total idiot" for having failed to get all the details.

"You're looking for the Holy Grail that doesn't exist," the adviser said flatly.

"What do you mean?"

"You're looking for the 'big bottom.' Well, there is no 'big bottom.' Each major sector hits bottom at a different time, maybe even in a different year. You know when utility stocks hit bottom in the twentieth-century Depression?"

"Around the early 1930s or something? 1931? 1932?"

"Surprise! It was 1942—almost 10 years after industrial stocks hit their bottom. Government bond prices hit an important bottom long *before* the stock market, and low-grade corporate bond prices at about the same time. It's all over the lot. This time, who knows what's going to touch down first. Actually, it's probably easier to look at which ones will *take off* first. I figure it will go more or less in *quality order.*"

"Say that again."

"In other words, line up all your asset classes and all your investments in order, starting with the highest-quality, most liquid investments and ending with the lowest-quality, most speculative, most illiquid investments. That's probably about the same order that people will start buying 'em in—and bid up their prices."

"For example?"

"For example, at the front of the line you've got Treasury bills. Then Treasury notes and Treasury bonds. Next—high-quality corporate bonds, followed maybe by preferred stocks in the companies with the strongest balance sheets and value. Then, common stocks in those same companies. Speculative stuff, like junk bonds and penny stocks are bound to be last."

"What about the convertible bonds? They give me a good yield now, and later I can convert them into common stocks. Are they safe?"

"Depends on the rating. High ratings—probably around the same time as the good corporate bonds. Low ratings will probably take a lot longer. All this is pure guess work, mind you. *You* will know a heck of a lot more about all of this *then* than *I* do *now*."

"What to do you mean by *that?*"

"I mean our conjecturing now may be fun and entertaining, but its value is inferior to what you'll be seeing with your own eyes on site—right there while it's happening."

"But I'm afraid I've *already* missed the bottom in the blue chips, in the Dow. Don't you agree? Don't you think that was *the* bottom we saw a couple of months ago, while Dad was testifying, and the sentiment was so negative?"

"Not necessarily. Many good investments could have multiple bottoms. So if you miss the first one, you probably can pick it up on the next round." He paused for a moment, then asked, "Have you ever taken a flight where they use a bus to shuttle people from the terminal to the aircraft?"

"Yeah, but—"

"It's the same thing. The shuttle bus keeps coming back several times to pick up passengers for the same flight. If you miss the first bus, no problem; you get on the next."

"Suppose you miss the flight?"

"You catch the *next* flight. So maybe it'll be more expensive. So what? You still get there, don't you?"

The adviser was right. As the market bounced wildly along the bottom, the trading volume in stocks was unprecedented. But after a few months, the indexes still had gone virtually nowhere. It was like the "great capitulation" everyone had been waiting for but *without* more significant price declines. And it was this not-so-little wrinkle that tripped up most of the gurus who tried to time the market.

Another aspect that threw these market timers off track was the cash position of mutual funds. The general rule of thumb they followed: If stock mutual funds had about 10 percent or more of their assets in cash, that was the sign of good potential buying power and a likely market bottom.

But at this point, the mutual funds could barely keep up with investors who wanted to yank their money out. So instead of building a cash position, they kept using up almost all their available cash just to meet investor demands. It wasn't until the market had bounced off the bottom repeatedly for several months and stabilized that the mutual funds started building cash again. And it wasn't until they had a few months of positive cash inflows that they started buying in any meaningful way.

Everywhere, there was still an unquantifiable amount of selling—investors who had held on till the bitter end and were now finally throwing in the towel . . . investors who sold because they needed the money to save their business or put food on the table . . . small investors and large investors . . . investors residing in the United States, Canada, Germany, Japan, Hong Kong, Singapore, Taiwan, and Latin America.

There were even many investors who sold just because they discovered that they were all alone and everyone else they knew was already out.

"I thought you said you were still hanging in there," one elderly retiree asked another by a Century Village swimming pool in South Florida.

"No, no. I've been out of the market now for a *long* time. Didn't I tell you?"

The fact is, he didn't. When these particular investors sold, they did so quietly, embarrassed to admit they had taken a beating. It was only after the market fell a lot further, making that decision look prescient, that they finally told their friends about it. What they didn't realize was that being "alone" was often a good thing, especially at critical turning points.

Despite all the selling pressures, however, equally strong buying appeared whenever the Nasdaq, Dow, or S&P indexes approached the bottom. It was indeed the beginning of the end for one of the greatest bear markets in American history. It was not, however, the end of the crisis—let alone the beginning of a new bull market.

Governments all over the world made announcements to rally their economies. Japan: "The pain does not end, but the time to heal has arrived." France: "It's time for all citizens of the Republic to reinvest their confidence in their country." Britain: "The real recovery will soon begin."

Markets ignored them. Rallies collapsed. Both the Nasdaq and the Dow bounced up and down off the bottom for many months.

GOLD

One day, when trading in some markets was temporarily halted and some banks had closed their doors, Johnston's secretary told him he had an urgent, almost frantic call from his son-in-law, Gabriel Dedini. Johnston picked up the phone immediately.

"What's up?" he asked.

"What's up? Nothing's up. Everything's down, and going down much, much, much further. I'm not talking just about the stock market. The stock market is already history and everyone knows that. I'm talking about real estate. I'm talking about the banks, the insurance companies, the government, the entire society. Remember, I'm a citizen now. I love this country. My children—your grandchildren—were born here. I get no satisfaction out of this, but I know what I'm talking about. I *know.* I was there with my parents when the economy—almost the whole society—collapsed in Argentina. Now, the same thing is going to happen here in America. I can feel it in my bones. Everything I see confirms it."

"Such as what?"

"Such as the demonstrations on Wall Street. The people marching down Wall Street shouting and banging their clipping machines or whatever that metal thing is. In Argentina, they did it with pots and pans. So what's the difference? And look at those mobs at that one bank in Los Angeles! This is just the beginning, I tell you."

"I can understand your sentiment. It's natural when things are this bad, but—"

"Hah! That's *exactly* what they said in Argentina. They said, 'Things are so bad, they couldn't possibly get any worse.' They were wrong. Things got much worse. When the government announced the biggest default in history, they said it couldn't get any worse. Then the government announced the biggest devaluation in history. When the banks closed down 'temporarily,' they said it couldn't get any worse. Then the banks swallowed our money *forever!* And, by the way, I'm talking about *American* banks with Argentinean subsidiaries, where we kept our money in *American* dollars! We lost three-quarters of our money!"

"Calm down, Gabriel. Let's look at this with more reason and less emotion."

"I know what you're thinking! It's what most people think. They think Argentina is just one of *those* "south of the border" places. I can assure you, it is not. It is—or at least was—an advanced, mostly middle-class, democratic, industrial, highly educated society, just like here in the United States. It happened there. It can happen here."

"Do you really believe that it can get worse?"

"There you go again—just like they did in Argentina! In Argentina, when the economy collapsed and jobs disappeared, they said it couldn't possibly get any worse. Guess what? Society collapsed. Kids out of college, even professionals went into the scavenging business. You know what that really means? That means spending 12, 14 hours a day with your little children by your side, digging through the muck and the grime of the city dump. Middle-class people! People with college degrees! So everyone said, 'Now it *certainly* can't get any worse than *this.*' But it did. Violence! Violence and bloodshed were next! The *narcotraficantes* took over. They shut down Buenos Aires. Over in Brazil, in the midst of a democratic presidential election, the *narcotraficantes* virtually shut down São Paulo. That's why I got my parents the hell out of there."

"I've read about some of that. Is it really that bad?"

"No! It's worse—much, much worse than what you read. There's nothing you can put on a printed page, nothing you can put into words that could possibly describe it. You have to see it to believe it. You have to be there in person to feel it in your gut, to understand it in your heart."

"How come you've never talked about this before?"

"Are you kidding? I've been telling Linda about this for many months. I told her it was coming—not just to Argentina, but also to Uruguay, Paraguay, Brazil, Venezuela, the Caribbean, Mexico, then here. At the reception, when your wife's father passed away, I practically was giving public speeches about this to anyone who would listen—by the pool, in the parking lot, all over the place. Didn't you see me? Didn't you hear me? You were there, weren't you?"

"I was, I was, but I was preoccupied with my draft proposal and . . ."

"*Jesus!*" Gabriel exclaimed. Then he was silent for a moment and made an attempt to shift to a less alarmist, more practical approach, slowing his tempo. "The real question now is, What are we going to do about it?"

"I honestly don't know. What do you have in mind?"

"Your committee! Your committee needs to give up trying to save people's money and start saving people's *lives*–starting with our family. We need to get as many people out of here as you can, out of the cities and into the countryside where they can at least defend themselves against the mobs. We sold our country home to play the stock market and lost it all. You still have a place in the . . . in the . . ."

"The Appalachians."

"Yes, the Appalachians. And the family inheritance! You need to help me–help us–persuade Linda to get the hell out of everything she's investing in now and move it to a safe haven, a *true* haven. What are those Treasury investments going to be worth when they shut down the Treasury Department? What are those puts going to be worth when they shut down the put exchange? *Una putaria!* That's what it will be–a whorehouse! And the mutual funds? Mutual funds will be worthless, and the managers will skip the country."

"I can't say I agree. But let's assume for a moment that you're right. What would *you* do with the money?"

"There's only one investment that will survive this. Gold. Bullion bars. Bullion coins. I wouldn't even trust rare coins. Did you see what gold has done already? It's gone *through the roof.* That's where I have my parents' money, and they're making a bloody fortune. When society collapses, that's the only thing that will have value, the only thing you'll be able to exchange for food and shelter and weapons to defend yourself. You talk about a recovery, but there will be no recovery. No one has any money to invest in a recovery. Soon, everyone will be running for the hills, literally."

Johnston was momentarily taken aback and said he'd think it over carefully. He went back to the round glass table by the pool, where the water reflected the rays of a quarter crescent. Yes, Gabriel's logic seemed clear: Argentina, a predominantly middle-class society, had suffered a financial collapse that had torn apart the fabric of their society. Now the United States, also a mostly middle-class, industrial, and educated society, has suffered a similar financial crisis. Ergo, what was to protect American society from a similar fate? Johnston understood the logic, but he still didn't agree.

Argentina, dependent on foreign capital, foreign trade, and foreign banks, had lost effective control over its own destiny. The United States, despite its dependency on the outside world, had a better opportunity to regain control. And, ultimately, there was also hope for Argentina.

If the U.S. Government had intervened too aggressively, dragging the crisis out for many years, Gabriel's arguments might have been more credible. But precisely the opposite was happening. The decline was relatively quick. The government had turned its focus primarily to meaningful reform. The dollar had stabilized. Overall, the actual events were conforming mostly to the *less* pessimistic scenario that Tamara had outlined in her report months earlier.

Yes, Gabriel was right about gold. It *had* surged in value. But it did not reflect the true inevitability of social chaos as Gabriel said. It merely reflected the spreading *belief* that such chaos was inevitable.

Yes, Gabriel was right about the danger of market shutdowns in futures, options, and stock markets. But the market shutdowns were not virtually permanent, as Gabriel implied. They were temporary, paving the way for solid bounce-backs.

It was also very true that most people did not have available funds to reinvest. There were, however, many individuals and institutions that had managed to stay out of risky investments throughout the decline, who were anxious for the right moment to jump in on the ground floor.

There was one more item Gabriel was right about. It was *not* the time to invest in put options and reverse index funds. Rather, it was *the ideal time to go back into high-grade corporate bonds and common stocks*–provided investors waited for the big dips.

They could pick up solid blue-chip companies at prices far below their book value. They could buy into firms with still-excellent prospects for growth at a time when they were shunned by the consensus of Wall Street analysts. And they could secure for themselves a big stake in America's future with a relatively small nest egg of cash. Many opportunities abroad—in some of the countries most devastated by the crisis—offered even greater profit potential.

In the United States, the biggest bargains of all were the few good apples in the most battered industries—including some high-tech companies. Earlier, near the market's peak, investors failed to notice that these companies were financially weak. All they cared about was sales growth. And so, when the first went bankrupt, they got caught by surprise.

Now, near the bottom of the market, investors made the same mistake—in reverse. They failed to consider that some companies had strong finances, and they continued to sell the stocks anyhow—just because it was in an industry that had gotten clobbered. However, if they had some cash readily available, they could buy the shares for a pittance and make a very handsome profit just as soon as the worst of the panic was over. Later, after a true recovery in the economy got underway, their investment would be worth even more.

Often they would find a company that held valuable patents and had an inside track on the most promising new technologies in the world—wireless, biotechnology, or fiber optics—but had floundered because of financial mistakes: A high-interest loan from a bank, a bond issue that it couldn't keep up with, uncollected bills from customers.

Or, better yet, they could occasionally find a firm that had an impeccable balance sheet but whose stock was battered simply because the nature of its business was similar to another, larger firm that had gone belly-up. In fact, it was this "panic by association" that helped to generate some of the greatest bargains of all.

Which ones were the best? Most of Wall Street was no longer able to give the answer, primarily because so many analysts, assuming they were still employed, were shell shocked by the panic. They weren't looking for bargains.

That was a shame. Back during the prepanic period, if investors had erred on the side of caution by placing their money into the safest possible investments, they could now afford to err somewhat in the opposite direction. With a modest portion of their assets, they could take some risks that most investors at the time might have considered "aggressive." With time, they would be richly rewarded with gains several times their initial investment.

However, it was absolutely essential that they continued to keep a portion of their money safe. In those final days of the panic, the nation was in unchartered waters. No one really knew what would happen next. Until they had solid confirmation that the economy was on the recovery track, it was unwise to commit all of their assets.

THREE INTEREST-RATE MOVES

Even while Gabriel was on the family line with her father, Linda was getting ready to call her new broker to give him a long list of buy orders. As she was put on hold for a few seconds, waiting for the broker to pick up, her mind flashed back to the final, critical meeting that triggered this momentous decision in her now-stellar investment career.

Her adviser had been ill and was unavailable. So, on the occasion of a holiday dinner at the Johnston residence, she asked her father for his opinion. "I'm afraid of stocks, Dad. I still can't shake off the experience I had with stocks last time, and I've done so well without them. Everything I see tells me it's time to go back into the market, but I also say to myself, 'my current program isn't broke—why fix it?' "

Johnston warmed up when he realized his daughter was finally asking his opinion about investments—or about anything, for that matter. "How well *have* you done?" he asked.

She fetched a file folder she had left on the China cabinet and pulled out a sheet printed from Excel. Down the left side were the investment categories, and across the top of the columns were headings such as "investment," "maturity," "purchase price," "current price," "closed or open," "gain/loss—percent" and "gain/loss—$." Down the right-hand side was a bolded number in the last column showing the total dollar gains for each investment category, plus another bolded number in the previous column showing the average percentage gains.

Johnston leaned over, gently placing his hand on his daughter's right shoulder while squinting at the spreadsheet. "I'll probably have to get my reading glasses, but what's this first investment category? Treasuries?' "

"Yes," she responded meekly.

"That's interesting. You have some *long-term* bonds in there. I was under the impression you said your adviser was against those. Or was it Oliver who was telling you not to buy them?"

"Actually, they both were, Dad. But I figured I needed the yield. So I bought a few anyhow. Did I do the wrong thing?"

"No, no! Look! Those bonds have just kept going up and up. We all thought they were going to tank, and they did for a while, but now they've come back nicely and you have nice capital gains in them. How did you know?"

"I didn't *know*. But about a year ago, while I was hanging around your office, I asked Oliver for his opinion on some old charts I had found on interest rates back in the 1930s. I also thought it would be something Tamara would be interested in. I left the charts on his chair for at least a week, but neither of them paid much attention. They were too busy working up their report on the stock market. So one day, I got tired of waiting and just went back into his office to retrieve my charts. Would you like to see them?"

"Yeah, sure."

"I love charts, and in my field I can't live without them. So a while back, while I was struggling to squeeze some more yield out of my portfolio, I started looking into interest rate charts and just happened to find these old ones from an old, dog-eared Federal Reserve chart book. It was sitting in the pile of things to be thrown out from the committee's research library." [See Figure 23.1.]

"What is it?"

"It's interest rates in the 1930s. Treasury bills, Treasury bonds, corporate bonds, etc."

"No kidding!"

"Yup. See? I drew some vertical lines in it. Those are the phases. Like phases in the moon—only there were just three."

"Tell me more!"

"OK. Phase 1 was a sharp decline in rates. Tamara told me that's when the Federal Reserve pushed interest rates down to soften the blow of the stock market decline, to avert a rapid fall in the economy. Tamara also told me the other day that history

Mass Interest-Rate Moves in the 1930s

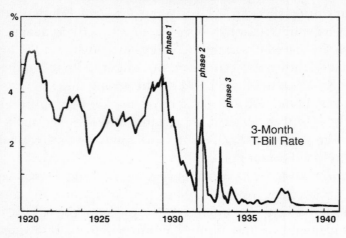

3-Month
T-Bill Rate

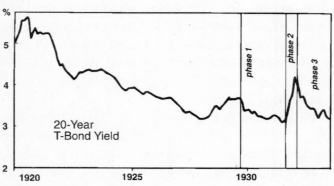

20-Year
T-Bond Yield

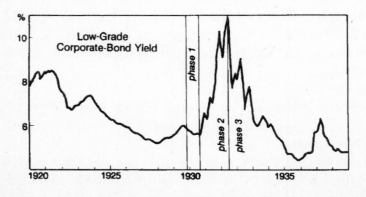

Low-Grade
Corporate-Bond Yield

blames the Fed for causing the Great Depression because they didn't do enough. But they sure got these Treasury bill, or T-bill, rates down there, didn't they? Look at those T-bill rates plunging in this chart during phase 1."

Johnston's mind drifted to the 'blame game' of the recent Congressional hearings. Did history also make a similar mistake about the 1930s—blaming the Fed for a depression that it couldn't have possibly prevented? But before he could explore an answer, Linda brought him back to the charts.

"Phase 2 was an upward spike in interest rates which no one expected—a big collapse in bond prices. Tamara says she's not sure what caused it. I figure it was because of some of the things my adviser told me about a long time ago—you know, the need, the fear, the envy."

"Huh?"

"Never mind that now. The main thing I wanted to show you was Phase 3. That's when the spike ended and interest rates fell back down to normal levels. That was the true end of the panic."

"Sounds like a darn important turning point to me."

"It sure was. And similar things seem to be happening this time too. Not just for the country but for me personally. When Phase 2 ended and Phase 3 began—that's when my bonds really started looking great. I bought them a bit early, granted. But I've locked in some truly nice yields—for decades. Then, when those yields plunged, just like they did in the 1930s, guess what happened to the value of my bonds?"

"I don't have to guess, Linda. It's right here in your spreadsheet. Your bonds soared in value. You've got huge potential capital gains in them. You really did great there. Congratulations! Good thing you didn't buy them *too* soon, or you would have gotten caught in

Figure 23.1 (p. 320) In the 1930s, interest rates moved down, up and then down again, in three distinct phases: In *Phase 1*, all interest rates declined due to deflation and the Federal Reserve's attempt to counter the deflation. In *Phase 2*, interest rates abruptly turned around and exploded. The 3-month Treasury-bill rate jumped by over sixfold—from about a half percent to 3 percent. Yields on the 20-year Treasury bonds surged beyond their pre-Crash peaks. And the yield on low-grade corporate bonds literally went through the roof, hitting 11 percent. In *Phase 3*, however, interest rates fell sharply. The best time to buy long-term bonds was at the end of Phase 2 or the beginning of Phase 3.

our modern-day version of this Phase 2–this period when rates surged and bond prices plunged. Great!"

Johnston leaned over a bit further, again squinting at the spreadsheet. "Uhm . . . let's see here, what else have you got . . . what the he—!"

A bolded number near the bottom right of the sheet caught his eye and his jaw fell open. "Are you sure you've got the decimal points right in this total?"

"It's gotta be right. It's an Excel formula that sums these ranges here."

"No kidding! Linda, this is incredible! Do you realize what you've done here? Do you realize that you and Gabriel are now wealthier than your mother and I?"

Linda was both proud and saddened. She folded the spreadsheet and turned to face him. "How can that be? You were with UCBS for years. Your total pay was several million before you retired! There's no way I could have more than you do. What did you do with all that money?"

"Unfortunately, I lost a lot of it in UCBS stock. Like a dummy, I held on to the bitter end. Plus, I've been a lousy fund-raiser for the committee. I knew how to do it for a regular corporation alright, but a nonprofit? I didn't have a clue. I should have hired someone to do that, but I kept thinking, 'I can do this myself. I know how to do this better than anyone.' Not very smart! In any event, I just kept making contributions out of my personal checking account, always figuring I'd raise funds from outside sources later. You'd be surprised how much you can chew up with a few years of big overhead, a bunch of big names, and heavy advertising. But forget about me! The more important question is, What are *you* going to do with all this money?"

"Let's not go there right now. You have your causes, I have mine," Linda responded softly.

"No, no. I'm not talking about what you're going to use the money for. I'm asking what you plan to reinvest in? You're not going to let it sit in Treasuries and these bear market investments forever, are you?"

"That's what I wanted to ask you about."

"Ask *me?* Are you joking? Look at those numbers again! I should be asking you for advice. No, your *adviser* should be asking you for advice! So let me throw the question back to you. What do *you* think you should be doing now?"

"Buying! Buying with both hands—and feet. Buying the bottom, even if it's not the exact bottom. I figure I should be going in there right now and buying every darn company I can lay my hands on that isn't going broke."

"You realize you'll be practically the only one buying right now. Practically everyone I know is still selling. Does that bother you?"

"No."

"Good for you, because it shouldn't! Your grandpa sure as heck didn't care who else was buying or selling when he bought his GMs and his IBMs for pennies on the dollar."

"No, I guess not." She saw no point in sharing her grandfather's secret.

"Plus, you've been alone on the way down, haven't you? Look at these weird mutual funds you've got! Look at these crazy put options! What percent of the population invested in this kinda stuff? What percent of those investors you think bought put options when this market was starting to crash? One percent? One-hundredth of a percent? And among those, how many actually knew what the heck they were doing? One-half? One-fourth?"

"I don't know," Linda responded.

"Well, isn't it true that 80 percent of the options in the market expire worthless? Obviously you've been very, very much alone all along. One of a very rare species. What did you use?"

"Mostly the reverse index funds. That's where I put the larger chunk of the money. The put options had the biggest percentage gains, but I couldn't see risking as much there, because they're so volatile."

"I understand, but what indicators did you use? How did you actually do it?"

"Overall, I'd say part luck, part just doing the same thing I do in lab—seek precision; expect errors. Talking about errors, my loss ratio on the puts was also pretty darn lousy—almost 70 percent. But among the 30 percent winners, I had some home runs; then those home runs gave me the capital to buy a few more good ones on the next rally, and the next rally, and on an on. But the main thing was that I was playing the market to go down, and that's what it did—it went down. I figure if I had been doing this in a bull market, I would have just poured more and more money down a drain, just like you did with the commit—. Oh, geez! I'm so sorry, Dad, I didn't mean for it to come out that way. I do respect—"

"Don't apologize! Look, lots of investors and regulators have been screaming bloody murder at CEOs like me, forcing them to give back their ill-gotten gains. Look at how much Spitzer sued them for! And they were my friends, my mentors—or my rivals. Hard to believe, isn't it? So I look back at my own not-so illustrious career as a CEO and I say to myself, 'Self, you gave back yours too—just in another way.' Getting back to you, though, are you going to go ahead with your stock-buying program?"

"Should I? I'm afraid."

"Afraid of what? Take a piece of this not-so-small fortune you have here. Take 10 percent, 20 percent. I don't know. Start small. If you feel that strongly about it, invest more. But if this is the real turn—in the markets, in the economy—you don't have to do all your buying now. You can do it in stages, one step at a time, adding as you go."

"Actually, I was thinking of 10 percent of our money in common stocks and 20 percent in convertible bonds?"

"What do the convertibles do for you?"

"I figure the convertibles are great when you're searching for a bottom but not sure you've found it. If the stocks go down, you still have a good yield. If the stocks go up, you participate in that too—maybe not as much as in the common stocks but almost."

Johnston nodded and smiled with pride. His daughter truly did not need his advice or anyone else's. She was doing just fine entirely on her own.

CHAPTER 24

THE DARKEST DAY

A furor of protest swelled up from every town and city in America. Again, you could hear the new word, the word that most people did not fully understand—"moratorium."

It appeared in the newspapers, on TV debate shows, on Internet chat rooms, and in the Congressional debt hearings. It was on the posters and placards of protesters. On Wall Street and on Main Street, and even from within the White House itself, the plea could be heard.

The Federal Reserve chairman retired. But his successor did little to stop the turmoil.

Municipal and federal employees walked out anytime a paycheck was late. The slogan was simple: "No pay, no work." They weren't bargaining for raises or better benefits; all they wanted was their regular paychecks.

In some states, banks suffering large withdrawals had gotten permission from the Federal Deposit Insurance Corporation (FDIC) to allow their depositors to take out no more than $100 each day. Mobs of depositors lined up at their banks, overflowing into the streets, protesting loudly if their money wasn't produced immediately. Some, taking a verse from the 1930s, chanted slogans: "This is not a bread line. No more crumbs!"

The nation appeared to be on the brink of total chaos.

All eyes focused on one man—the president of the United States. In the months following his decision to abandon the Harris–MetroBank rescue plan, he had grown increasingly frustrated with the advice he had been receiving from his closest aides. On several occasions, he was said to have banged his fist on his desk in an unusual expression of presidential anger, saying: "I want an alternative plan! I want a constructive, rational plan!"

None was forthcoming.

It wasn't until the crisis literally spilled over onto the streets that the president appointed a new group of lenders and experts to various high government posts. He had already appointed a new Fed chairman. In addition, key posts were given to Paul E. Johnston, the founder of CECAR; Tamara Belmont, the widely respected chief economist at CECAR; and others from independent think tanks. They met with the president for a weekend of intensive talks at Camp David.

The peaceful tranquility of the Maryland mountain retreat belied the economic confusion in the world at large. But the president made no effort to mask his desperation.

"The people say they want a 'moratorium,' " the president said, "but no one seems to know what a moratorium really is or what its true consequences would be."

The newly appointed Fed chairman was the first to respond. "A moratorium is a suspension of debt payments. But that is impossible. As my predecessor repeatedly warned, people have to realize that they are not just debtors. They are also creditors. If you have money in a bank, you're a creditor. If you own shares in a money market mutual fund, you're a creditor. And creditors don't get paid during a blanket moratorium. No, a moratorium is absolutely out of the question. It cannot and must not be allowed!"

"What we need," continued the chairman, "is a *general holiday*. In a general holiday, nothing is forgiven. Quite the contrary, we will all have to meet our obligations. But we stop the panic. We stop this madness before it causes social and political chaos."

"I don't understand," said the president.

"Instead of just shutting down one market, we shut down everything."

"Everything?"

"Everything! Markets, factories, banks. Everyone is running around like a madman. There is no order. We've got to step in there and shout out 'freeze!' That way, we stop the withdrawals on banks and other bank-like financial institutions. Simultaneously, we impose a coordinated freeze on all financial markets and transactions—a temporary stoppage that will last for no more than a few days, perhaps a week at the outside. Then, while all is quiet, while you can hear a pin drop and we have everyone's attention, we map out a plan to restore confidence, just like FDR did when he first stepped into office in the early 1930s."

The president slumped back into his armchair. "It's a final act of desperation."

"Yes, it is. But there are no other solutions."

The president disregarded the last comment. "I'm afraid it would be a dark tunnel, and that the only light at the end of that tunnel will be the headlight of a speeding locomotive. How could we ever survive it?"

The new Fed chairman spoke emphatically. "Sir, you have no choice. You are already in the tunnel. You already have a de facto banking holiday, a de facto production holiday, a de facto market holiday. In addition, you have agricultural surpluses in rural areas and acute shortages in urban areas. Why? Because you have transportation bottlenecks, communication failures, World Wide Web shutdowns, and excessive cutbacks of essential services in financially troubled municipalities. All because they ran out of money! Because credit was destroyed. You have to do something drastic to slow down the maddening pace of the panic, to gain control, to smooth it out, to restore faith."

The president nodded slowly and deliberately. "But what do you suggest we do to get the country going again?" he queried.

"First, let me cite what we cannot do. Many people in debt hope that the moratorium will get them off the hook. This cannot be. We cannot suspend—let alone wipe out—real contractual relationships between real institutions with a wave of the magic wand. To clean out debts, all of us—businesspeople, bankers, bureaucrats—have to meet face-to-face and hash it out. We must reorganize and rebuild, even if it means big cutbacks and greater sacrifices—a long, arduous process we won't accomplish overnight."

Paul Johnston and Tamara Belmont glanced at each other. The

Fed chairman was saying very much the same things that had been in the committee's reports, in Johnston's speeches, and in his Congressional testimony. So they let the new chairman do the talking and said very little.

"Now here's what we *will* do," the Fed chairman continued. "We will honor—at all costs—the government's obligation to the public. That is the absolute minimum requirement, our financial system's last flame of life that must not be extinguished. President Carter's 1980 experience demonstrated that. The budgetary battle that nearly shut down our government in the late 1990s proved it too. Our experience with the aborted Harris–MetroBank rescue plan proved it again. We must retain—at all costs—the government's ability to borrow money in the open market."

"Go on, please," said the president.

"That's one market that can never close down, one debt that must always be repaid no matter what. No matter where you live and no matter who you are, if you are an investor or saver who has bought Treasury securities, you will get your money back—promptly and on time. And no matter how you bought your Treasuries—through a money fund, a broker, a bank, or directly through our Treasury Direct program—you are guaranteed equal treatment."

"And if we don't have the money?" asked the president.

"We borrow more."

"And if we can't borrow more?"

"We raise the rate."

"What about the rest of the economy?" the president asked.

"The Treasury must come first; the rest of the economy comes second. Except for essential goods and services, our efforts must be focused not on production, but on communication and transportation. While other institutions are down, the web of relationships between friends, relatives, and neighbors will be needed as society's second line of defense. Telephone networks, TV newsrooms, the Internet, and printing presses—plus, minimal land-, sea-, and air-transportation facilities—must be kept functioning, regardless of financial difficulties.

"Second," he continued, "Congressional debates must be open to the public, regardless of possible inconveniences. Third, the lines of communication between nations must be used to their utmost to coordinate an international holiday, regardless of current trade disputes. You have to—"

Johnston, silent during most of the discussions, broke in. "I'm not convinced you should shut anything down. But if you do, don't forget one thing: Even a disorderly market is a thousand times better than no market at all. Before you close down the markets, you must make sure there is a mechanism in place for opening them back up again. You must find liquid buyers who have been standing on the sidelines and attract them back into long-term Treasuries, corporate bonds, stocks, and so forth."

"Easier said than done" was the skeptical response from all those present. "Where are the buyers? Where is the liquidity? Who has the cash?"

On this particular day, no one had the answers. But the president felt that he had no other choice. He set out to engineer a full-scale national holiday—a temporary shutdown of nearly all financial markets and all nonessential production. It was the greatest peacetime risk ever taken by any president in the history of the nation.

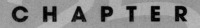
A TRUE
RECOVERY

The panic selling stopped. An eerie tranquility spread across the globe. But in the hearts and minds of the people, fear lingered.

The average citizen imagined that some faceless bureaucrat, in a final act of desperation, might set off the money presses . . . or that some terrorists, the survivors of the world's war on terror, would embark on a suicide mission to set off a nuclear bomb.

Authorities were concerned that the general holiday would be haphazard and unregulated.

Giant manufacturers feared that the shutdown might be permanent, while foreign competitors continued to dump their goods into the United States.

Political analysts predicted that the dizzying economic crises overseas might bring to power a new breed of quasi dictators backed by military juntas, that rogue nations might blackmail the world with a secret cache of biological weapons, that any recovery would be sabotaged by religious, ethnic, and racial wars. Fortunately, none of these feared events materialized in any significant way.

The president and his new advisors convened again at Camp David. Johnston brought his chief of staff, Oliver Dulles. And, in response to the question "Where is the cash?" the new Fed chairman brought a personal assistant with a laptop and a database of all the most liquid public companies. The assistant also had a hard-copy printout, which he placed on the table.

Dulles and Johnston glanced anxiously at the names and numbers on the list. Then the assistant stood up and helped them unfold the long sheets across the table and onto the floor. One column showed cash resources, one showed current debts, and a third showed quick-liquidity ratios—the dollars in cash or equivalent per dollars of current debts.

However, after scanning it for a few minutes, they were not enthusiastic and Dulles verbalized their concerns. "You can take all these horses to the water hole. But if they decide not to drink or, worse, if they decide to dump their loads, you're back to where you started. If this list is typical, the task ahead of us will be more difficult than I imagined. Look," he said, stabbing his finger at the printouts as he held them up in the air, "when the ratios are good, the quantities are small, and when the quantities are big, the ratios are not so good. This is a far cry from the days of J.P. Morgan, when all the reserves needed to piece things together after a panic could be scribbled on a napkin."

No matter how big the names and no matter how impressive the numbers, they recognized that it was still just a spit in the ocean compared to the debts that surrounded them. On the other hand, no matter how daunting the task ahead, they also recognized that *something* was infinitely better than nothing.

Later, they also recognized that they had made a grave error in their analysis. The data in the Fed's spreadsheet included strictly publicly traded companies. That meant they had overlooked a large number of insurance companies, banks, and brokerage firms that were not listed on any exchange but *did* have substantial capital and liquid resources.

Life and health insurers topped the list—Teachers Insurance & Annuity Assurance of America, based in New York, with over $130 billion in total assets; Northwestern Mutual Life Insurance in Wisconsin, with over $105 billion; New York Life ($79 billion); Massachusetts Mutual ($71 billion); Pacific Life, headquartered in California, with $53 billion; State Farm Life, from Illinois ($30 billion); and many more. Persuading them to commit their liquid

Table 25.1   Strongest Large Life and Health Insurers

Company Name	Weiss Safety Rating	Total Assets (millions)
Teachers Ins. & Annuity Asn. of Am. (NY)	A+	$132,059
State Farm Life Ins. Co. (IL)	A+	$30,859
Country Life Ins. Co. (IL)	A+	$4,236
American Family Life Ins. Co. (WI)	A+	$2,683
State Farm Life & Accident Asr. Co. (IL)	A+	$1,046
Northwestern Mutual Life Ins. Co. (WI)	A	$105,535
New York Life Ins. Co. (NY)	A	$79,010
Massachusetts Mutual Life Ins. Co. (MA)	A	$71,654
Pacific Life Ins. Co. (CA)	A	$53,416
Guardian Life Ins. Co. of America (NY)	A	$20,639
Minnesota Life Ins. Co. (MN)	A	$16,776
Jefferson-Pilot Life Ins. Co. (NC)	A	$11,938
American Fidelity Asr. Co. (OK)	A	$2,067
United Farm Family Life Ins. Co. (IN)	A	$1,392
Physicians Mutual Ins. Co. (NE)	A	$1,047
Principal Life Ins. Co. (IA)	A–	$77,869
John Hancock Life Ins. Co. (MA)	A–	$65,040
New York Life Ins. & Annuity Corp. (DE)	A–	$36,791
USAA Life Ins. Co. (TX)	A–	$8,156
Southern Farm Bureau Life Ins. Co. (MS)	A–	$6,910
Midland National Life Ins. Co. (IA)	A–	$6,589
Farmers New World Life Ins. Co. (WA)	A–	$5,845

Table 25.1 *(Continued)*

Company Name	Weiss Safety Rating	Total Assets (millions)
Farm Bureau Life Ins. Co. (IA)	A–	$4,226
Mutual of Omaha Ins. Co. (NE)	A–	$3,617
United Ins. Co. of America (IL)	A–	$2,769

Even in a worst-case scenario, there are always many companies able to stay intact financially by avoiding excess debts, maintaining strong capital, and continually taking steps to protect themselves. These institutions can (1) serve as a model for others that may be concerned about future declines in the economy (2) play a constructive role in any subsequent recovery, and (3) act as a relatively safe haven for consumers seeking to protect their capital. Ratings scale: A = excellent; B = good; + = high end of grade range; – = low end of grade range. For a complete listing, refer to the Weiss Ratings' *Guide to Life, Health and Annuity Insurers,* available at many public libraries or at www.weissratings.com.
Source: Weiss Ratings, Inc., Palm Beach Gardens, FL, based on second-quarter 2002 data filed with state insurance regulators, as well as some data provided by the companies directly.

resources to help lift common stocks or corporate bonds out of the abyss, however, was still a serious challenge. (See Tables 25.1 and 25.2.)

"Before any liquid resources are committed," said the head of ACLI, the American Counsel of Life Insurers, in a letter to the president, "certain conditions have to be met." What were these conditions? The letter referred repeatedly to the "housecleaning process" but complained about the slow progress that was being made. Here are some further excerpts:

Many are hoping that the latest round of casualties will be the last casualties, that there will be no more need for liquidation. But this is questionable. By the end of the boom, there were approximately $25 trillion in interest-bearing debts outstanding in the United States, over $50 trillion if you include Western Europe and Japan, and close to $100 trillion if you include all derivatives and non-interest-bearing commitments or guarantees. Many of those debts have now gone bad—they are nonperforming. But, to date, only one-fourth of bad debts have

Table 25.2 Strongest Large Banks

Name	Weiss Safety Rating	Total Assets (Millions)
World Savings Bank FSB (Oakland, CA)	B+	$62,342
Fifth Third Bank (Cincinnati, OH)	B+	$41,623
Mellon Bank NA (Pittsburgh, PA)	B+	$24,841
Fifth Third Bank (Grand Rapids, MI)	B+	$24,579
Hudson City Savings Bank (Paramus, NJ)	A	$12,843
Commerce Bank NA (Kansas City, MO)	B+	$10,300
Bancorpsouth Bank (Tupelo, MS)	B+	$9,932
Bank of Hawaii (Honolulu, HI)	B+	$9,673
Emigrant Savings Bank (New York, NY)	A	$9,065
Capitol Federal Savings Bank (Topeka, KS)	A–	$8,834
Valley National Bank (Passaic, NJ)	B+	$8,597
Fifth Third Bank of Indianapolis (Indianapolis, IN)	A–	$8,591
Washington Federal S&L (Seattle, WA)	A+	$7,117
Whitney National Bank (New Orleans, LA)	B+	$6,925
Trustmark National Bank (Jackson, MS)	B+	$6,693
Israel Discount Bank of New York (New York, NY)	B+	$6,131
Citibank–Delaware (New Castle, DE)	B+	$6,047
Apple Bank For Savings (Scarsdale, NY)	A–	$5,927
Republic Bank (Lansing, MI)	B+	$4,342
Mercantile Safe Deposit & TC (Baltimore, MD)	A	$4,170
Comerica Bank –Texas (Dallas, TX)	B+	$4,066
Columbus Bank & TC (Columbus, GA)	A–	$3,878

Table 25.2 *(Continued)*

Name	Weiss Safety Rating	Total Assets (Millions)
Silicon Valley Bank (Santa Clara, CA)	B+	$3,609
Fulton Bank (Lancaster, PA)	B+	$3,595
Texas State Bank (McAllen, TX)	B+	$3,508

These banks are currently the strongest among the large banks, based on their Weiss Safety Ratings, which consider the bank's capital, earnings, liquidity, and many other factors. It is believed that these institutions will be among those that fare best in a worst-case scenario for the early 2000s and will, it is hoped, play a constructive role in any subsequent recovery. Ratings scale: A = excellent; B = good; + = high end of grade range; – = low end of grade range. For a complete listing, refer to the Weiss Ratings' *Guide to Banks and Thrifts,* available at many public libraries or at www.weissratings.com.

Source: Weiss Ratings, Inc., Palm Beach Gardens, FL, based on second-quarter 2002 data filed by the institutions with the Federal Deposit Insurance Corporation and the Office of Thrift Supervision.

been liquidated thus far. How many more debts will go bad? It is unclear, but there is one thing we can say for sure: Until we see more concrete progress in the liquidation of nonperforming debts, the large life insurance companies will not reinvest in the institutions currently burdened with those debts. Until we ourselves have completed our own bad-debt liquidations, we will not be able to participate in your recovery program, except in token amounts.

Despite their hesitation, however, many strong insurers and banks would soon pour money into stocks and bonds of worthy companies. Meanwhile, back at Camp David, one Administration official was visibly upset by the slant of the debate. Echoing a widespread concern throughout Washington for the free enterprise system, he raised his voice in protest. "Are you gentlemen implying that the president should assume dictatorial powers under the cloak of a national emergency? Are you saying he should take over private industry, preside over market transactions?"

What he failed to realize was that the panic had made—for better or for worse—those arguments academic. Because of the sharp declines in tax revenues, many government programs had been reduced to almost empty shells, and the government's power—to tax less, spend more, tighten money, or ease money—was reduced to a mere shadow of its former self. To think that the government could now assume dictatorial powers was completely out of tune with reality.

The president was particularly conscious of this change. "The government cannot call a national emergency," he replied, "because we *already* have a national emergency. All the government can do is guarantee law and order, set parameters for fairness, and help provide the information needed to put the pieces back together."

The Administration official also complained bitterly about one more key factor—the extremely high real cost of money. The cost of consumer goods was going down. The cost of money—interest rates—was going up. In other words, the inflation rate was well below zero and, at the same time, interest rates were far *above* zero. The gap between them, the *real interest rate,* was at the highest level in American history.

Suddenly, everyone was talking at the same time—all saying different things, but all related to this one subject: high real interest rates. The president tapped deliberately on the table like a stern schoolmaster until the room was quiet. Turning philosophical, he responded with this comment: "This is the first time in our history that the cost of money and the cost of things have taken such widely divergent paths. Could it be that the market is trying to tell us something?"

The others stared solemnly.

"I'm not an economist," the president continued, "but one thing I have learned in recent months is that interest rates represent more than just the market value of money. They also represent the value we assign to credit, faith, and trust. The market is telling us that it needs more trust and more faith. At the same time, falling consumer prices are telling us that we live in an era of abundance, that we have an almost unlimited ability to produce material goods but have often been producing the wrong ones. Could it be that this crisis is a flash of lightning giving us a brief glance into a future of more faith and more abundance? I only hope we can make a more conscious distinction between the two. Clearly, to force interest rates down artificially at this juncture would be tantamount to . . . would be like . . ." The president groped for the appropriate simile.

REOPENING

At last, the market reopened. Unlike the reopening after the previous market shutdown of September 17, 2001, however, there was no big volume. No fanfare. But when you looked at the prices, you saw a huge jump. Thus, there was a big gap from the last day before the forced holiday and the first day after the market reopened. Although it was certainly not too late to buy, it was too late for the lowest prices of the entire century.

Separately, the Federal Reserve made it clear that any attempts to lower real interest rates artificially would be tantamount to "barking at the thunder."

As confidence returned, the big action began. Despite the lack of government intervention, the dollar recovered smartly. The very fact that the markets were functioning smoothly again was, in itself, hailed by overseas investors. A sudden flush of funds, hoarded in cash and Treasury bills, returned to the equity markets.

Many high-net-worth invididuals put up more than half their fortunes to rescue their country. And, most important, a not-so-small minority of investors with crash profits began pouring their gains back into the stock market. Still, most investors were extremely skeptical, asking, "Will this be a real recovery? Or will the market fall back down again, plunging the nation into a financial morass for many years to come?" No one knew.

With time, however, the U.S. and world economies did recover. There were conflicts and accidents along the way. There were more errors. But the most fatal mistakes were avoided.

At CECAR, the leadership changed and pursued new goals as the former leaders completed successful careers in government and private enterprise.

Linda Dedini and her husband, however, stayed out of politics. Instead, they continued to teach. And they invested in a diversified portfolio of domestic and international companies, including some unique start-up ventures.

Many years later, when their grandchildren reviewed the portfolio, they marveled at how much had been made, but they couldn't quite understand many things about it. For example, how did Grandma Dedini ever discover those self-sustaining forestry conglomerates that grew out of nothing in the faraway State of Acre in northwestern Brazil?

Where did she find that small Japanese software company that used advanced game technology to teach the history of the Meiji era to the children of Hokkaido and, later, the history of the world to all children everywhere?

How did she learn about that large global publisher that started out as a mom-and-pop early-learning center in Pennsylvania?

How did she learn about the new biotech companies that turned complementary medicine into a trillion-dollar industry?

No one in the family knew, and she was no longer around to explain. She obviously must have been a visionary and an investing genius from her earliest years.

For regular updates to this book or to contact the author, visit www. crashprofits.net.

ENDNOTES

Chapter 1. The Broker's Hidden Agenda

Page 4: The myth of long-term investing. Although some brokers bend over backwards to do the right thing for their customers, Linda Dedini's encounters with her broker are typical of the experiences of millions of investors. The broker's hidden agenda is *to get you to buy what they want to sell,* and therein lies a fundamental conflict of interest, which prompts many brokers to promote ideas that are good for them but not always good for the customer. Case in point: the idea that investing in stocks for the long term always pays off.

Consider virtually any guide to investing. With rare exceptions, they advise investors to hold onto sinking stocks, implicitly disregarding the possibility of a deep, multiyear stock market decline that could wipe out the wealth of virtually everyone who pursues such a strategy.

Page 4: The myth of paper losses. Like thousands of brokers around the country, the broker in this story, James Dubois, regularly tells his customers that "paper losses" are not real until they actually sell the stock and take the loss. However, brokerage firms themselves mark their securities to market—recognizing their own so-called paper losses every day. If they did not, they would be in violation of Exchange Rule 440 and SEC Rules 17a-3 and 17a-4, causing false entries to be made to books and records.

Chapter 2. The Bubble

Page 7: Nasdaq bubble. The 1990s craze over tech stocks was easily the greatest speculative bubble of all time, with initial public offerings (IPOs) of companies attracting the most funds in history. For more details on the boom and bust of IPOs, see www.marketdata.nasdaq.com/asp/Sec3IPO.asp and www.ipohome.com/default.asp.

Page 10: Executive pay. It is now obvious that even the honest CEOs of America were routinely paid excessive salaries, while the less honest often plundered the wealth of shareholders and trashed the good effort of employees. For some classic examples, see "Enron's Many Strands, Excerpts From Testimony Before House Subcommittee on Enron Collapse," *New York Times,* February 5, 2002. See also "Business Week Special Report–Executive Pay," *Business Week,* April 16, 2001, also available at www.businessweek.com/pdfs /2001/0116comp.pdf.

Page 10: WorldCom. The executives at WorldCom were among the most guilty, but they were by no means unique, as you can see from "What's Wrong? Deadbeat CEOs Plague Firms As Economy and Markets Roil," *Wall Street Journal,* August 1, 2002, and from "The Board Of WorldCom Begins Search For Next Chief" by Simon Romero, *New York Times,* September 11, 2002.

Page 12: Boards of directors did little or nothing to stop the plundering. The board of directors of a corporation has the responsibility to keep wayward officers of the company in check, firing those that are not acting in the best interests of shareholders. But in too many cases, they have sat by passively while officers continued to manipulate the books, falsify records, and/or run the company into the ground. See, for example, the Hearing of the Permanent Investigations Subcommittee of the Senate Governmental Affairs Committee, chaired by Senator Carl Levin (D-Mich), in 2002 regarding the role of the Enron board in the collapse of the Enron corporation.

Chapter 3. The Wall Street Hype

Page 15: Pension fund data source. Annual reports and 10K filings, Standard & Poor's Compustat database.

Page 20: Unanimously wrong till the bitter end. It is very common for Wall Street analysts to unanimously continue to heap lavish praise on a particular stock, even if the company is on the verge of bankruptcy. Weiss Ratings examined 19 companies that filed for Chapter 11 bankruptcy in the first four months of 2002 and that were rated by Wall Street firms. Among these 19 companies, 12 received a "buy" or "hold" rating from *all* of the Wall Street firms that rated them. Furthermore, they continued to receive those unanimously positive ratings right up to the day they filed for Chapter 11 bankruptcy. Thus, even diligent investors who sought second or third opinions on these companies would have run into a stone wall of unanimous "don't sell" advice. The Wall Street firms led them like lemmings to the sea, with not even *one* dissenting voice in the crowd. See "47 Brokerage Firms Recommended Shares of Failing Companies Even as They Filed Chapter 11 in 2002," Weiss Ratings, Inc., June 3, 2002, www.weissratings.com/crisis_of_confidence.asp.

Page 22: Dropping coverage. While "buy" recommendations were announced with great fanfare, analysts were often mute when their opinion of a company turned negative. In many cases, they simply dropped coverage without informing investors. For details see "Crisis of Confidence on Wall Street:

Brokerage Firm Abuses and the Worst Offenders," Weiss Ratings, Inc., July 24, 2002, p. 6, www.weissratings.com/crisis_of_confidence.asp.

Page 24: Grubman's bad ratings. According to the *Wall Street Journal,* prior to October 1998, Grubman did not include AT&T in his list of key players in the telecom industry. In fact, on numerous occasions, AT&T management complained about his treatment of the company. Then, in a 1998 speaking appearance, Grubman again failed to identify AT&T as a rising telecom star. In response to renewed complaints and a demand for an apology from AT&T's CEO, Grubman wrote an interoffice memo that could serve as the basis for an apology. He stated, in part, that he viewed "AT&T as one of the most significant companies in the industry." Later, he raised his rating to a "strong buy." AT&T then gave Salomon a major role in the offering. See "Wildcard: Citigroup Now Has New Worry: What Grubman Will say," *Wall Street Journal,* October 10, 2002. See also "Grubman May Turn on Citigroup," *CNN Money,* October 10, 2002, http://money.cnn.com/2002/10/10/news/companies/grubman/index.htm.

Page 24: Blodget ratings. Prior to his forecast for Amazon, Henry Blodget was essentially unknown. Following this prediction, however, he was recruited by Merrill Lynch. See "Oh, Henry!" *Red Herring,* December 2000.

Page 25: An outrageous betrayal of trust. One of the first official recognitions of the great Wall Street scam came on July 31, 2001, in testimony before the House Financial Services Capital Markets Subcommittee. Acting SEC chairperson Laura S. Unger testified to the effect that nearly all major Wall Street firms were guilty of serious conflicts of interest. However, in the wake of the September attacks, the issue was shelved, not to reappear until Elliot Spitzer, the attorney general of New York State, filed suit against Merrill Lynch, as reported in "Merrill Lynch Under Attack As Giving Out Tainted Advice" by Patrick McGeehan, *New York Times,* April 9, 2002.

Page 26: UBS Paine-Webber silences employee giving sell advice on Enron. In August of 2001, several months before Enron's failure, a UBS analyst sent an e-mail to Enron employees warning them that holding the company's stock, then worth almost $37 a share, could "cost you a fortune." Wu was fired immediately because his message ran contrary to UBS's current recommendation concerning Enron stock, which was urging investors to buy. *USA Today,* March 14, 2002.

Page 27: Spitzer and Washington attack Wall Street. After months of turf battles, federal and state regulators agreed to divide up the intense labor of investigating Wall Street firms, attacking them in one united front. Patrick McGeehan of the *New York Times* reports that "a posse of state regulators from Sacramento to Boston . . . are hurriedly investigating conflicts of interest within more than a dozen of the biggest securities firms in the country, including Morgan Stanley, Lehman Brothers, Bear Stearns and UBS PaineWebber." *New York Times,* October 20, 2002.

Page 30: Make Merrill Lynch's shenanigans appear tame. See "Salomon's Woes Multiply," *CNN Money,* September 3, 2002, http://money.cnn.com/

2002/09/03/news/companies/salomon/; "Spitzer Raises the Heat on Citi-group," *Business Week Online,* October 2, 2002, www.businessweek.com/bwdaily/dnflash/oct2002/nf2002102_2153.htm; "City of Schemes," *New York Times,* October 6, 2002.

Page 30: Wall Street firms backslide and make lame excuses. In early June 2002, the CEO of Goldman Sachs, in a speech at the National Press Club, boldly placed the blame for Wall Street's crisis of confidence on corporate CEOs and their accountants, including some of his firm's top customers. But in the process, he minimized the responsibility of his own firm and the brokerage industry. Similarly, on the CNBC program *Louis Rukeyser's Wall Street,* the chief executive of Merrill Lynch, fresh out of a settlement with New York State, brushed off the entire matter by asserting the offenders were just a "few bad apples." These industry denials were nonproductive, calculating, and disingenuous. Until the industry leaders fully recognized their own offenses, real solutions would continue to elude them.

Page 30: Merrill Lynch not the worst. Although Merrill Lynch was the first target of regulators, it was, by far, not the worst. The offenses committed by the likes of Salomon Brothers Smith Barney and Morgan Stanley were worse, according to testimony by New York State Attorney General Elliot Spitzer before the House Committee on Commerce, Science and Technology. www.oag.state.ny.us/press/2002/jun/testimony7.pdf.

Page 31: Wall Street "Mafia." William F. Galvin, the chief Massachusetts official investigating Credit Suisse First Boston, seems to agree with the author's view that the Mafia would be green with envy, saying "You almost have to treat these people like drug dealers. You have to confiscate all their ill-gotten gains." *New York Times,* October 20, 2002, p. BU 12.

Page 32: Hauled off in handcuffs. See "2 Ex-Officials at WorldCom Are Charged in Huge Fraud," *New York Times,* August 2, 2002; "Founder of Adelphia and 2 Sons Arrested," *New York Times,* July 25, 2002; and "Former Chief of ImClone Systems Is Charged with Insider Trading," *New York Times,* June 13, 2002.

Chapter 4. The Bubble Bursts

Page 33: Offshore escapes. Many U.S. corporate giants have headquarters or subsidiaries in offshore locations such as Bermuda, including Tyco International, and in many cases these offshore entities were used to hide certain accounts from shareholders or U.S. authorities. For a listing of Bermuda-based operations, see: http://bermuda-online.org/intcoys.htm.

Page 35: Pension scam unravels. For additional data, refer to Watson Wyatt, a global consulting firm focused on human capital and financial management, at www.watsonwyatt.com.

Page 40: Waste Management. The case of Waste Management, which came to light well before Enron, WorldCom, and other major accounting scandals, should have served as a warning to both investors and regulators of more troubles to come. However, it was largely pooh-poohed at the time. See SEC Press Release, dated March 26, 2002, "Waste Management and Five Other Former Officers Sued For Massive Fraud," www.sec.gov/news/press/2002-44.txt.

Page 40: Auditors fail to warn about accounting troubles. The auditing process suffered a broad breakdown with disastrous consequences:

First, auditing firms almost universally failed to warn the public, giving a clean bill of health to 93.9 percent of public companies that were subsequently involved in accounting irregularities. These companies had a total peak market value of over $1.8 trillion, but by June 2002 were worth only $527 billion, implying an aggregate loss to shareholders of up to $1.276 trillion, due to a variety of factors including accounting issues.

Second, the auditing firms also had a poor track record in warning of future bankruptcies, giving a clean bill of health to 42.1 percent of the public companies that subsequently filed for bankruptcy between January 1, 2001, and June 30, 2002. Nevertheless, at 88.9 percent of the companies that were given a clean bill of health, there were at least two negative financial indicators that were evident in their accounts at the time of the audit—indicators that should have alerted auditors to future troubles.

For details, see *The Worsening Crisis of Confidence on Wall Street: The Role of Auditing Firms,* submitted by Martin D. Weiss, Ph.D., of Weiss Ratings, Inc., to the U.S. Senate as input for the Public Company Accounting and Investor Protection Act (S. 2673), introduced by Sen. Paul Sarbanes (D-Md), July 5, 2002, www.weissratings.com/worsening_crisis.asp.

Page 44: SEC Chairman Arthur Levitt warned of coming accounting disaster. See, for example, "SEC Chairman Arthur Levitt, Concerned that the Quality of Corporate Financial Reporting Is Eroding, Announces Action Plan to Remedy Problem," September 28, 1998, www.sec.gov/news/press/pressarchive/1998/98-95.txt.

Page 44: Public Company Accounting Reform and Investor Protection Act. In 2002, Congress passed this new law, making it more difficult for companies to cook their books. However, three months later, the Bush administration threatened to undermine the legislation in two ways: first, by slashing the funding needed to implement the law, and, second, by appointing an industry-friendly official to head the public company accounting board that would oversee the industry. See "Bush Tries to Shrink S.E.C. Raise Intended for Corporate Cleanup," by Stephen Labaton, *New York Times,* October 19, 2002, and "Ex-Director Of FBI, CIA Could Be Accounting Top Cop," by Greg Farrell, *USA Today,* October 25, 2002.

Chapter 5. The $17,000 Toilet Kit

Page 51: Commission on Public Trust and Private Enterprise. See "Expert Business Panel Puts Stock Options on a List of Reforms," by Kenneth N. Gilpin, *New York Times,* September 18, 2002.

Page 52: IT spending survey by Goldman Sachs Global. This was conducted at the end of June 2002 on a panel of 100 IT executives from Fortune 1000 companies. For details see www.gs.com/insight/research/reports/it_spending_survey.pdf.

Page 53: Garnter Dataquest comment. "Quarter sees fall in EMEA PC shipments," *Financial Times,* July 18, 2002. See also "Gartner Dataquest Says Worldwide PC Shipments in Second Quarter of 2002 Dampen First Quarter Optimism," www.gartner.com, July 18, 2002.

Page 53: Telecom companies in bankruptcy. For the latest on failures in the telecom industry or other industries, go to www.bankruptcydata.com and click on "find a bankruptcy," selecting an industry in the box labeled "business type."

Chapter 6. Sell These Stocks Now!

Page 57: WorldCom fraud over $9 billion! See "WorldCom Wins Approval To Borrow up to $1.1 Billion," *Wall Street Journal,* October 15, 2002, and "Two Ex-WorldCom Execs Plead Guilty To Fraud," *Financial Times,* October 10, 2002; See "WorldCom Strikes a Deal With SEC," *New York Times,* November 27, 2002.

Page 57: Merrill Lynch not alone. In addition to Merrill Lynch, 46 other major Wall Street firms continued to recommend the shares in companies going bankrupt, even after it was obvious to everyone, including the major rating agencies, that these companies were failing.

Not only are there many more pending actions against brokerage firms, but those actions seem to be getting far more aggressive. On October 21, 2002, Massachusetts regulators filed an administrative complaint against Credit Suisse First Boston, contending that the firm's investment advice had been tainted by its hunger for fees from corporate clients.

Meanwhile, Bear Stearns was under investigation by the state of New Jersey and also by the NYSE. Credit Suisse First Boston was being investigated by Massachusetts and the NASD; Goldman Sachs, by Utah and the NYSE; JP Morgan Chase by Texas and the NYSE; Lehman Brothers, by Alabama and the SEC; Morgan Stanley and Salomon Smith Barney, by New York State and the NASD; UBS Paine-Webber, by Arizona and the NYSE; UBS Warburg, by Illinois and NYSE; and US Bancorp Piper Jaffray, by the state of Washington and the NASD.

See "States Talk Tough. Wall Street Sweats," *New York Times,* October 20, 2002, and Weiss Ratings White Paper, "Crisis of Confidence on Wall Street: Brokerage Firm Abuses and the Worst Offenders," July 14, 2002, www.weissratings.com/crisis_of_confidence.asp.

Page 60: 25 years before you recoup your losses? This was certainly the case after the 1929–1932 bear market. At its peak in 1929, the S&P 500 index traded at 31.83. It did not recover to that level until September 22, 1954, a full 25 years later. Data: Bloomberg.

Chapter 7. Get Your Money To Safety

Page 82: Bonds in default. For the latest listing similar to the one shown to Linda Dedini by her advisor, go to http://riskcalc.moodysrms.com/us/research/defrate.asp.

Page 83: What would happen to your bonds if yields doubled? Gabriel Dedini's guess is very close to the mark. For example, in late October 2002, a 5.38 percent U.S. Treasury bond of 02/15/2003 with a face value of $10,000 was selling for $10,359. In the event that rates doubled, the bond's price would decline to approximately $5,500.

Chapter 8. The Ballooning Budget Deficit

Page 92: Complacency about deficit. America's complacency toward budget deficits and lax accounting in the early twenty-first century contrasts dramatically with the great sense of alarm that prevailed in the late 1950s.

At that time, the author's father, Irving Weiss, founded two nonprofit organizations: the Businessman's Committee for Seasoned Management and the Sound Dollar Committee.

The former, comprising prominent chief executives and business leaders, such as James M. Kemper of the Kemper Insurance group, lobbied successfully for sound accounting and management practices.

The latter, with support from presidential adviser Bernard Baruch and former president Herbert Hoover, organized a mass media campaign, urging the public to support a balanced budget. In response to the Sound Dollar Committee's ads and press releases, voters sent an estimated 12 million postcards, letters, and telegrams to Capitol Hill, swaying Congress to vote for a balanced budget in 1959.

Page 93: Raiding social security funds. See "Budget Scramble—Social Security, Programs and Borrowing from the Social Security," *AARP Bulletin,* www.aarp.org/bulletin/departments/2002/news/0405_news_1.html.

Page 93: Fed chairman's testimony encouraging the tech boom. In the late 1990s, Mr. Greenspan apparently gave up fighting the tech bubble and decided to support it instead, saying ". . . our economy is still enjoying a virtuous cycle, in which, in the context of subdued inflation and generally supportive credit conditions, rising equity values are providing impetus for spending and, in turn, the expansion of output, employment, and productivity-enhancing capital investment. The hopes for accelerated productivity growth have been bolstering expectations of future corporate earnings and thereby fueling still further increases in equity values." Testimony of Chairman Alan Greenspan, "An update on economic conditions in the United States, before the Joint Economic Committee, U.S. Congress, June 10, 1998.

Page 94: Government economists miss the recession. See "Forecast Too Sunny? Try the Anxious Index," by David Leonhardt, *New York Times,* September 1, 2002.

Chapter 9. The Bond Market Bubble

Page 98: Uncle Sam crowding out other borrowers. In the second quarter of 2002, the U.S. government borrowed new funds at the annual rate of $948.4 billion, or 39 percent of all the funds raised during the period. In contrast, in 1997, the government borrowed $236 billion, or only 15 percent of the total funds raised. See www.federalreserve.gov/releases/Z1/Current/z1r-3.pdf, Table F.4, "Credit Market Borrowing, All Sectors, by Instrument."

Page 102: Bond market paralysis of February 11, 1980. According to the *Wall Street Journal* of February 7, 1980, the flood of sell orders in the bond market prompted all except four or five of the largest, best capitalized bond houses to effectively abandon their market-making role. Five days later, the *Wall Street Journal* of February 12 reported that "traders at major institutions yesterday were unable to find buyers for amounts as little as five million dollars of Treasury bonds."

Page 102: President Carter's response to the bond market collapse of 1980. With the full blessing of the president, the Federal Reserve took the following actions: It (1) raised key interest rates, (2) imposed stiffer controls on borrowing by U.S. banks, and (3) slapped unusual controls on the creation of new credit–from credit card borrowing by consumers to money funds. The immediate result was a dramatic recovery in the bond market, plus one of the steepest plunges in the economy in decades.

Chapter 10. The Real Estate Bubble

Page 104: Federal Reserve lowers interest rates dramatically and pumps money into economy. Fearing something akin to the worst-case scenarios to be discussed in subsequent chapters, the U.S. Federal Reserve pumped unprecedented amounts of money into the economy, and *Business Week* commented as follows: "Even as the global economy slows to a halt, liquidity is surging worldwide. In the U.S., repeated interest rate cuts by the Federal Reserve mean that M3 (the broadest indicator of money supply, including bank deposits and money-market mutual funds) rose by almost 14 percent, year-on-year, to the end of October. That's the fastest rate of growth in more than 20 years." See "Money, Money Everywhere," *Business Week,* December 17, 2001.

Page 105: Housing boom. It was the Fed's aggressive money pumping that spurred the latest housing boom. For details on home price rises, see Office of Federal Housing Enterprise Oversight, House Price Index, Second Quarter 2002, pp. 19ff; "Frenzy Returns to California Housing Market," by Broderick Perkins, *Realty Times,* May 29, 2002, http://realtytimes.com/rtnews/rtcpages/20020529_calfrenzy.htm; "As safe as what? Global house prices," *The Economist,* August 29, 2002, p. 2; and "Housing Boom Breeds New Mortgage Deals," *USA Today,* October 25, 2002, p. 1.

Page 107: Housing bust? See Jim Scott, "Waiting for the Shoe to Drop," www.sqre.com/report_april01.html.

Page 108: Average home equity down to 55. Source: *Flow of Funds for the U.S.,* Table B.100, "Balance Sheet of Households and Nonprofit Organizations," Section 102, Federal Reserve Statistical Release, Z.1, www.federalreserve .gov/releases/Z1/Current/data.htm.

Page 111: Mortgage delinquencies. See "A Record Percentage Of U.S. Home-owners Are Facing Foreclosure, And Many More Are Falling Behind On Monthly House Payments," *USA Today,* September 10, 2002.

Page 111: Stock market losses make real estate investing more difficult. The Nasdaq Composite Index declined from a peak of 5,132 to 1,119 on October 7, 2002, a 77 percent plunge; the S&P 500 fell from a peak of 1,553 to 785 in the same period, a 50 percent drop; and the Dow Jones Industrials fell from its peak of 11,750 to 7,423, a 27 percent decline. With these losses, few people would be willing to shift from the stock market to real estate. Instead, it appears that the bulk of new money going into real estate came from new borrowing, further inflating the real estate bubble.

Chapter 12. The Team

Page 127: Savings rate. U.S. Department of Commerce, Bureau of Economic Analysis.

Page 128: Large burden of corporate debts. Source: Federal Reserve's *Flow of Funds,* B.102, Balance Sheet of Non Farm Nonfinancial Corporate Business," www.federalreserve.gov/releases/Z1/Current/z1.pdf.

Page 129: Tamara Belmont quits. A *Wall Street Journal* article from as far back as 1992 demonstrated that brokerage industry insiders have known for a long time what happens to uncooperative analysts: The analysts often find them-selves blackballed by the industry, their careers destroyed. See, for example, "Under Pressure: At Morgan Stanley, Analysts Were Urged To Soften Harsh Views," *Wall Street Journal,* July 14, 1992, p. A1.

Page 133: Plunge Protection Team. See "Plunge Protection Team," by Brett D. Fromson, *Washington Post,* February 23, 1997; and "In '87 Crash, All Eyes on Greenspan; Two Months Into Job, Fed Chairman Faced Ultimate Chal-lenge," by Bob Woodward, *Washington Post,* November 13, 2000.

Page 135: Japanese bond market collapse of 1987. The Japanese bellwether 5.1 percent bond of 1996, which had reached a historic high of 125 (12,500 yen for each 10,000 yen face value bond) plunged to 100. Meanwhile, the yield, which had dropped to a historic low of 2.6 percent, jumped to 4.6 per-cent, an amazing 77 percent increase.

Page 139: Cash settlements in the stock market. Pursuant to Sections 220.8(b)(1) and (4) of Regulation T of the Federal Reserve Board, a bro-ker/dealer may wait for five business days after the date of purchase before paying for the securities purchased.

Page 140: New York Stock Exchange curbs. For the most recent rules, go to www.nyse.com/press/press.html, check under "press information," and then see "Circuit Breakers and Trading Collars."

Page 140: Program trading. For a concise definition, see Investopedia.com. Click on "Dictionary."

Page 141: The fair value of a mutual fund in a crash. The SEC states: "If fund assets are incorrectly valued, shareholder accounts will pay too much or too little for their shares. In addition, the over-valuation of a fund's assets will overstate the performance of the fund, and will result in overpayment of fund expenses that are calculated on the basis of the fund's net assets, such as the fund's investment advisory fee. The Investment Company Act requires funds to value their portfolio securities by using the market value of the securities when market quotations for the securities are 'readily available.' When market quotations are not readily available, the 1940 Act requires fund boards to determine, in good faith, the fair value of the securities." This would be extremely difficult in a crash, and many mutual funds may have no choice but to use the most recent closing price, which could greatly overstate the net asset value of the funds' shares. Source: www.sec.gov/news/speech/spch517.htm.

Chapter 13. Hidden Risks

Page 145: Long Term Capital Management debacle. For further details, see www.erisk.com/LearningCenter/CaseStudies/ref_case_item.asp and "Hedge Fund Debacle Offers a View of a Secret World," by Joseph Kahn and Laura M. Holsom, *New York Times,* September 30, 1998.

Page 148: Enron derivatives. Not only did the esoteric nature of the derivatives make it possible for Enron to deceive shareholders regarding the true size of its debts, it also made it possible for Enron's traders to engineer the greatest energy market conspiracy of all time. Indeed, on October 17, 2002, Timothy N. Belden, the former head of trading at Enron's Portland, Oregon's office "admitted to working with others on trading tactics that effectively transformed California's complex system for buying and transmitting energy into a fictional world, complete with bogus transmission schedules, imaginary congestion on power lines and fraudulent sales of 'out of state' energy that in fact came from California itself." *New York Times,* October 18, 2002, p. C1.

Page 149: Big banks taking big risks with derivatives. The Office for the Comptroller of the Currency monitors outstanding derivatives contracts each quarter. The relevant table referred to here, entitled "Percentage of Credit Exposure to Risk Based Capital," shows that for each dollar of risk-based capital, JP Morgan Chase had $5.89 in credit exposure related to derivatives. Bank of America had $1.69, and Citibank had $1.99. These are excessive risks in any scenario. See www.occ.treas.gov/ftp/deriv/dq202.pdf.

Page 156: High-net-worth individuals bailed out corporate America after previous crashes. For more background, see Harry Schultz, *Panics and Crashes* (New Rochelle: Arlington House, 1972) and Alfred Sloan, Jr., *My Years with General Motors* (Garden City: Doubleday, 1969) and Lewis Corey, *The House of Morgan: A Social Biography of the Masters of Money* (New York: AMS, 1969).

Page 158: Japan's economic collapse. There have been thousands of major articles in the Japanese and U.S. press documenting the economic collapse in great detail. Specifically, consider National Center for Policy Analysis, Oct. 14, 2002, www.ncpa.org/edo/bb/2002/bb101402.html; "Global economy to grow 1.7 percent in 2002, Japan to fall 0.7 percent: UN," *Kyodo News,* Oct. 9, 2002; and Bank of Japan Acts to Shore Up Banks Against Market Swings," Mariko Sanchanta, *New York Times.*

Page 159: Winning a game of poker on the Titanic. A casual visitor to Japan would still see most of the trappings of prosperity, despite more than a decade of rolling depression and stock market declines. See "Japan Markets Resume Their Search For Bottom," by James Brooke, *New York Times,* September 26, 2002.

Page 163: Four and a half years of sinking balance sheets. Source: *Moody's Global Credit Trends: Weekly Commentary,* October 14, 2002.

Page 164: Big debts: At the end of June 2002, corporate debt in the United States totaled $4.9 trillion, or 57.1 percent of corporate net worth. See Federal Reserve's *Flow of Funds,* Table B.102, "Balance Sheet of Non Farm Nonfinancial Corporate Business," www.federalreserve.gov/releases/Z1/Current/z1.pdf; and Table D.3, "Debt Outstanding by Sector," www.federalreserve.gov/releases/Z1/Current/z1r-2.pdf. These show that total corporate debt outstanding on June 30, 2002, was $4.876 trillion, compared to total net worth of $8.573 trillion.

Page 164: Total private debt. Total private debt outstanding in the United States on September 16, 2002, was $20.023 trillion. In contrast, total gross domestic product was $10.376 trillion. Data: Federal Reserve's *Flow of Funds,* Table L.4., "Credit Market Debt, All Sectors, by Instrument"; www.federalreserve.gov/releases/Z1/Current/z1r-2.pdf; and U.S. Department of Commerce, Bureau of Economic Analysis.

Chapter 14. Deflation!

Page 167: Deflation in the United States. See, for example, "Bargains for Buyers May Also Hold Risk of Slower Recovery," by David Leonhardt, *New York Times,* November 25, 2001, and www.nvca.org/ "Venture Capital Investments in Q2 2002 Continue To Slide Back Toward Pre-Bubble 1998 Levels," July 2002.

Page172: Safeguard scientifics. Data: Bloomberg.

Page175: Bought and paid for. Both Standard & Poor's and Moody's provide fee schedules upon request. Standard & Poor's charges 3.25 basis points for ratings of bonds and preferred stocks. The minimum fee is $25,000, but for issues larger than $500 million, the fee is $162,500. Moody's charges 3.30 basis points, with a minimum of $33,000. On large issues, it charges a maximum fee of $250,000.

Chapter 15. The Fall of the Blue Chips

Page 200: The weakness of banks. As of September 30, 2002, there were 2,016 banks and thrifts receiving a Weiss Safety Rating of B+ or higher, meriting inclusion in the Weiss recommended list. The number of banks and thrifts receiving a D+ or lower was 1,748, implying a warning of vulnerability.

Page 203: The bankruptcy tripwire. In the case of WorldCom, 10 days prior to filing for bankruptcy, lenders froze loans to the group of $2.65 billion. Five days later, S&P cut the company's credit rating to the lowest possible level amid allegations of corruption by a Californian pension fund. In the case of Enron, energy competitor Dynergy, also based in Dallas, sought to purchase the ailing energy trader on November 9, 2001. When Dynery withdrew from that agreement at the end of the month, it left Enron no choice but to file for bankruptcy one week later.

Page 203: Commercial paper. These are very short-term borrowings that can become a serious trigger point in a crash. The largest issuers are General Electric, General Motors, and Ford. For details, see www.tradeweb.com, www.nact.org/US_Commercial_Paper–A_Shrunken_Market.pdf, and www .gtnews.com/articles6/4537.pdf.

Page 205: Who's to blame for outdated ratings? When it was pointed out that many large brokerage firms maintained "buy" and "hold" ratings on failing companies right up to their date of failure, some of the firms responded with the excuse that the ratings were out of date and should have been withdrawn from circulation, blaming the major data distributors, such as Bloomberg, for the lapse. However, in an e-mail to Weiss Ratings, Bloomberg stated: ". . . We receive all analyst coverage directly from the analysts themselves and/or from the firm they represent. . . . As long as the analyst is actively covering a security and is still considered active at the firm they represent, we leave their coverage up on the system. Finally, we remove coverage from an analyst if they leave the firm they are representing or if they drop their coverage of the security."

For similar reasons, Yahoo.com and other major sources continued to disseminate the "buy" and "hold" ratings with no notification from the brokerage firms that the ratings had changed.

Chapter 16. Move Your Account!

Page 209: James Dubois's shoes. A broker being forced to take off his shoes may sound ludicrous, but fact is stranger than fiction. A very similar tactic was described in a 16-page report by the National Endowment for Financial Education (NEFE). However, the report barely saw the light of day because major Wall Street firms apparently threatened to sue, and the NEFE immediately pulled its report out of circulation.

Page 209: Was it Linda's fault that she lost money? Absolutely not–for the simple reason that she was deliberately and knowingly misled about the stock's prospects. In other words, the broker lied. How common are such lies? For an answer, consider a survey of the industry conducted by the *Washington Post,* from which it was concluded that stockbrokers regularly lie as a "pervasive and routine part of doing business." *Washington Post,* June 16, 2002.

Page 212: 10,000 brokers caught in the act. The GAO study on brokers that Dubois found is entitled *Actions Needed to Better Protect Investors against Unscrupulous Brokers,* GAO/GGD-94-208 9/14/1994. In it, the GAO concluded that 10,000 brokers active at the time had been caught swindling their clients in some way.

Page 212: File of infractions and legal actions against firms too big for e-mail. Among the largest Wall Street firms, such as Morgan Stanley Dean Witter, Prudential Securities, and Merrill Lynch, the list of legal actions taken against them is so large that the NASD has decided the computer files are too large for an e-mail. Therefore, the NASD's policy is to send those reports to investors via first-class mail. In 2002, a report on Lehman Brothers had 550 pages; Prudential Securities, 500 pages; Merrill Lynch Pierce Fenner and Smith, 450 pages; Salomon Smith Barney, 350 pages; Morgan Stanley Dean Witter, also 350 pages. The reason James Dubois is so pleased is that he realizes it would be almost impossible for the average investor to make use of this mass of data.

Chapter 17. An Appeal to Action

Page 228: Innumeracy. See *Innumeracy: Mathematical Illiteracy and Its Consequences* by John Allen Paulos (Hill & Wang, 2001).

Chapter 19. The Big Bailout

Page 252: Japanese government bond auction collapses. See "Not Enough Bidders for Bond Auction in Japan," *New York Times,* September 21, 2002. This was easily the starkest and clearest warning of the dangers facing U.S. authorities if they try to intervene to support the U.S. stock market.

INDEX

www.CrashProfits.net

At the dawn of the new millennium, just when idyllic prosperity seemed guaranteed, the technology bubble burst and the stock market began a deep decline. Similarly, at some point in the not-too-distant future when it might appear that the financial world is "coming to an end," it could actually be a bottom in the market and the time when a firm foundation can be laid for a better future. However, there could also be many deceptive short-term rallies in the stock market and temporary recoveries in the economy, raising false hopes and trapping investors into more losses.

To help provide continuing updates during critical turning points such as these, the author and his staff have created www.CrashProfits. net, dedicated primarily to readers of this book. Readers and non-readers alike are encouraged to visit for the following:

- The author's analysis of new developments such as war, economic initiatives by the administration, meaningful reforms on Wall Street, the failure of a major institution in the United States or overseas, and other critical events that can impact your finances today or alter the future scenarios outlined in this book.
- Free step-by-step instructions on what to do to protect yourself and even benefit from these events.
- Free updates to instructional guides and tables contained in this book.
- Free but valuable supplemental information that, because of space limitations, could not be included in this book.
- Free consumer and investor guides to help you make better financial decisions.
- Links to contact the author and to reach the Weiss companies.

CrashProfits.net is an educational Web site for consumers, and all material posted is free of charge. For more information, call (800) 814-2451 or write to Crash Profits, 4176 Burns Road, Palm Beach Gardens, FL 33410.